When is it proper to s you use numerals?

Should it be "A crow waiting"?

Do you write "He *flied* out to center field" or "*flew* out"?

When is it best to use a comma, a colon, or a semicolon?

How has the rule concerning "will" and "shall" changed?

How can you overcome writer's block?

What quality must a letter possess to be truly effective?

If you've ever found yourself at a loss for words, or unable to recall a specific nuance of grammar or punctuation, you'll find all the information that any professional or aspiring writer could need in—

THE WRITER'S HOTLINE HANDBOOK

MICHAEL MONTGOMERY, a native of Knoxville, Tennessee, taught at the University of Arkansas at Little Rock and worked with the Writer's Hotline from 1978 to 1979. Currently he is on the faculty of the University of South Carolina, where he teaches freshman composition and linguistics and has set up an answering service for writers. He holds a Ph.D. in linguistics from the University of Florida and enjoys doing research in American dialects.

JOHN STRATTON, a native of the Los Angeles area, received his doctorate in English from the University of Nebraska at Lincoln. He has been on the faculty of the University of Arkansas at Little Rock since 1970, where he has taught courses ranging from freshman composition to Shakespeare and the experimental novel, and served for five years as Director of Freshman Composition. He also conducts special writing projects with elementary school children.

THE WRITER'S HOTLINE HANDBOOK

A Guide to Good Usage and Effective Writing

BY MICHAEL MONTGOMERY
AND JOHN STRATTON

A MENTOR BOOK

NEW AMERICAN LIBRARY

NEW YORK AND SCARBOROUGH, ONTARIO

*To the people who have made
this possible—those who called
and those who answered the calls—
and to all those setting up
their own hotlines*

Copyright © 1981 by Michael Montgomery and John Stratton

Library of Congress Catalog Card Number: 81-81583

MENTOR TRADEMARK REG. U.S. PAT. OFF. AND FOREIGN COUNTRIES
REGISTERED TRADEMARK—MARCA REGISTRADA
HECHO EN WINNIPEG, CANADA

SIGNET, SIGNET CLASSIC, MENTOR, ONYX, PLUME, MERIDIAN AND NAL
BOOKS are published in the United States by
NAL Penguin Inc.
1633 Broadway, New York, New York 10019,
in Canada by The New American Library of Canada Limited,
81 Mack Avenue, Scarborough, Ontario M1L 1M8

First Printing, June, 1981

5 6 7 8 9 10 11 12 13

PRINTED IN CANADA

Contents

[v]

Appendices

Foreword

The University of Arkansas at Little Rock sees itself as an urban university, serving night and part-time students, ethnic minorities, senior citizens, and other groups who are not likely to attend the more traditionally oriented branches of the university system. In addition to serving its diverse student body, UALR perceives its "urban mission" as consisting in part of serving the business, professional, governmental, and private sectors of the Greater Little Rock area.

We in the English Department judged contests and gave readings and talks to groups in the community, but we had the uneasy feeling that we were not "relevant" in the way that our colleagues in the sciences, social sciences, and technologies were. We felt that we should offer the community what we offer our students: help with basic writing skills.

Phone calls occasionally came into the department from people needing assistance in matters of grammar, punctuation, diction, spelling, or style. We sometimes joked about the questions, the need to ask them, or both. But we were glad to have contact with the "outside," and we did our best to help the callers.

So it was only logical that one day I conceived of a new service to fulfill the English Department's part of the "urban mission." I christened it the "UALR Writer's Hotline" and secured the approval of the department. The University News Service distributed a notice of the service to the local media late in January 1978. On February 23, 1978, the Writer's Hotline opened for business at 9:00 A.M., CST.

During the weekend before the hotline opened, at least three radio stations called me at home to tape phone interviews explaining the service to listeners around the country. As the service got under way, those taped radio interviews were being aired not only across the United States but across Canada as well. Paul Harvey praised the service on his radio show, and several radio networks carried reports of the hotline's operation. One of the three major television networks did a feature on this newest in telephone services; it was aired in the Midwest and as far away as northern Michigan. The *Atlanta Constitution* published a story on the first page of its feature section. And many papers across the nation ran versions of wire-service stories.

The caller response was even more amazing. The Greater Little Rock community used the service from the beginning. But soon people were calling from around the country. A woman called from Punxsutawney, Pennsylvania (as W. C. Fields is my witness), began a conversation by stating that she assumed the service was run on an incoming WATS line (it wasn't—and isn't), nearly choked when she was informed that she was paying for prime-time long-distance phone service, and gasped that she would mail her question, hanging up immediately thereafter. A secretary working for the Veterans Administration in the Chicago area, and obviously feuding with her male boss over sexism in pronouns, called up to have us discipline him. There were callers who had hoarded idiosyncratic questions which they used on our volunteers, to "test" their knowledge.

The service worked and worked well. Individual callers were grateful to a fault, often sending me "fan mail." The university administration sent memos of praise and paraded me before their advisory board.

Of all the forms of flattery accorded the hotline concept, however, the most sincere has been the spread of the idea. The original hotline in Little Rock still operates, and others now operate at campuses and community education centers across the country. One can only conclude that these hotlines are working because the concept works—because a grammar hotline is a cheap, easy, low-stress method of giving and receiving help with the fundamentals of writing. The advice is personalized, and it is task-oriented. The individual who makes a request accomplishes a fixed goal by learning the answer. Under such circumstances, learning is usually effective.

An editorial in the *Arkansas Democrat* observed, "[The hotline service] sends you forth armed for grammatical combat." So what follows is something of a "military manual," a collection of tactics and strategies for coping with the unending battle to express oneself well. The battle for self-expression is what William Blake called "ceaseless mental fight." It takes place in the arena of the mind. And victory is not the raising of a single voice but the raising of many, engaged in "conversation," in the fullest sense of that word's meaning.

STUART PETERFREUND
Boston, Massachusetts

Introduction

Why another English handbook?

A year or two ago we at the Writer's Hotline would have asked ourselves the same question. In fact we did ask ourselves that question when Gerry Howard, then an editor with New American Library, first approached us with the idea of writing up the questions that callers frequently asked. Most questions the hotline received were answered quickly and directly with information that we writing teachers keep in the tops of our heads—information about basic word choice, punctuation, and grammar. Other problems required our discussing individual sentences with callers, and still other questions required us to search through dictionaries and usage guides, and to debate among ourselves.

Contrary to what is implied by some well-known doomsayers, who seem to feel that they alone stand between English as we know it and love it and a mass of illiterate and insensitive writers of the Mother Tongue, hotline callers have convinced us that Americans are serious about their writing. They may occasionally have a problem writing, but they want to be read and understood. They want to be informed so they can make intelligent, defensible choices about their writing, but they do not always have all the information they need.

Our callers invariably want rules and often an explanation for the rule. Rules are crucial to them; rules are often the authorities cited in the debates between office colleagues and between bosses and secretaries. (Secretaries are usually right.) Our callers, like many teachers and critics of current language, sometimes equate "correct" writing with effective writing. But following the rules does not, of itself, lead to effective writing, that is, writing that clearly and vividly explains a subject. For proof of this, one has only to look, for instance, at a few college textbooks, particularly for advanced courses. The grammar, punctuation, and spelling are correct throughout, but more than likely the book is filled with jargon-packed sentences that often lose the struggling reader. But while following the rules does not necessarily lead to fluent writing, the rules for using English are to be ignored only at the writer's peril. Readers expect writers to follow the rules.

Rules and Usage

What are these rules actually? First, it must be admitted that rules are sometimes made up and perpetuated by grammarians. In the eighteenth century, for instance, grammarians took a rule that made perfect sense for Latin—a sentence should not end with a preposition—and applied it to English. This "rule" reflected the way grammarians wanted English to be, not the way it was or is. In the nineteenth century, Noah Webster, America's first noted maker of dictionaries, removed the *u* from numerous words ending in *our,* such as *colour* and *humour.* (These words are spelled today in Britain with the *u,* in the United States without.) And even today grammarians are attempting to impose rules (see *that/which,* pages 76–78). Thus some rules do come from grammarians trying to tidy up the language in one way or another.

But most rules come from usage. These rules codify and reflect the usage of educated writers, editors, and speakers. (Yes, editors play a significant role in determining rules and usage.) Once a rule is codified, however, it takes on a life of its own. It appears in grammar books, is taught in schools, is argued about by editors, and is abused by writers. Usage (especially in speech) continues to evolve, but now the rule acts as a restraint, reminding users of what readers expect and serving as a brake on idiosyncratic tendencies. Writers and editors examine writing with the rule in mind. And writers begin to follow this particular practice simply because it is now a rule, and they don't want to be called down. Eventually a rule may lose its force in usage and may begin to die out, but this takes time. It is important to recognize that language is a complex, living thing, and as it changes, our description of its patterns and rules changes also.

Formal and General Writing

Although many of our writer-callers may not think about it, there are two basic levels of writing—formal and general. These are two different styles of standard English. Formal writing—the writing of legal documents, some scholarly journals, and "official" publications—gives utmost importance to form. Its grammar is conservative, and it adheres to many distinctions (e.g. *shall/will* and *may/can*) for the special effect they seem to create. Formal writing does not need to be dull and pompous, although it often is; it can be graceful and precise.

General writing is the writing that most writers write and most readers read. It is the writing found in annual reports and in interdepartmental memos, in magazines and newspapers. It is the only style of writing most writers ever use. It is less formal in tone, usually livelier, and more varied in texture. It usually contains fewer abstractions and more concrete examples. It may contain contractions and first- and second-person pronouns. Writers of general writing may use formal writing for a special effect; they may make occasional use of slang and colloquialisms and may bend rules for dramatic effect. Thus, in general writing, a writer has more choices and more possibilities for expression than in formal writing. General writing should be lively and brisk, but it need be no less precise, nor are there any fewer possibilities for expressing complex, abstract thoughts in general writing than in formal writing.

This Book

We take general writing as our reference point throughout the book because it is the writing style that most writers use. It is with these daily situations that writers need most information. We tell writers when adhering to a certain rule is a matter of style, representing a choice between formal and general English. Rarely, very rarely, does this difference in style affect meaning in any way. Writing formally is a matter of tone and style. It is not a matter of being correct or incorrect, although it sometimes seems so because we are all preoccupied with rules.

Our discussions of rules are presented against a background of varied usages and against a background of language that is constantly changing. We tell readers when rules are dying (the distinctions between *will* and *shall*, for instance) and when rules have simply been forgotten (nearly all uses of the subjunctive, for instance), and we try to warn readers against the temptation to overcorrect for something they are unsure of. We try never to leave readers caught in a dilemma between writing "correct" English in a formal sense and writing idiomatic, natural-sounding English. We spend much time indicating to writers how to write around problem situations, such as "Everybody brought *his/her/their*. . . ." (See pages 69–75 for our discussion of this problem and our suggested solutions.) In doing this we give writers additional resources to draw on.

Giving writers tools with which to express themselves is the ultimate goal of this book. We give them the information so that they can make choices for themselves. And, because we are concerned too about helping writers develop good habits, we have also added some thoughts about writing well and about writing in spite of mental blocks.

We have kept grammatical terminology to a minimum, bringing it in only with reference to a specific writing problem and never dwelling on grammatical distinctions that are of little use to a writer. We end up covering as much grammar as most other books, but we do this on location, so to speak, only when directly relevant to a matter at hand. We think writers understand grammar more easily this way. Yet we have avoided simplifying. We discuss differences in usage and try to be forthright about differences between various authorities. We have tried to be authoritative without being authoritarian.

Because of our experience in answering many hundreds of hotline questions, we know what problems writers actually have. We kept these in mind as we wrote, and we think this is a better book because of it.

The one great drawback to a book, as opposed to the telephone, is that we cannot get the immediate response of the people being helped. So we invite your reactions and comments, sent to us in care of the publisher. These will help us to improve future editions of this book.

MICHAEL MONTGOMERY
Memphis, Tennessee

JOHN STRATTON
Little Rock, Arkansas

Acknowledgments

Many people have contributed to this book. Our colleagues in the English Department at the University of Arkansas at Little Rock, who set up and continue to staff the hotline, have supported us with numerous discussions and examples. Gerry Howard, an education editor with New American Library, conceived the idea of a handbook based on information requested by hotline callers. Nick Bakalar succeeded Gerry Howard as our editor and has kept the project moving along. Bill Reynolds, our copy editor, saved us from many blunders and infelicities. And Dotty Stratton, who provided meals and encouragement, but more than that, demanded that sentences make sense and be readable, put up with more annoyances from the book and its authors than anyone else. Without these people the book would not have been possible.

Whatever problems remain are strictly the authors'.

PART ONE

Grammar

1

Verbs:
The Essential Words

Simply put, verbs are the most important parts of sentences. Sentences are built around them, and a writer who can handle verbs with skill and accuracy has traveled a long way toward becoming an effective writer. On the other hand, the writer who wrote *A decision with regard to the investigation of public misconduct has been made* doesn't appreciate what a verb can do in a sentence and still has a long way to go toward writing effectively.

Verb comes from the Latin word meaning "word." This etymology reflects the importance of the verb in a sentence. It is the one part of speech that every sentence must have. Grammarians and linguists in writing grammars of English have found that verbs require more time and space to cover than any other part of speech.

Verbs have many grammatical properties (number, mood, tense, voice, and others) and hotline callers ask questions involving most of them: Do my subject and verb agree? When do I use the subjunctive? What's the past participle of *prove*?

Most verbs have a property called "number," which means that they are singular or plural. Verbs must agree with their subjects in number. In earlier stages of English, verbs had different forms for singular and plural in every tense, but in Modern English, verbs change number only in the present tense and only when subjects are in the third person. Exceptions are *was* and *were* (the forms of *be* in the past tense) and the helping verb *have* in the present perfect tense (*he has had, they have had*). Still, subject-verb agreement is a complicated matter today, and we have dealt with it in a chapter of its own (see Chapter 3).

Most verbs also have a property called "voice," which means that they are active or passive, that they let their subjects either perform an action (*The police caught the suspect*) or receive an action (*The suspect was caught by the police*). The choice between an active verb and a passive verb is one of style, and we deal with this choice in detail in Chapter 14. Most English verbs express action, but a few only connect or link subjects with other parts of a sentence (as in *Taxes are high* and *Cocaine is addictive*). The writing problem associated with linking verbs involves choosing between adjectives and adverbs that follow them (see pages 80–82).

Principal Parts of Verbs

To express their many grammatical properties, verbs have four different forms called their "principal parts": the present or infinitive (*look, see*), the past (*looked, saw*), the past participle (*looked, seen*), and the present participle (*looking, seeing*). The present form can function by itself or can appear with such helping verbs as *do, may,* or *will,* and when it appears with *will* or *shall,* it forms the future tense. The past form must stand alone. The past participle and present participle occur with one or more helping verbs, always including a form of *have* (*she has looked*), a form of *be* (*she is looking*), or a form of each (*she has been looking*). In speech, many verbs have more than one past form and more than one past participle, and sometimes past forms are used for past participles and vice versa. Most, but not all, of this variation in past and past-participle forms is unacceptable in writing.

The vast majority of verbs in English are regular verbs, forming their principal parts in an entirely predictable manner. They add *ed* to form the past and the past participles and add *ing* to form the present participle. The *ed* ending may be pronounced in various ways, but the only regular verbs that writers ever have much trouble spelling are *used to* and *supposed to* (the *d* is always required when *to* is used). Dictionaries do not list the principal parts of regular verbs unless they have both a regular and an irregular past-tense or past-participle form.

The approximately two hundred irregular verbs often cause trouble because their past-tense and past-participle forms occur in many unpredictable patterns (the present participles are always regular and add *ing* to the present form). Some change only a vowel to form their past and past participles (*ring, rang, rung, ringing*), while others neither change a vowel nor add an ending (*put, put, put, putting*). Other irregular verbs follow still other patterns. Irregular verbs are fewer in number than regular ones, but they are the verbs that occur most frequently in English. They often have equally correct and acceptable alternate forms for the past tense and past participle, and writers often have problems with them.

Below we list the principal parts of the irregular verbs that sometimes give writers trouble. We give only the widely acceptable alternate forms that writers may safely use. Writers will find the principal parts of these and all other irregular verbs in any dictionary. Dictionaries usually give alternative forms alphabetically and not in their order of acceptability (they are usually equally acceptable).

PRESENT	PAST	PAST PARTICIPLE	PRESENT PARTICIPLE
awake	awoke	awaked	awaking
awaken	awakened	awakened	awakening
begin	began	begun	beginning
bet	bet or betted	bet or betted	betting
bid (to request)	bade	bidden or bid	bidding
bid (to make an offer)	bid	bid	bidding
break	broke	broken	breaking
bring	brought	brought	bringing
broadcast	broadcast or broadcasted	broadcast or broadcasted	broadcasting
burst	burst	burst	bursting
cling (to hold on to)	clung	clung	clinging
come	came	come	coming
dive	dived or dove	dived	diving
do	did	done	doing
dream	dreamed or dreamt	dreamed or dreamt	dreaming
eat	ate	eaten	eating
fly (except in baseball)	flew	flown	flying

PRESENT	PAST	PAST PARTICIPLE	PRESENT PARTICIPLE
fly (in baseball)	flied	flied	flying
forbid	forbade	forbidden or forbid	forbidding
get	got	got or gotten	getting
give	gave	given	giving
go	went	gone	going
hang (a picture)	hung	hung	hanging
hang (a criminal)	hanged	hanged	hanging
hide	hid	hidden or hid	hiding
lay	laid	laid	laying
lead	led	led	leading
learn	learned or learnt	learned or learnt	learning
lie (to recline)	lay	lain	lying
lie (to tell an untruth)	lied	lied	lying
light	lighted or lit	lighted or lit	lighting
plead	pleaded or pled	pleaded or pled	pleading
prove	proved	proved or proven	proving
ride	rode	ridden	riding
rise	rose	risen	rising
run	ran	run	running
set	set	set	setting
shine	shined or shone	shined or shone	shining
sing	sang	sung	singing
sink	sank or sunk	sunk	sinking
sit	sat	sat	sitting
slay	slew	slain	slaying
smell	smelled or smelt	smelled or smelt	smelling
sneak	sneaked	sneaked	sneaking
spell	spelled or spelt	spelled or spelt	spelling

PRESENT	PAST	PAST PARTICIPLE	PRESENT PARTICIPLE
spoil	spoiled or spoilt	spoiled or spoilt	spoiling
spring	sprang or sprung	sprung	springing
sting	stung	stung	stinging
stink	stank or stunk	stunk	stinking
strike	struck	struck or stricken (different meanings)	striking
strive	strived or strove	strived or striven	striving
swim	swam	swum	swimming
swing	swung	swung	swinging
take	took	taken	taking

Lay/lie and *set/sit*

Lay/lie and *set/sit* are the two pairs of verbs most often confused in English, without doubt because their principal parts look and sound so much alike. *Lay* (principal parts *lay, laid, laid, laying*) means "to put something down"; *lie* (principal parts *lie, lay, lain, lying*) means "to recline." *Sit* (principal parts *sit, sat, sat, sitting*) means "to be seated"; *set* (principal parts *set, set, set, setting*) means "to put or place."

Lay and *set* are transitive verbs, which means they take direct objects (the receivers of the action of the verb). If there is no direct object, then *lie* and *sit* are the proper verbs to use. (See *lay, lie* and *set, sit* entries in the Glossary of Usage for sample sentences.)

Tense in English

The most important property that the principal parts of verbs show is tense, which refers to the time distinctions that verbs express. While English is usually said to have six tenses (we display these below), English verbs can take many more forms than we show here. Each of the six tenses has a corresponding set of progressive forms—forms using the present participle to express a continuous action or state of being (*I am going, I was going, I will be going,* etc.). Many verbs have a corresponding set of passive forms (*I am hit, I was hit, I will be hit,* etc.). In addition, some of the tenses below have uses that are not apparent from the forms themselves; for instance, the present tense can express habitual action. One tense, the future perfect (which indicates an action or state of being that will have been completed at a future time), occurs very infrequently.

	SINGULAR	PLURAL
Present	I, you/go, walk he, she, it/goes, walks	we, you, they/go, walk
Past	I, you, he, she, it/went, walked	we, you, they/ went, walked
Future	I, you, he, she, it/will go, will walk	we, you, they/will go, will walk
Present Perfect	I, you/have gone, have walked he, she, it/has gone, has walked	we, you, they/have gone, have walked
Past Perfect	I, you, he, she, it/ had gone, had walked	we, you, they/had gone, had walked
Future Perfect	I, you, he, she, it/ will have gone, will have walked	we, you, they/will have gone, will have walked

The problems that hotline callers have with verb tenses are relatively few, and these involve special uses of the present tense and the proper sequence of tenses in sentences.

Uses of the Present Tense

The simple present tense usually expresses an action or a state of being that occurs or is true in the present. Anything not specifically limited in time is expressed in English in the present tense. This may be a general or universal truth (*Two plus two is four* and *An apple a day keeps the doctor away* and all other proverbs) or a habitual action or state of being (*The sun sets in the west* and *Diabetics avoid carbohydrates*). Present tense forms (with the aid of adverbs) may also express future time (*The delegation leaves for Moscow Monday*).

Tense Sequence

Ordinarily a writer chooses one tense to write in. All the actions or states in each sentence occur or are true roughly at the same time, and the tenses of all verbs in each sentence usually conform to the dominant tense.

> The competition *is playing* the same game they always *do*. (Both verbs are in the present tense.)
> The competition *was playing* the same game they always *did*. (Both verbs are in the past tense.)

So strong is this dominant tense that considerations of real time may be subordinated to it, and the verb of a subordinate clause made consistent in tense with the main-clause verb.

> What *did* he *say* his qualifications *were*? (Presumably they still are his qualifications.)

Sometimes, however, a writer needs to indicate clearly that actions or states in a sentence occur or are true in sequence (one ends before the other begins). This sequence can be shown either by a change of tense of one verb within a sentence, by the addition of an adverb or prepositional phrase referring to time, or sometimes by both. There are several minor exceptions too, so we provide below a summary of possible tense sequences within a sentence.

Main-Clause Verb in a Present Tense

When the main-clause verb is present (*needs*) or present perfect (*has needed*), the verb tense to be used in the subordinate clause depends on the meaning the writer intends. The subordinate verb may be in any tense.

> The steel industry *needs* tariffs because Japanese imports *are* so cheap.

The steel industry *needs* tariffs because Japanese imports *have been* so cheap.

The steel industry *needs* tariffs because Japanese imports *will be* so cheap.

The steel industry *has needed* tariffs because Japanese imports *are* so cheap.

and so on.

When the subordinate clause has an adverb or prepositional phrase expressing time, writers have a choice of which tense to use.

We *hope* that it *is* (or *will be*) available by Christmas.

Main-Clause Verb in a Past Tense

When the main-clause verb is past (*was*) or past perfect (*had been*), writers may usually choose either a past or a past-perfect verb in a subordinate clause, regardless of whether it refers to the same or to a later time.

It *was* a long time before we *forgot* the favor.

When a sentence must clearly indicate a sequencing of time, writers can use either of two options, or sometimes both. They can put one verb of the sentence in the past tense and the other in the past perfect (the function of the past-perfect tense in English is to indicate when one event occurs before another). Or writers can rely on a time adverb or a prepositional phrase expressing time to show the sequence.

Jackson *said* that he *had been* an alcoholic. (He wasn't at the time he made the statement.)

Jackson *said* that he *was* an alcoholic for fourteen years. (He wasn't at the time of the statement.)

Jackson *said* that he *had been* an alcoholic for fourteen years. (He may or may not have been at the time of the statement.)

Jackson *had said* that he *was* an alcoholic. (He may or may not have been at the time of the statement.)

Jackson *said* that he *was* an alcoholic. (He was at the time he made the statement.)

Jackson *said* that in all likelihood he *would remain* an alcoholic. (Even a statement referring to a possible

future must use a verb that is past-tense in form—
would.)

When the subordinate clause begins with *when*, either one
verb in the sentence should be put in the past perfect or *when*
should be changed to *after* or *before* to clearly show the
sequence.

> He *had lived* (not *lived*) in Memphis only two weeks
> when the accident *happened*.
> He *lived* in Memphis only two weeks *before* (not *when*)
> the accident *happened*. (The past perfect *had happened*
> is unnecessary since the time sequence is clear.)

When the subordinate clause expresses something long-
lasting or universally true, its verb can either be in the present
tense (regardless of the tense of the main-clause verb) or
agree with the main-clause verb in tense.

> In the Middle Ages, astronomers *believed* that the earth
> *was* (or *is*) round.
> In the future, astronomers *will say* that the earth *is* (or
> *will be*) pear-shaped. (*Will be* in this case is per-
> missible, but not idiomatic.)

Main-Clause Verb in a Future Tense or Imperative

When the main-clause verb is future (*will be*) or future
perfect (*will have known*), the subordinate-clause verb is
usually in the present tense. Occasionally the meaning demands
that it be in a past tense. When the main-clause verb is
imperative (expressing a request or a command), the
subordinate-clause verb is in the present tense.

> It *will be* a long time before we *forget* the favor.
> They *will* soon *discover* that Ace *canceled* the merger.
> *Ask* the Writer's Hotline when you *need* the best answer.

Subjunctive Mood

The subjunctive mood, used for nonfactual statements (such
as wishes and beliefs), hypothetical statements, and other

expressions, is alive and well in French, German, and several other languages related to English. But the English subjunctive has largely disappeared, having been replaced by other constructions. Its present-day use is inconsistent and confined to the few situations we describe below.

The Writer's Hotline receives more questions about the subjunctive than about any other aspect of verb use, for several reasons. Since it occurs even less in speech than in writing, the subjunctive is only partially idiomatic and often cannot be successfully sounded out. Occasions when the subjunctive still occurs are relatively rare, giving writers little practice in using it. In addition, many writers believe that the subjunctive gives writing a desirably formal tone, so they want to use it. However, this desire to use the subjunctive, along with the somewhat complicated rules showing where it does and does not belong, causes writers to use it often when it is unnecessary.

In some cases, using the subjunctive in Modern English is a matter of style. Either it is optional or writers can paraphrase their ideas without the subjunctive. In other cases, writers must decide whether a sentence expresses an unlikely condition (which requires a subjunctive) or a possible condition (which does not require a subjunctive). A writer should not use a subjunctive verb unless it is grammatically and logically needed. When one is unsure whether or not to use a subjunctive, it is safer not to do so. Using a subjunctive verb to express a possible condition or a fact, no matter how formal a tone is desired, is incorrect.

Below are the current uses of the subjunctive in English.

Set Phrases

The subjunctive occurs in certain set phrases and idioms for wishes and other expressions.

> God bless America. (*That is,* May God bless America.)
> Far be it from me to say that you should do it.
> Be that as it may, I will go.

That Clauses

The subjunctive occurs in subordinate clauses beginning with *that* when the main clause is or contains a demand, a request, a wish, a recommendation, or a similar expression. The main clause has either a verb such as *ask, insist, command, order, wish,* or *suggest* or an adjective such as *important, essential, urgent,* or *necessary.* In such sentences, writers often try to make the verb of the *that* clause agree with its subject, but the verb is subjunctive and does not agree with its subject as an indicative verb does.

> We ask that the following procedures *be* (not *are*) implemented.
> I request that he *report* (not *reports*) directly to me. ·
> The judge ordered that the remarks *be* struck from the record.
> It is suggested that each employee *receive* (not *receives*) due process.
> It is essential that each member *have* (not *has*) a role to play.

Such sentences can often be rephrased more idiomatically by using an infinitive to replace the *that* clause or by inserting *should* before the subjunctive verb.

> We ask the following procedures *to be* implemented.
> I request him *to report* directly to me.
> The judge ordered the remarks *to be* struck from the record.
> It is suggested that each employee *should* receive due process.
> It is essential that each member *should* have a role to play.

The Subjunctive Following *wish, as if,* and *as though*

In formal writing, the subjunctive is required after the verb *wish.* In speech and in general writing, use of the subjunctive is usually optional (*I wish I was/were going with you*), especially if the verb following *wish* is negative (*I wish I wasn't/weren't going with you*).

> I *wish* I *were* going with you. (referring to a future or present event)
>
> I *wish* I *had been* going with you. (referring to a past time)
>
> Their fifteen-year-old *wishes* he *were* old enough to drive. (referring to a present time)
>
> Their seventeen-year-old *wishes* she *had been* allowed to drive at sixteen. (referring to a past time)

In formal writing, the subjunctive is also required after the subordinating conjunctions *as if* and *as though*. It is usually optional in speech and in general writing.

> The experience seemed almost as if it *were* a dream. (*Was* is acceptable in general writing.)
>
> The milk tastes as though it *were* spoiling. (*Was* is acceptable in general writing.)

The Subjunctive Following *if*

A subjunctive verb is not always required in a subordinate clause beginning with *if;* determining when it is the proper choice is quite simple. If the *if* clause expresses a contrary-to-fact or a highly unlikely or doubtful condition and if *would* is a part of the main verb of the sentence, then the *if*-clause verb should be subjunctive (*If I were you, I wouldn't go*). However, if the *if* clause expresses a likely or possible condition and if *would* doesn't appear in the main-clause verb, the subjunctive should not be used (*If he comes, I won't go*). Unsure writers may be tempted to always use a subjunctive in an *if* clause, but they should check for *would* in the main clause before they do.

Use the subjunctive *were* to refer to a present or future event and the subjunctive *had been* to refer to a past event.

Incorrect

> If the Missouri *were* to rise, much of central Missouri *will be* flooded.

Revised

> If the Missouri *were* to rise, much of central Missouri *would be* flooded. (The use of *would* indicates a

contrary-to-fact condition; the river hasn't risen and no rain is forecast.)

Revised

> If the Missouri *rises,* much of central Missouri *will* be flooded. (This is a possible fact and *would* is not used in the main clause; storms are predicted for the next three days.)
>
> If the deadline *were* missed, the publisher *would* withdraw the contract. (A contrary-to-fact or hypothetical condition.)
>
> If the deadline *is* missed, the publisher *will* withdraw the contract. (A possible fact.)
>
> If I *was* (not *were*) there last month, I *don't* remember it. (A possible fact.)

In a past-subjunctive sentence, one with *would have* (rather than *would*) as part of the main-clause verb, the subjunctive verb in the *if* clause is also past, and the writer must use *had,* not *would have.*

> If her report *had* (not *would have*) come earlier, the plans *would* not *have* been delayed.
>
> If the police *had* (not *would have*) been there, they *would have* stopped it.

A final note on the subjunctive: Never use *be* in an *if* clause. This is a use of the subjunctive sometimes still heard but no longer a part of written English practice.

> If it *is* (not *be*) true, we are all in trouble.

Shall and *Will*

Many of us had teachers who tried to instill in us the fine distinctions between *shall* and *will.* According to the prescriptions, these two words complemented one another but were never interchangeable. So many were the distinctions between *shall* and *will* (and their related forms *should* and *would*) that it took H. W. and F. G. Fowler twenty-one pages in *The King's English* to discuss them. Despite these authorities of school and scholar, today most of the distinctions between *shall* and *will* simply no longer exist (although they are still often maintained in Britain). *Will* has so thoroughly replaced *shall* that contemporary writers are safe to go by the following simple rule: If it sounds natural, use *will*.

To express simple futurity, *shall* was at one time commonly used with first-person subjects and *will* with second- and third-person subjects. One or two remnants of this distinction remain, but *will* is now the normal future form for all levels of writing and for all subjects. *Shall* can still be used to express futurity when an especially formal effect is desired, as in legal documents. It is also used in formal and polite first-person questions (*Shall I be seeing you tomorrow?*). Use *shall* for the future conservatively; it often sounds affected.

Traditionally, to express determination that something must or should be done, *will* was required with first-person subjects and *shall* with second- and third-person subjects (the inverse of their use for simple futurity). But now to express obligation, warning, determination, or prohibition in statements about the future, both *shall* and *will* are acceptable. *Shall* is usually more forceful and is typically used in government and legal documents.

> At the end of the year, division chiefs *will* (or *shall*) submit inventory statements.
> The accused *shall* (or *will*) stand trial on March 15.
> Only tennis shoes *shall* be worn on the courts. (*Will* seems to lack the force required here.)

Often futurity and obligation or determination become indistinguishable. Use either *shall* or *will* in the following sentence.

> All employees with more than two years of service *will* (or *shall*) receive a longevity payment on September 30.

Shall is still used in first-person questions where its use indicates a request for permission and not simply an inquiry about the future. (*Shall I see you tomorrow?* requests permission. *Will I see you tomorrow?* does not.)

In choosing between *shall* and *will*, several things may come together in a writer's mind: a hazy recollection of the "rules," a sense of how formal the writing should be, and an attempt to convey determination or futurity. All these needlessly complicate the choice. Except when it sounds quite unnatural (as sometimes in first-person questions), writers will always be safe in using *will*.

Should and *Would*

Should and *would* are still distinct in English in several ways. *Should* expresses obligation (*You should go home now*) and probability (*The letter should be typed by noon*) and is equivalent to "ought to." *Would* expresses a habitual action or state in the past (*We would often work on weekends*). A verb with *would* expressing something habitual is usually better phrased with the simple past if there is an adverb expressing time in the sentence (*In the fall, we often worked on weekends*).

The Overuse of *would*

Normally a sentence with *would* implies a hypothetical condition or a habitual state of affairs. A hypothetical condition is stated either in a subordinate clause beginning with *if* when *would* is the verb in the main clause (*If you were fired, I would resign*) or with certain verbs such as *like* (*I would like you to do this for me*).

Would is used in speech, when a condition isn't indicated, to be polite and circumspect (*I would suggest you take a day off* is less direct and more polite than *I suggest you take a day off* or *Take a day off*). But often in modern-day writing *would* is added to a sentence needlessly when a condition is not stated. This not only adds an extra, meaningless word to a sentence, it also creates a more hesitant and often deceiving sentence that leaves readers in the dark, unsure under what conditions the sentence is true. Cut it out of sentences wherever possible.

Original

> It would appear that there is a discrepancy between these
>   accounts. (Under what conditions does it appear?
>   *Would* makes this statement needlessly indirect.)

Revised

> It appears (*or* seems) that there is a discrepancy between
> these accounts.

or more directly

> There is a discrepancy between these accounts.

Original

> Our preliminary studies would suggest that wood cannot
> be burned efficiently. (Under what conditions do the
> studies suggest this?)

Revised

> Our preliminary studies suggest (*or* indicate) that wood
> cannot be burned efficiently.

2

Plurals:
S and Other Endings

Writer's Hotline callers and writers in general often have a problem spelling the plural forms of nouns. This problem has many sides to it. We'll deal with it here rather than in Chapter 9, on spelling, because our callers usually ask "What's the plural of ———?"

Each noun and pronoun in English has a property called "number," which means it is either singular or plural. There is usually no difficulty in telling which number any given noun or pronoun has. *Handbook* is singular, of course, and *handbooks* is plural. *Handbook* and most other nouns in English form the plural by adding *s* or *es* to their singular forms. Only a small percentage of nouns are exceptions to this very general rule.

The Correct Plural Forms of Nouns

A good dictionary (see Chapter 18) will spell out any plural which is not formed regularly. Most nouns simply add *s* to the singular. Nouns ending in *s*, *z*, *x*, *sh*, or *ch* are regular exceptions to this, and these always add *es*. If a dictionary entry does not show a plural form, you should assume it is formed in one of these two regular fashions.

The *s* is added to form the plural even in those cases when the additional sound is difficult to hear, as it is in nouns ending in *sp*, *st*, or *sk*.

> The mud dauber and the yellow jacket are types of *wasps*.
> All members of the society born in March will be *guests* of honor.
> Both *pathologists* arrived at the same diagnosis.

The school board will buy nine hundred new *desks* for the school.

Proper nouns (names of specific persons, places, organizations, etc.) are made plural in the same manner that common nouns (names of unspecific persons, places, organizations, things, etc.) are, with the exception of proper nouns ending in *y* (common noun: *duty, duties;* proper noun: *Murphy, Murphys*).

Plurals Ending in *es*

Because of their endings, four classes of nouns require the addition of *es* to form their plurals. In some cases, the endings of their singular forms must also be changed. A dictionary will usually give the correct spelling.

Nouns Ending in *s, z, x, sh,* or *ch*

Except for some words of foreign origin that have retained their original plurals, such as *axis* and *crisis* (see pages 28-30,) nouns ending in an *s* sound, whether spelled *s, z, x, sh,* or *ch,* add *es* to form the plural. The plurals are pronounced with an added syllable. A few English words (*stomach* may be the only one) end in the letters listed, but do not end in an *s* sound and are not pronounced with an added syllable when plural; these words add only an *s* to form the plural (*stomachs*).

SINGULAR	PLURAL
address	addresses
waltz	waltzes
box	boxes
ambush	ambushes
match	matches

Hotline callers often ask about the correct plurals of surnames with one of these endings. Is it the *Jones'* or the *Joneses*? Neither looks quite right, callers sometimes insist. But the correct answer here is *Joneses*; the apostrophe in such a case indicates possession, not plurality.

The *Essexes* (not *Essex's*) send season's greetings to all their friends.

The Malcolm *Thomases* (not Thomas' or Thomas's) have bought the house on the corner.

Nouns Ending in *y*

Nouns ending in a *y* which is not preceded by a vowel change the *y* to *i* before adding *es*. Thus, *duty, duties; quantity, quantities; policy, policies;* but *donkey, donkeys*. This rule has no exceptions among common nouns, but for proper nouns this rule hardly operates at all. Proper nouns ending in *y* almost never change to *ies*; personal names never do, and apparently the only exceptions are the names of mountain ranges: the *Rockies*, the *Smokies*, the *Alleghenies*.

SINGULAR	PLURAL
Kennedy	Kennedys
Murphy	Murphys
Chomsky	Chomskys
Peggy	Peggys
Mary	Marys

Nouns Ending in *o*

Nouns ending in *o* frequently add *es* to form the plural, but because some nouns add only *s*, writers should consult a dictionary to be certain. Whereas *echo* and *tomato* add *es, radio* adds only *s*. Many other nouns, *volcano* and *zero*, for example, have two equally acceptable plural forms, *volcanos* and *volcanoes, zeros* and *zeroes*. Either form is acceptable.

Nouns Ending in *f* or *fe*

Nouns ending in *f* or *fe* that are native to English (that is, they have not been adopted from French, Norse, or another language) change their ending to *ves* to form the plural.

	SINGULAR	PLURAL	
	half	halves	
	knife	knives	
	leaf	leaves	
	life	lives	
	self	selves	
	thief	thieves	
	wolf	wolves	
but			
	belief	beliefs	(from French)
	chef	chefs	(")
	chief	chiefs	(")
	grief	griefs	(")
	reef	reefs	(from Norse)

Compound Nouns

Perhaps the most intricate pluralization problem is presented by compound nouns, that is, nouns of more than one word. What is the correct plural of *attorney general*? *Attorneys general* or *attorney generals*? The correct plural of *runner-up*? *Runners-up* or *runner-ups*? The plural of *time-out*? Some compounds are pluralized at the end and others are not, and the spelling of a compound noun frequently gives no clue about how to proceed. As a guide, the writer should rely on the principles presented here, on a dictionary when possible, and on modern idiomatic usage.

Most compounds form plurals in the normal English manner by adding *s*. Thus, *water fountains* and *salad dressings* are the plurals of *water fountain* and *salad dressing*. Many other compounds have evolved or are currently evolving toward forming their plurals in the same way.

In modern usage, compounds of nouns and prepositions or adverbs are generally pluralized by adding the *s* in the middle rather than at the end of the compound. *Hangers-on* and *runners-up* remain the preferred plurals of *hanger-on* and *runner-up*. The same is true for *passersby*. However, *times-out* was the preferred plural form not so very long ago, and although it is still fancied by a few sportscasters, it has inevitably given way to *time-outs*.

Semilegal and similar compounds are changing. *Courts-martial*, *attorneys general*, and *mothers-in-law* are still the preferred plural forms in educated usage, but the tendency to add the *s* at the end is very strong. Many of us have had to be specifically instructed in school about the proper plurals of such compounds. Even so, *attorney generals* has become generally acceptable as an alternative to *attorneys general*. The writer is best advised to consult a dictionary for alternate spellings and, when in doubt about the formality of the writing demanded, to use the conservative form, making the plural in the middle.

Compounds consisting of a verb and a preposition are always pluralized by adding a final *s*, as *walkout, walkouts; walk-on, walk-ons; go-between, go-betweens.*

A final type of compound consists of two nouns, the second one limiting or modifying the first. The writer usually creates a new and unintended meaning by making the second noun plural.

> There are actually two government *forms* 2095A.
> Please note that there are two proposed *exhibits* A.

The first sentence, referring to two different kinds or versions of a form designated 2095A, has the correct plural *two government forms 2095A*. If the writer wants to refer to two copies of the *same* form, the correct plural is *two government form 2095A's* (or, as better rephrased, *two copies of government form 2095A*). By the same token, *two proposed exhibits A* in the second sentence refers to two different exhibits, but *two proposed exhibit A's* refers to two copies or examples of the same one.

Plurals with the Apostrophe

A final category of items requiring the *s* to form the plural includes letters, cited words and phrases, abbreviations, dates, numerals, and figures. These items have conventionally been made plural by adding an apostrophe and the *s*. Thus the conventional plurals in the following sentences are *i's, t's, Ph.D.'s, IOU's, 20's,* and so on.

> You should remember to clearly dot your *i's* and cross your *t's.*

Today some universities will hire only *Ph.D.'s.*
The salesman was left with only a handful of *IOU's.*
The temperature in Orlando rarely reaches into the *20's.*
During the *1970's,* the oil companies assumed increasing
control.
The prosecutor interrupted any *"if's," "and's,"* or *"but's"*
in the testimony.

The apostrophe has actually become optional in most of
these cases. In the modern-day thrust toward economy, spear-
headed by journalistic usage, the apostrophe is preferred only
when lower-case letters (*p's and q's*) and abbreviations with
periods are made plural. The apostrophe in all other cases is
optional, but the writer should feel free to put it in if it lends
an aesthetically satisfying appearance to what is being written.
Thus either plural form is correct.

Every child is taught the *ABCs* (or *ABC's*) in the first
grade.
The baby boom lasted through the *1950s* (or *1950's*).
To the report's final sentence the manager added two *l*s
and three *?s* (or *l's* and *?'s*).

(In the last sentence, the writer chose to use symbols for
greater visual impact. The names of symbols could have been
spelled out.)
We advise writers to be consistent above all. Using the
apostrophe is the more conventional practice, but neither
practice used conscientiously should confuse the modern-day
reader.

Mistakes with Apostrophes

Hotline callers are frequently tempted to use the apostrophe
in two situations they shouldn't: with proper nouns and with
clipped nouns. Because possessive forms and plural forms of
proper nouns sound alike (*Jones'* and *Joneses*), it is tempting
to spell them alike. Writers sometimes want to use an apostrophe to make *Jones* plural because they feel the integrity of
the name is respected that way. *Jones'* and *Lewis'* are the correct possessive forms of the singular but not the correct plurals;
Joneses and *Lewises* are the correct plurals. Nor are *auto's*

and *disco's* the correct plurals of *auto* and *disco* (these nouns are formed by "clipping" off part of the original noun—*automobile* and *discothèque*). The correct plurals are *autos* and *discos*. With proper nouns and clipped nouns the apostrophe is *not* optional.

Plurals Without *s*

More than ninety-nine percent of the nouns in English form their plural with *s* or *es*. All newly created words in the language and most nouns borrowed from foreign sources (except the few discussed in Foreign Plurals, pages 27–31) form their plurals this same way. But English does have several small classes of "irregular" nouns which don't add *s* or *es*.

Plurals with *en*

Only three nouns in Modern English add *en* to form the plural: *ox, oxen; brother, brethren; child, children. Brethren* is used today only in religious contexts; otherwise, *brothers* is the plural. *Children* is etymologically a double plural, the only one in English (adding *r* was one way of forming plurals in Old English).

Vowel-Changing Plurals

A small number of nouns in English form their plurals by changing their internal vowels. The most common of such nouns are these eight:

SINGULAR	PLURAL
foot	feet
goose	geese
louse	lice
man	men
mouse	mice
titmouse	titmice
tooth	teeth
woman	women

but

Churchmouse, dormouse, and other nouns whose last element is a member of this class are pluralized in this irregular fashion.

SINGULAR	PLURAL
mongoose (not etymologically related to *goose*)	mongooses

Unchanged Plurals

The plurals of some nouns, especially those denoting animals of the field (*quail, snipe*), wood (*deer, moose*), or stream (*fish, trout, salmon*), remain unchanged. The context usually reveals whether these nouns are singular or plural.

The problems with these unchanged plurals are threefold. The first problem occurs because we remember that under some conditions nouns like *deer* and *fish* can take *s* or *es*. This is true; they take the *s* or *es* when referring to kinds, types, or species of an animal. Thus *the deers of America* refers to the various species of deer in the country and not to the sum total of individual creatures. To refer to the individual creatures, use *the deer of America.*

A second problem is that a few nouns have an unchanged plural when the animal referred to is huntable but a normal plural ending in *s* or *es* in other contexts. Compare *waterfowl* to *barnyard fowls. Buffalo* may be unchanged in the plural in the hunting context, but not in other contexts. Both of the following are correct.

On the hunt, the hunters bagged two *buffalo.*

but

The most popular animals in the zoo are two new *buffalos.*

Several other nouns (e.g. *quail, snipe*) have an unchanged plural in the hunting context, but when the birds are on the table, they add *s* or *es*.

A third problem arises when a writer is uncertain and

assumes that other animal names have unchanged plurals. This can lead to

The municipal zoo has acquired three *bear* and two *lion*.

which is clearly incorrect.

With nouns referring to animals, the dictionary will indicate which nouns have alternate plurals. When an unchanged plural and an *s* or *es* plural are both cited, assume that the unchanged plural is appropriate for specialized contexts such as hunting. Use the "regular" plural in other contexts.

Foreign Plurals

When English adopts a noun from another language, it normally borrows the singular form and then makes it plural in the appropriate English fashion. Nouns have entered English from dozens of other languages, from Algonquian (*hickory*) to Yurak (*parka*). But the plurals of these borrowings do not usually enter English. We form the plurals by English rules. The plural of *bratwurst*, for instance, is *bratwursts* in English and not *Bratwürste* as in the original German.

But in some cases, particularly nouns borrowed from Greek and Latin, both the singular and the plural forms have been adopted. Thus we, as students in school, were faced with learning "irregular" plurals (irregular in English, that is). We learned to use *crises*, not *crisises*, as in

International *crises* always affect stock market prices.

and *alumni*, not *alumnuses*, as in

The *alumni* of the university have a history of generous financial support.

Memorizing these irregular plurals was simplified if we learned that they follow six or seven basic patterns or if we knew a smattering of Latin. But knowing both Greek and Latin thoroughly will not solve all the problems, because English is neither Greek nor Latin. (As words are borrowed from other languages, we begin to Anglicize them; that is, we turn them into English words. Anglicization can be a long process affecting the spelling, the pronunciation, and even the meaning of words. Usually we ignore such changes. We no longer spell *premiere* with an accent mark (') over the middle *e*, nor do we spell *role* with a circumflex (^) over the *o*.)

Basic Principles

There are two important points to remember when choosing the proper form of a noun adopted from a foreign language:

1. Keep in mind that nouns from foreign languages are Anglicized at different rates. Some have entirely lost, while others are losing, their original plurals. Others have preserved them. Determine which category discussed below includes the noun you are using.
2. In many cases you should use the foreign or irregular plural form in more formal writing situations, especially for a specialized audience or in a specialized context. For a nonspecialized audience and in general writing, the English regular plural form, if there is one, is acceptable. *Formula,* for instance, has two acceptable plurals: *formulae* for scientists or in a scientific context; *formulas* for general use.

In some cases Greek and Latin plurals have been retained as the plural forms in English, but in some other cases the foreign singular-plural distinction has been lost altogether. In still other cases foreign plurals alternate with English plurals, or foreign plurals have evolved into English singulars.

Preserved Foreign Plurals

These nouns have kept their original foreign plurals intact in English. Many of them are generally restricted to scientific and scholarly usage.

SINGULAR	PLURAL
addendum	addenda
alumnus	alumni
appendix	appendices (or appendixes)
diagnosis	diagnoses
erratum	errata
hypothesis	hypotheses
series	series
species	species
stimulus	stimuli

This category includes all nouns derived from Greek that end in *is* (*thesis, basis,* etc.). As a noun with a true foreign plural becomes more generally used, it usually acquires a regular English plural.

Regularized English Plurals

Many borrowed nouns are now pluralized by adding *s* to their singular form, in the regular English manner. These should give the contemporary writer of English no trouble. Only the Latinist or Hellenist would likely know the foreign plural forms. Nouns that have lost the foreign plural form include the following.

SINGULAR	ENGLISH PLURAL	LOST FOREIGN PLURAL
dogma	dogmas	dogmata
gymnasium	gymnasiums	gymnasia
opus	opuses	(opera)
stadium	stadiums	stadia
status	statuses	status

(*Opera* remains in English as a singular referring to a play set to music; it has an English plural, *operas*. *Opus* remains in English as a singular used to number musical compositions; its English plural is *opuses*.)

The foreign plural forms of a few nouns have become singular in English. Their foreign singular forms have disappeared.

LOST FOREIGN SINGULAR	FOREIGN PLURAL/ ENGLISH SINGULAR	ENGLISH PLURAL
agendum	agenda	agendas
insigne	insignia	insignias
(opus)	opera	operas

Alternate Foreign/English Plurals

The nouns which give writers problems involve a choice of usage. Some have two plural forms, one in specialized usage and another in general usage. One should be used in specialized writing; the other is otherwise used. For example, the plural of *formula* is *formulae* for chemists but *formulas* for nonscientists and in nonscientific contexts. For the botanist, *fungi* is the plural of *fungus;* for nonscientists, the plural is *funguses.* The music devotee uses *celli* and *concerti* as the plural forms of *cello* and *concerto,* but most of us use *cellos* and *concertos.* For most words in this category, specialists use the foreign singular and plural, but nonspecialists use the Anglicized plural.

Some words in this category have different plurals when they have different meanings. The more restricted and specialized meaning employs the foreign plural; the more general meaning employs the English one. Here we detect the dynamics of the language at work. When we refer to the appendages on the tops of our houses which receive television signals, we use *antennas,* the plural of *antenna.* When referring to the appendages on an insect, we use *antennae.* The foreign plural has been preserved for restricted use, while a new plural has been created for other meanings. Specialized usage is always more conservative than usage in the everyday workaday world. A form which is acceptable in a scientific, technical, or scholarly context may not be in general usage, and vice versa. This is why a dictionary frequently lists two forms.

The following nouns have two alternate plural forms in English:

SINGULAR	SPECIALIZED/ FORMAL PLURAL	NONSPECIALIZED PLURAL
antenna	antennae	antennas
cactus	cacti	cactuses
cello	celli	cellos
concerto	concerti	concertos
curriculum	curricula	curriculums
focus	foci	focuses
formula	formulae	formulas
larva	larvae	larvas
memorandum	memoranda	memorandums
referendum	referenda	referendums
syllabus	syllabi	syllabuses
vertebra	vertebrae	vertebras
virtuoso	virtuosi	virtuosos

Alternate Foreign/English Singulars

As far as we can determine, only one noun has a specialized/formal plural form that is regularly used as the nonspecialized singular.

SPECIALIZED/ FORMAL SINGULAR	SPECIALIZED FORMAL PLURAL/ NONSPECIALIZED SINGULAR	NONSPECIALIZED PLURAL
bacterium	bacteria	bacterias

Two other nouns, *criterion* and *phenomenon*, are sometimes treated similarly in speech. Thus, the actual plural forms, *criteria* and *phenomena*, are assumed to be singular, and the forms *criterias* and *phenomenas* are assumed to be the appropriate plurals. These plurals are unacceptable, however, in both formal and general writing, and they should be avoided. For further information on these two nouns, see below.

The Exceptions—*data, media, criterion, phenomenon*

Four of the most commonly used nouns from Latin and Greek are exceptions to the patterns we have discussed. In the specialized usage of chemists, linguists, and other scientists, *data* is a plural (the singular is *datum*) meaning "pieces of information." But in general usage, *data* has become a mass noun (like *information*) meaning "a mass of facts or information." *Data* is now generally used as a singular. In general usage, there is no plural; the word *datas* doesn't exist.

Media is a plural form of *medium* and refers to the agencies of mass communications, especially television, radio, and newspapers. Although there is a tendency to treat *media* as a collective singular noun (a noun that groups together several like people or things), this is not yet acceptable in writing.

Use a plural verb with *media* and avoid the form *medias* altogether.

Criterion and *phenomenon* each have two plural forms, the original forms *criteria* and *phenomena* and the more recent *criterions* and *phenomenons*. *Criteria* and *phenomena* should be used in specialized writing, but all four forms are acceptable in general writing.

Mistaken Plurals—Mass Nouns and Measure Nouns

Pluralizing a noun in English is not as easy as merely discovering its correct plural form. One class of nouns—mass nouns, such as *luck, water, information, equipment*—cannot be made plural, but hotline callers frequently want to do so. Another class of nouns, those that measure distance, time, volume, and weight (such as *foot, mile, week, gallon, ton*) are usually not made plural when they are used as part of an adjective (*a seven-foot-tall basketball player, a three-week vacation, a five-gallon can, a hundred-ton load*. See pages 33–34.

Mass Nouns

Mass nouns refer to things that cannot be divided into discrete units—*sand, water, knowledge, air, music, leisure,* and so on. They differ from collective nouns, which refer to groups of things considered as a single unit—such as *committee, jury, flock,* and *family* (for a full discussion of collective nouns, see pages 44–46). Mass nouns take singular verbs and are *always* singular in form except in some poetic or idiomatic phrases (*the sands of time, the Father of Waters, to give oneself airs,* etc.). And a few mass nouns such as *love* and *experience* can be made plural when the writer wants to refer to individual instances, as *many loves* and *many experiences*.

The only idiomatic way to pluralize most mass nouns is by including them in a plural phrase such as *types of, pieces of,* or *sets of*. Rather than adding an *s* to *equipment* and changing *is* to *are* in the following sentence,

> Some equipment is manufactured by the company; others are purchased.

the writer should first paraphrase *equipment* as *type of equipment* and then pluralize *type*, changing *is* to *are*.

> Some *types of equipment* are manufactured by the company; others are purchased.

For the same reason, *clienteles* should not be used as the plural form of *clientele* in

> The bank offers many services to its various *clienteles*.

The idea in this sentence is better phrased by the addition of *kinds of* or *types of* or a similar phrase.

> The bank offers many services to its various *types of clientele*.

The result is a much smoother and more logical sentence.

Measure Nouns as Modifiers

The nouns that refer to distance and area (*mile, foot, acre*), time (*minute, month*), and weight and volume (*ton, gallon, bushel*) are called measure nouns. When they stand alone in a sentence and are not part of an adjective preceding a noun, they are usually made plural in one of the ways already discussed in this chapter.

> Surrounding the house was a stone wall which was five *feet* high.
> The weight capacity of many elevators is only two thousand *pounds*.
> The lake in Riffley Park is seven *acres* in area.

(The only exception in Modern English is *foot*, as in phrases like *five foot ten* and *six foot one*, which measure feet and inches. This reflects a special grammatical case in Old English, but using *feet* in such phrases is also acceptable, as in *six feet one*.)

However, if sentences with measure nouns are phrased so that these nouns become parts of noun modifiers and precede other nouns, several problems arise: Is the measure noun plural? Is it possessive? Does it take a hyphen? In other words, if we wish to rephrase *a layoff of three weeks*, should it be *a three-week layoff, a three-weeks layoff, a three-weeks' layoff,* or *a three week layoff*? Which is correct?

Measure nouns appearing in modifiers should always be hyphenated. They may or may not be plural and they may or may not be possessive, depending on what is being measured.

With a noun that measures distance or area and that is not preceded by a numeral, either the possessive (*a mile's drive*) or the simple (*a mile drive*) form of the noun is acceptable. With a numeral, the noun must be singular and cannot be possessive.

> A five-*foot*-high stone wall surrounded the house.
> Riffley Park has a seven-*acre* lake.
> a twenty-*mile* race
> a three-*meter* jump

With a noun that measures time and that is not preceded by a numeral, either a possessive (*a year's delay, an hour's walk*) or a simple (*a year delay, an hour walk*) form of the noun is acceptable. With a numeral, writers can choose either a singular or a possessive plural noun, whichever is more idiomatic. *An eight-hour day* requires the singular, but *six-months' pay* requires the plural and is possessive. Either *a three-weeks' vacation* or *a three-week vacation* is idiomatic and permissible. If either a singular or a possessive plural can be used, the possessive plural is more often preferred by style guides. Grammatically, it makes no difference whether one writes *a three-week vacation* or *a three-weeks' vacation*, but a writer who chooses the possessive must remember to put the apostrophe after the *s*. At the Writer's Hotline, we usually advise using the singular because the added *s'* makes sentences look cluttered.

With a noun measuring quantity or volume, only the singular, nonpossessive form can be used, whether or not a numeral is also used.

> Many elevators have only a two-thousand-*pound* capacity.
> a ten-*ton* truck
> a fifty-*gallon* drum

3

Subjects and Verbs: Be Sure They Agree

In English the subject and verb of a sentence or a clause should agree in number. Singular subjects require singular verbs. Plural subjects require plural verbs. Simple enough, but agreement is often not as simple as it is in

> The corporation's *vice-president has* taken a long vacation.

or in

> *Birds fly* south for the winter.

In English, problems of subject-verb agreement occur only when subjects are in the third person and verbs are in the present tense (except for the verb *be* in the past tense *was/were* and the verb *have* in the present perfect tense *has/have*). Yet these problems are plentiful. Theodore Bernstein, longtime contributing editor and language watchdog of *The New York Times,* once concluded that "errors in agreement between subject and verb are the most common ones that writers make." Why?

Sometimes the subject and the verb are separated by intervening, distracting prepositional phrases or even entire clauses. Sometimes the subject follows the verb, and sometimes it is difficult to know whether the subject is singular or plural. However, if you take a problem sentence step by step through this chapter, perhaps consulting a good dictionary for nouns or verbs with special problems, you should be able to solve any problem you have with subject-verb agreement. If a problem still remains, or if the sentence sounds awkward, it is time to rewrite.

The first and most important step in dealing with a problem

sentence is to identify the subject. The subject is the thing the sentence is about, the WHO or the WHAT, whether the WHO is a person, several people, or a company, whether the WHAT is a building, a concept, or something else. The easiest way to locate the subject is to put Who? or What? in front of the verb to see what the answer is. For example, in the sentence

> Only one *person* in the executive branch *was* available for comment.

Who was available? One person. *Person* is the subject of the sentence.

And in

> The *typewriter* that the Smiths bought *costs* five hundred dollars.

What costs five hundred dollars? The typewriter. *Typewriter* is the subject of the sentence.

Finding the subject is frequently easy, but not always. This chapter will be concerned with those cases in which picking out the subject is tricky for some reason.

Locating the Subject

In many sentences the problem is to find exactly where the subject is located. Subjects don't always come immediately before verbs, so find the subject wherever it appears in a sentence. Don't let any other part of a sentence affect your choice between a singular and a plural verb. (The exceptions to this—verbs that have indefinite subjects—are dealt with below, pages 49–52.)

We are frequently tempted to make a verb agree with an object of a preposition next to a verb when the subject is several words away from the verb. But we can resist this if we take care to locate the subject of the verb first and to see whether the subject is singular or plural. For example, in

> The *date* of these invoices *is* January 21.

even though the plural noun *invoices* is closer to the verb, it is the object of the preposition *of* and not the subject of the sentence. We can easily see this by finding the WHO or WHAT word of the sentence. What is January 21? It is the date. *Date* is the subject, not *invoices.* Thus the correct verb is the singular *is.* Many other sentences are like this:

> Principal *interest* on federal securities *is* not guaranteed.
> The high *incidence* of hypertension, obesity, and heart disease *has* been attributed to dietary conditions.
> Which *one* of the envelopes *contains* the lucky number?

The WHATs of these sentences are the *interest,* the *incidence,* and *one.* Each of these subjects is modified and explained and added to by the prepositional phrase that follows it, but the subjects are the single words underlined. The verbs should agree with these words. Only *one* of the envelopes *contains* the lucky number. So do not be confused by prepositional or other phrases or by clauses that intrude between the subject and the verb.

Sentences with Inverted Word Order

Subjects are sometimes not easily identified because they follow verbs. One kind of sentence with inverted subject-verb order is called a "there" or existential sentence because it begins with the word *there* and expresses the existence of something. For example, in

> There *were* three disheveled old *men* on the bench outside.
> There *is* a *need* for more volunteers at the local veterans hospital.

the word *there* only introduces these sentences. We must look beyond the verb to find the subject before deciding to use a singular or plural verb. Often (but not always, and not in the second sentence above) the subject can be identified by turning a *there* sentence around, putting the subject before the verb, as

Three disheveled old *men were* on the bench outside.

When this is impossible, you can identify the subject by asking what the WHO or WHAT of the sentence is. In the second sentence above, it is the *need*. In the sentence below, it is a *flood*.

> There *is* likely to be a *flood* of complaints about the snow cleanup.

Note: When the subject is compound, having two or more parts joined by a conjunction, and the first element following the verb is singular, most grammarians allow the writer a choice between a singular and a plural verb.

> There *is/are* a *Xerox Sigma Nine* and an *IBM 8000X* at your disposal.

Of course, if the sentence is written with the subject first, the verb must be plural to match the compound subject.

> A *Xerox Sigma Nine* and an *IBM 8000X* *are* at your disposal.

And if the first element following the verb is plural, the verb must be plural.

> There *are* two *Xerox Sigma Nines* and an *IBM 8000X* at your disposal.

There are two minor exceptions to this. One occurs when the phrase *one or two* modifies the subject.

> There *are* one or two *items* left on the agenda.

The other occurs when the subject is singular in form but plural in interpretation (see pages 45–46).

> There *were* a *number* of expensive tools stolen over the weekend.

Style Note: As you may have noticed, sentences with *there* are less effective and less direct. Turn them around and re-phrase them without *there*, when this is possible.

> A *number* of expensive tools *were* stolen over the week-end.

The subject-verb pattern may also be inverted when phrases or words other than *there* begin a sentence.

> First among the people who benefited *were* the *ones* he trained.
> Among the services provided *are* risk *management* and financial *planning*.
> Not included in this report *are* any waste treatment installation *laboratories*.

In each of these cases, *were* or *are* is chosen because the subject is plural. Such sentences often present a pleasant change of pace to the reader.

Sentences with Normal Word Order

We have now examined two types of sentences whose subjects do not come directly in front of their verbs, but unfortunately there are pitfalls even in sentences whose subjects precede their verbs, as many Writer's Hotline callers have discovered. In some sentences, what follows the verb may seem to dictate the verb choice as much as the subject does, and neither a singular nor a plural verb is entirely satisfactory.

> The major factor for the success of the show *is* (or *are?*) the journalists who ask the questions. (*Is* is correct: there is only one factor.)
> Our greatest problem *is* (or *are?*) the long vacations our employees take. (*Is* is correct: there is one problem.)
> Share drafts *are* (or *is?*) one of the nation's most innovative programs for saving money. (*Are* is correct here.)

You will notice that the verbs here are forms of the verb *be* and that these sentences equate or identify two things, one singular and one plural, with each other (*factor = journalists, problem = vacations, drafts = one*). While the correct verb choice in these sentences depends, strictly speaking, on the nouns which precede them, the logic of sentences like these can always be improved by rewriting them to get rid of *is* or *are* (see pages 266–68) or by otherwise revising them.

The show's *success is* due primarily to the journalists who ask questions.

Our *employees take* long vacations, and that is our greatest problem.

The share *draft is* one of the nation's most innovative programs for saving money.

Often making both nouns (or a noun and a pronoun) singular or plural or turning the sentence around will create a better sentence.

Original
> The first *group* I want to discuss today *is* the professionals.

Improved
> The *professionals are* the first group I want to discuss today.

In helping hotline callers solve subject-verb agreement problems we have learned that apparent problems with subject-verb agreement are often caused by illogical or unidiomatic sentence. Rather than forcing a verb choice in such cases, the writer should restructure the sentence.

What Clauses as Subjects

One type of sentence is almost ready-made to present agreement problems: sentences whose subjects are clauses beginning with *what*. Normally, these sentences require a singular verb, even if a plural noun follows the verb and an awkward-sounding and unidiomatic sentence results. Here are some examples.

> *What is especially annoying about our chairman is* his bad manners. (One thing is annoying—his bad manners.)
> *What hotline callers want is* good answers. (Hotline callers want one thing.)
> *What seem to be accidents are* actually deliberate provocations. (Clearly *are* sounds better here than *is*.)

When, as in the last sentence, only a plural verb sounds

natural, the writer should choose it. Otherwise a singular verb is the better choice. A helpful rule of thumb we give callers is

> If *what* can be replaced by *the thing that,* use a singular verb.
> If *what* can be replaced by *the things that,* use a plural verb.

Fortunately, sentences with *what* clauses as subjects can easily be revised to create better, more direct sentences.

> Our chairman's bad *manners are* especially annoying.
> Hotline *callers want* good answers.
> The seeming *accidents are* actually deliberate provocations.

Compound Subjects

Compound subjects have two or more parts joined by a conjunction (*and, or,* or *nor*). A compound subject with *and* is nearly always plural, no matter if any or all of its parts are singular.

> Your *interest* and *concern are* appreciated by all of us.
> That *kind* of duty and that *kind* of status *are* being phased out.
> The *knowledge* and *technology* which would permit the development of nuclear fusion *are* not available at this time.

Only when a seemingly compound subject with *and* functions as a unit or when the parts of the subject are identical in meaning is a singular verb required.

> *Chicken and dumplings is* a favorite dish in the South.
> The *chairman* of the board and the chief *stockholder* of the company *is* Dr. Roger K. Easson.

Subject-verb agreement with compound subjects joined by *or* or *nor* is quite a different story, however. Several hotline callers have had the notion that any subject having two or more parts joined together must logically be plural and thus require a plural verb, but they have been wrong. In sentences whose subjects are joined by *or, either . . . or, nor,* or *neither . . . nor,* regardless of how many parts the subject has and even though some of the parts are singular and some are plural, the verb agrees with the part of the subject *closest* to it. For example, in

> Either the athlete or the *agents are* holding up negotiations.

and

> Neither the plaintiff, the defendant, nor the *lawyers were* present at the final ruling.

agents and *lawyers* are closest to the verbs, and therefore the verbs are plural. If the sentences are rewritten as

> Either the agent or the *athlete is* holding up negotiations.

and

> Neither the lawyers, the plaintiff, nor the *defendant was* present at the final ruling.

athlete and *defendant* are closest to the verbs and dictate that the verbs be singular.

Style Note: When a singular and a plural subject are joined by *or* or *nor,* the preferred style places the plural subject next to the verb, as in the first examples directly above. This makes the sentence sound more idiomatic. It also agrees with our intuition that subjects with *neither . . . nor* are in some sense plural; in the examples with *neither . . . nor* above, all the individuals were absent.

When two or more singular nouns are joined by *neither . . . nor,* most grammarians advise a singular verb but leave the choice up to the writer. Most writers choose the singular verb, so that they treat *either . . . or* and *neither . . . nor* consistently.

> Neither the generator nor the carburetor *was* (or *were*) in good working condition.

Complex Subjects

At first glance, complex subjects look very much like the compound subjects we have just looked at.

The pickups, but not the van, *were* demolished in the pileup.

The entire *family,* including both of the children and all of the dogs, *is* going on vacation.

The *producer,* as well as all the actors, *was* pleased.

But look at the logic of these sentences and examine closely what the basic idea of each sentence is. The *pickups were* demolished. The *family is* going. The *producer was* pleased. The phrases following the subjects provide additional information, but they are not crucial parts of the subject. They are added on as a kind of afterthought.

The most frequent phrases found in complex subjects are *as well as, together with, along with,* and *in addition to.* Whereas the conjunction *and* joins whatever follows to a subject, these phrases do not, and nouns introduced by these words should not influence the choice of verbs. For example,

The *design* of the magazine, as well as its content, *has* been devised for a specialized audience.

has as its basic point that the design of the magazine has been specially devised. The comment about the magazine's content is only an additional or parenthetical remark.

To show that such phrases are not parts of subjects, we can shift them around in sentences.

Objectivity, together with independence, *is* the hallmark of our profession.

Together with independence, *objectivity is* the hallmark of our profession.

Objectivity is, together with independence, the hallmark of our profession.

Each of these sentences emphasizes the objectivity. If a writer wishes to state that both objectivity and independence are the hallmarks of the profession, the conjunction *and* should be used. Rephrasing sentences with conjunctions changes the emphasis.

Objectivity and *independence are* the hallmarks of our profession.

The *design* and *content* of the magazine *have* been devised for a specialized audience.

To show that such a phrase as *together with independence* is not part of the subject, the writer should set it off clearly from the rest of the sentence with commas.

Collective Subjects

Frequently difficulties with subject-verb agreement arise because we cannot decide whether the subject word is singular or plural. The two groups of words that present problems in this regard are collective nouns and indefinite pronouns and nouns.

A collective noun is one which groups together several like things or people. If the individuals making up the collective term are thought of separately, the verb should be plural; if they are being viewed as a group, the verb should be singular. In the following sentences, the words *crowd, flock, tribe,* and *Board* each refers to a group, but each group is treated as a single set, rather than as a collection of individuals.

> A *crowd* of hungry men *is* waiting at the front of the building.
> A *flock* of snipe *descends* upon the park every spring.
> A *tribe* of Indians *was* to send a delegation to Washington.
> The Tennessee State *Board* of Regents *is* to meet at noon today.

The men are gathered into one crowd, the snipe into one flock, the Indians into one tribe, and the regents into one board. The verbs should be singular, and we see this quite clearly when we remove the prepositional phrase that follows the subject word to get *A crowd is waiting, A flock descends, A tribe was to send,* and *The Board is to meet.*

Typical collectives are words like *team, committee, family, jury,* and *group.* Each of these words requires a singular noun when the group, as a group, is being discussed.

> The *team has* a long winning streak. (the team as a group or unit)
> The *committee is* taking its final vote now. (the committee as a group)

But sometimes we may wish to consider the team members or committee members as individuals. In such a case a plural verb is required, and it is usually more idiomatic to add a phrase to indicate that the individual members of the group are meant.

> The *members* of the team *are* playing to their fullest potential.
> The committee *members are* taking a roll-call vote.

We have changed the subject word of each sentence to *members*. This avoids the grammatically correct but unpleasing sound of *The committee are taking a roll-call vote*.

To test whether a subject requires a singular or a plural verb, try to add a phrase to your sentence. If such a phrase as *the members of* or *the parts of* seems appropriate, the emphasis of your subject is plural and you need a plural verb. If *as a whole* or *together* seems appropriate, the emphasis is singular and you should choose a singular verb. Thus, the difference in verb choice is often a matter of emphasis, not one of right and wrong. The same action may be construed either as singular or plural grammatically:

> Member by member, the entire *jury* is being polled by the judge.
> The *members* of the jury *are* being polled by the judge.

The action may be viewed as collective or as individualized. The form of the verb and sometimes an added phrase or two will reflect the writer's choice.

As we were writing this section, we became increasingly impressed by the number of nouns which can be used as collectives. Even such ordinary words as *row* and *dish* often act as collective nouns.

> That *row* of onions *is* doing well.
> A *dish* of peas *was* spilled on the floor.

But don't panic. When these words act as collectives, they do not present any problem. Simply ignore the prepositional phrase that intrudes between the subject and the verb.

Exceptions: A small group of collective nouns, including *number*, *total*, and *variety*, take a singular verb when preceded by the definite article (*the*); *number* takes a plural verb when preceded by an indefinite article (*a* or *an*).

> A large *number* of trailers *were* demolished by the storm.
> The *number* of trailers demolished in the storm *stands* at thirty.

Total and *variety* are not so clear-cut. While always singular when preceded by *the*

> The *total* collected in the fund drive *was* $10,000.
> The *variety* of emergency equipment aboard the plane *was* astounding.

they are only sometimes plural when preceded by *a*.

> A *total* of fifteen prizes *were* awarded at the annual banquet.
> A *total* of ten thousand dollars *was* collected in the fund drive.
> A *variety* of life-insurance plans *is* (or *are*) available.

The emphasis of the last sentence will be changed slightly by your choice of verb, throwing the weight onto the range of plans (*A variety of plans is available*) or onto the number of plans (*A variety of plans are available*).

Collectives Expressing Amounts

Collective subjects having to do with sums, measurements, and quantities are seemingly plural in form but must be viewed as singular for agreement purposes. These subjects involve something which is measured or counted but which is treated as a unit. A recent hotline caller who was writing a letter to a television network wanted us to support her claim that the titles of two programs, *Three's Company* and *Eight Is Enough*, had subject-verb agreement errors. We finally persuaded her that this was not true, since the subjects are collective, indivisible units and must take singular verbs.

When the subject expresses a specific amount, the verb is normally singular.

> Seven thousand eight hundred *feet is* considered a long walk.
> Twenty *yards* of concrete *was* poured at the front of the building.
> Three *days* of snow *has* left Buffalo paralyzed.
> Thirteen million *dollars was* the low bid.

We can write *twenty yards of concrete were poured* only if there were several separate pourings. We can test whether such subjects are singular by adding a phrase like *one at a time* or *one by one* to the sentence in question. If the sentence makes sense with the added phrase, the subject is not collective and a plural verb is required; otherwise, the subject is collective, and it requires a singular verb.

> Five hundred *bushels* of corn an acre *is* a good harvest. (We certainly cannot insert *one at a time* or *one by one* here.)
>
> Five hundred *bushels* of corn *were* sold at the market yesterday. (The bushels were sold one at a time or in several groups.)

In the first sentence, the five hundred bushels is viewed as a unit, but in the second sentence, they are not.

If two specific amounts are added together, the writer may choose either a singular or a plural verb. Both are acceptable.

> *Eight and eight are* (or *is*) *sixteen.*
> *Two and two is* (or *are*) *four.*

Collectives Ending in *s*

Most nouns ending in *s* take plural verbs, even those such as *trousers* and *scissors*, which refer to single objects. But many nouns ending in *s* (such as *news*) are collective and take singular verbs. Names of diseases (e.g. *measles, rickets, mumps*) often end in *s* but are always singular. *United States* is normally singular but is often plural (as in *these United States*) in legal documents and in political rhetoric.

The real troublemakers are the nouns ending in *ics* such as *politics, statistics, mathematics, linguistics, graphics,* and *athletics.* When these words (and others such as *public relations*) refer to a field of study or to a body of knowledge, they are singular and require a singular verb:

> *Ethics is* a demanding subject.
> *Physics is* considered an exact science by some people.
> *Athletics is* compulsory at most colleges.

When these words refer to the specific practice of the art or science, they require a plural verb:

The *ethics* of the committee's decision *are* questionable.
Outdoor *athletics are* enjoyable.

Generally, if the *ics* word is modified in some way, it will take a plural verb. When it is modified (whether by an adjective, a prepositional phrase, the article *the,* or anything else), it refers to the practices in a specific time or place or under specific circumstances. Note the following comparisons.

Politics is a dirty business.

but

Politics in 1972 *were* dirtier than usual.

and

The *politics* in Washington, D.C., *are* always unpredictable.

and

Mathematics has never been clear to many people.

but

The *mathematics* of stellar gases *are* clear to only the experts.

and

Statistics is a branch of mathematics.

but

The congressman's *statistics were* too confusing to be of any help.

A Reminder: Consult the usage notes of a good dictionary if you think a particular word may require special handling. Somewhere in the body of the definition or in a usage note preceding or following the definition, a good dictionary will steer you to the usual usage of a word. For instance, if you look up *scissors,* your dictionary should say that the word is always plural in form and takes a plural verb, as *The scissors were lost.* It should also indicate, perhaps through an example, that the only way to have more than one scissors is to have two or three *pairs* of them.

Did your dictionary tell you all of that? Most of it? The word *trousers* works exactly the same way.

Indefinite Subjects

Perhaps the most perplexing subject-verb agreement problems involve sentences with indefinite subjects. Such words as *each, someone, all, none*, along with fractions, are indefinites because they do not refer to one definite person or thing. For our purposes here we'll divide indefinites into four classes.

The first class of indefinites includes the following words:

anybody	everybody	no one
anyone	everyone	one
anything	everything	someone
each	much	something
either (when there is no following *or*)		

When used as subjects, these words always require singular verbs.

> *Someone* in each department *has* the responsibility of writing a weekly progress report.
>
> *Everything* the industry proposed *was* rejected by the union.
>
> *Either* of the candidates *is* capable of keeping his temper during a debate.
>
> *Anything* you want *is* in Alice's restaurant.

These indefinites are singular because they make a statement about one person or one item at a time. (*Everyone* and *everybody* are sometimes exceptions to this for purposes of pronoun agreement, but see pages 70–73.) Each verb is singular, even if the prepositional phrase following contains a plural noun, as in *either of the candidates*. This statement refers to each candidate; either *one* is able, in other words. The sense of the subject is thus singular. This becomes clear when *of the* is deleted and the *s* on the end of *candidates* falls away:

> Either *candidate is* capable of keeping his temper during a debate.

Often, however, rephrasing the sentence with either *each* or *both* produces a more idiomatic wording.

> Both *candidates are* capable of keeping their tempers during a debate.

Note on *each*: When *each* is the subject by itself, a singular verb is required.

> *Each* of us *is* asked to contribute five dollars to the fund.

(This is made even clearer if *one* is added: *Each one of us . . .*) But when *each* follows the subject, it does not affect the choice of verb. Often a plural verb is required.

> *We* each *are* asked to contribute five dollars to the fund.

Note on *neither*: When neither alone functions as the subject and is followed by a prepositional phrase, it can be construed as either singular or plural. The choice of verbs is up to the writer.

> *Neither* of the candidates *are* capable of holding their tempers.

or

> *Neither* of the candidates *is* capable of holding his temper.

Often using indefinite pronouns in the first group can force a writer into an undesirable pronoun usage, as in the last sentence above (one of the candidates may be female). On pages 73–75, we have presented several ways to write around such problems.

The second class of indefinites includes words which may refer to groups of things, to single things, or to parts of things. Among the indefinites in this group are the following:

all	none	some
any	one-half	two-thirds
more	percentage	other fraction
most	(percent)	words

These words may be singular or plural, depending on the context. And the context which must be considered is the word or phrase the indefinite subject refers to. Look at these two sentences:

> *One-half* of the class *is* sick with the flu.
> *One-half* of the students *are* sick with the flu.

These sentences say basically the same thing, of course. But in the first sentence, *one-half* refers to one *class*, a single thing. A singular verb is thus needed. In the second sentence, *one-half* refers to many (i.e. more than one) students. A plural verb is required.

The number of the subject can frequently be determined by referring to the word or the phrase which explains the subject. But this is true only if the subject is an indefinite; otherwise the prepositional phrase should be ignored (see pages 36–37).

> *Most* of the tree *has* been cut up for firewood.
> *Most* of the trees *have* been cut up for firewood.
> *All* of the cheesecake *has* been eaten.
> *All* of the cheesecakes *have* been eaten.
> Seven *percent* of the budget *has* been spent already.
> Seven *percent* of the voters in this country *are* Chicano.
> *Some* of the material *is* defective.
> *Some* of the materials *are* defective.

These indefinite pronouns are singular when a mass or a group is viewed as a whole but plural when the individual units are being considered. When an indefinite pronoun stands alone as a subject and there is no clue to its number either from a prepositional phrase or from anything else in the sentence, writers must ask themselves what a subject implies. A handy way to do this is to decide whether the subject has the sense of "much" or "many" (or "several"). If the subject is equivalent to "much," as in *all of the tree*, the subject is a collective, and a singular verb is required. But if the subject is equivalent to "many" or "several," as in *all of the trees*, a plural verb is needed.

Majority and *minority* can take either a singular or a plural verb in a given sentence.

> Barely a *majority* of Americans *have* (or *has*) graduated from high school.
> A *minority* of those polled *favor* (or *favors*) capital punishment.

Technically, *a lot* should not be in this second list of indefinites, but it works in the same way. It is plural when it is equivalent to "many."

> *A lot* of the products our company sells *are* unavailable elsewhere in town.

But it takes a singular verb when it means "much."

> *A lot* of the stolen money *was* never recovered.

The third class of indefinites includes only *none*. Because the word originated from the words *not one*, a few grammarians still insist that it should take only a singular verb. Most grammarians, however, rely on modern idiomatic usage and other criteria for determining whether a word is singular or plural, and these grammarians explain that *none* is more often plural than singular.

None should be handled in the same way as any of the indefinites in the second class above, which can be either singular or plural, except when a writer wants to be emphatic by using a singular verb with *none*.

> *All* of the pines *have* been cut for firewood.
> *Some* of the other pines *have* been cut for firewood.
> *None* of the pines *has/have* been cut for firewood.
> *None* of the cast *has/have* arrived on location yet.

In some cases it is more emphatic to replace *none* by *not one* or *no one*.

> *Not one* of the pines *has* been cut for firewood.
> *Not one* of the cast *has* arrived on location yet.

And how should the following sentence be handled?

> *None is/are* left on the table.

Here you must decide what *none* refers to before choosing the verb, as only you, the writer, know what was left on the table.

The fourth group of indefinites includes words that are always plural such as *both, few, many,* and *several*. When used as subjects, these words always take plural verbs.

> Very *few were* expected at the grand opening.
> *Both* of the candidates *have* assured me that they are willing to serve.

Titles, Names, Phrases

The names of companies and organizations, the titles of books and movies, and phrases or words which are being discussed as phrases or words are always singular.

> *Merrill, Lynch, Pierce, Fenner and Smith is* doing the audit.
> *A Tale of Two Cities was* written by Charles Dickens.
> *"Over the fence is out" was* our only rule.
> The word *"both" refers* to two items.
> *Davis Camper Sales brings* you the RV highlights of the day.

Phrases that act as subjects are always singular.

> *Leaving early is* considered poor manners.

Some phrases which look like compound phrases act as units.

> *Wear and tear* on the car *is* not tax-deductible.
> *Cash and carry is* an efficient way to conduct business.
> *Chicken and dumplings is* a favorite in the South.

If such a phrase (e.g. *chicken and dumplings*) can be preceded by *both*, it is not singular and requires a plural verb.

Agreement in Relative Clauses and Following *one of the . . .*

Verbs in relative clauses (clauses introduced by relative pronouns such as *who* and *that*) should agree in number with the subjects of the relative clauses. But since relative pronouns have no number, the verbs agree instead with the antecedents of the pronouns.

> The *people* who *are* fishing off the pier are not catching much.
> *Women* who *wish* to be more than secretaries make enemies.

Every *employee* who *desires* a better job should read the "Jobs Available" section of the company newsletter.

The verb in each clause agrees with the antecedent of the pronoun that introduces it. The verb can almost always be checked by inserting the antecedent for the pronoun in the clause and then choosing the proper verb.

Relative clauses involving *one of the . . .* or *the only one of the . . .* are not so straightforward. A plural verb is required after the phrase *one of the . . .* , even though there is a great tendency to use a singular verb, especially in speech.

> One of the things that *aren't* (not *isn't*) cheap is labor.
> If you are one of the members who *haven't* (not *hasn't*) paid, please call us immediately.
> Jane is one of the girls who *work* (not *works*) in the office.

In the above examples, the italicized verbs agree with the subjects of the relative clauses: *that* (which stands for *things*), *who* (which stands for *members*), and *who* (which stands for *girls*). They do not agree with *one* or anything else in the sentence. We at the hotline have had to settle several arguments over the correct subject-verb agreement in this kind of sentence, one a dispute between a husband and wife in Massachusetts that had lasted years. To be sure a plural verb is needed, a writer can turn a sentence around by starting it with *of*.

> Of the things that *aren't* cheap, labor is one.
> Of the members who *haven't* paid, if you are one, please call us immediately.
> Of the girls who *work* in the office, Jane is one.

If *only* precedes *one of the . . .* , a singular verb is needed.

> Carpentry is the only one of the careers presented in the home show that *appeals* to me.

When turned around, this sentence clearly requires *appeals*.

> Of the careers presented in the home show, carpentry is the only one that *appeals* to me.

4

Proper Substitution:
Being Choosy About Pronouns

Pronouns, the words that take the place of and refer to nouns, are the most common substitute words in English. Writer's Hotline callers more frequently ask about the proper use of pronouns than any other part of speech.

Pronouns are of seven different types: personal, interrogative, demonstrative, indefinite, reflexive, intensive, and relative. Each type has an indispensable function.

Personal pronouns stand for and refer to persons or things. Their use allows us to avoid the cumbersome repetition of nouns. Among the personal pronouns are *I*, *you*, and *they*. (See the complete list on page 57.) Other than *who* and *whoever*, personal pronouns are the only ones to have different "case" forms; that is, the form of the pronoun changes when its function changes (*I* is used as the subject, *me* as the object in a sentence).

Interrogative pronouns, those used in asking questions, are *who*, *whom*, *what*, and *which*.

Demonstrative pronouns allow a writer to point toward something mentioned elsewhere. The demonstrative pronouns are *this*, *that*, *these*, and *those*. When modifying nouns, they are sometimes called demonstrative adjectives (*this typewriter*, *these securities*).

Indefinite pronouns refer to one or more than one indeterminate person or object. Among the many pronouns of this type are *some*, *all*, *every*, *each*, *something*, *anybody*, *both*, and *everyone*.

Reflexive and intensive pronouns are those ending in *self* or *selves*, such as *myself*, *ourselves*, *himself*, *itself*, and *herself*. A reflexive pronoun refers and reflects back to the person(s) who or object(s) that are the subject of the sentence or clause. (*The senators voted themselves a raise*). Intensive pronouns are used to strengthen or emphasize an action or a statement (*The children themselves decorated the tree*). Like reflexive pronouns, they can be used only when they refer to what has already been mentioned in the sentence.

Relative pronouns (*who, whom, which, that, whose, whoever*, and sometimes *where* and *when*) relate one clause either to a noun (*The corporation that lost the most money was Chrysler*) or to the rest of the sentence (*Chrysler lost millions in the third quarter, which was entirely unexpected*).

Pronouns for Animals and Countries

The most frequent problem writers encounter with personal pronouns is whether to use the objective- or the nominative-case form (*he* or *him, I* or *me*), but our hotline callers have other pressing questions about personal pronouns as well. A woman phoned us one day to ask whether personal pronouns should be applied to animals. She was writing a note complaining about a neighbor's dog that was constantly getting into her garbage. Should she call the dog *he* or *she,* or could she refer to it as *it*? Use *it,* we advised her, because the animal's sex was clearly irrelevant to the point she was making. The pronoun *it* is appropriate for all animals and for infants up to about six months old whose sex is unknown or not relevant to the context and for those animals and infants who have not been referred to specifically by name. Another question is whether countries, ships, and similar entities should be referred to as *she* or *it*. Both are acceptable, but the use of *she* in reference to the United States, a ship, a plane, the moon, or another entity is a literary device that may lend to a piece of writing an unwanted flavor of being old-fashioned. Modern fashion is to use *it,* especially in reference to ships and planes.

Case of Pronouns

"Case" refers to the form of a pronoun (e.g. *I, me,* or *my*). This form varies with the function of a pronoun in a sentence. Modern English has only three cases—nominative (sometimes called subjective), objective, and possessive—and that is enough to confuse many of us writers. But Old English, used a thousand and more years ago, had five cases, and many other modern-day languages have half a dozen cases or more (Finnish, believe it or not, has fifteen).

Most pronouns in Modern English have nominative- and possessive-case forms, but only the pronoun *who* and the personal pronouns (except *it* and *you*) have distinct objective case forms:

NOMINATIVE CASE	OBJECTIVE CASE	POSSESSIVE CASE
I	me	my, mine
you (singular and plural)	you	your, yours
she	her	her, hers
he	him	his
it	it	its
we	us	our, ours
they	them	their, theirs
who	whom	whose
whoever	whomever	whosever

The nominative-case forms should be used when the pronoun is the subject of a sentence or of a clause (*I read the report, I read the report that she wrote*) and, in formal English, when it is a predicate nominative (as *she* in *It was she who had the accident*). The possessive-case forms are used to modify nouns by either directly preceding them (*our commitment, his memorandum*) or directly following them (*a commitment of ours, a memorandum of his*). The objective-case forms are usually used on all other occasions—when the pronoun is a direct object (*The market report upset us*), an indirect object (*The boss told us the news*), or an object of a preposition (*The story was told to us*). When a pronoun is the object of one verb but the subject of another, its proper case form depends on its function within its own clause (normally the subordinate one).

I hit the ball that *she* threw to me.
All candidates will support *whoever* wins the election.

As subjects of the subordinate clause, *she* and *whoever* are the proper choices.

There is one very general rule for when to use the nominative form of a pronoun. That rule is this:

Use a nominative pronoun as the subject of a verb, even if the verb is only implied (see pages 60–61). The exceptions to this, both minor, involve pronouns following forms of the verb *be* (see page 62) and pronouns which are the subjects of infinitives (see page 68).

In *all* other instances, the objective form of the pronoun is the proper choice. It sounds so simple, doesn't it? Clearly the correct pronoun is *me* in *John took a seat behind Doris and me* because the pronoun *me* (along with *Doris*) is an object of the preposition *behind* and is not the subject of any verb. The subject of the verb *took* is *John*. Where's the difficulty?

The problems arise when a writer doesn't use this rule carefully to test for every pronoun or forgets that the rule says "*a* verb." A sentence has as many subjects and verbs as it has clauses. This rule demands special attention when a pronoun occurs in a compound, when a pronoun may have an implied verb after it, and when the pronoun is either *who* or *whom*.

Pronouns in Compounds

A pronoun is in a compound when it is joined with a noun or another pronoun: *Sergeant MacDuff and I, my husband and me, them and us, my wife and I*. It is a careless, but often-made, mistake to assume that one form of a pronoun is always correct in a compound. Whereas nouns in compounds (*Mr. Jones and Ms. Baker*) never change their form, a pronoun or pronouns in a compound will change case depending on the compound's function. First you must determine what function the compound has in the clause: Is it the subject of a verb? Is it the object? The caller who asked whether *Johnny and I* or *Johnny and me* is correct couldn't be given an answer. We had to ask him to read his sentence, which turned out to be *Johnny and I will be out of the office this afternoon*. His pronoun was part of the subject of the verb *will be*, and thus *I* was required. If the sentence had been *The lawyer talked an hour with Johnny and I*, the caller would have been using the wrong case.

The easiest way to test your choice of pronouns in compounds is to cross out all of the compound except the pronoun and then read your sentence.

We ask you to assist Mr. Morris and *him/he.*

should be thought of as

We ask you to assist *him.*

and so the sentence becomes

We ask you to assist Mr. Morris and *him.*

And

The boss wants Tom Fowler and *me/I* in the field.

should be thought of as

The boss wants *me* in the field. (*Me* is the direct object of *wants.*)

and so the sentence becomes

The boss wants Tom Fowler and *me* in the field.

Isolating the pronoun before making the choice of forms allows you to use your ear, usually a dependable guide for choosing a pronoun that is used alone.

Undoubtedly the phrase which most often violates proper pronoun choice is *between you and I.* Educated people often use this, either because it is supposedly more elegant than *between you and me* or more polite, but the problem with the pronoun in the phrase is one of case, not one of politeness.

Besides isolating them, correct pronouns can be found either by reversing them or consolidating them. By reversing them, we have *between me and you,* which is obviously preferable to *between I and you.* By consolidating them, we have *between us,* clearly preferable to *between we.* Substituting the singular pronouns in the same case as *us* gives the correct *between you and me.*

Possessive Pronouns Used Jointly

When two possessive pronouns modify a noun, a writer can either put both pronouns before the noun or put one before and one after.

Your and *my* savings are being shrunk by inflation.
Your savings and *mine* are being shrunk by inflation.

Note: Do not use the awkward and incorrect *Yours and my*

savings here. If both of these sentences seem awkward (they do to us), the writer should either repeat the noun being modified or recast the sentence so that it has no possessive pronoun.

> *Your* savings and *my* savings are being shrunk by inflation.
> Inflation is shrinking what you and I have saved.

Consolidate the pronouns and write *Our savings* only if all your readers will know whose savings are whose.

Sentences with Implied Verbs

Sentences with compounds sometimes have too many words to allow quick and accurate pronoun choice, but some sentences have too few words. These sentences, including those that make comparisons with *than* or *as*, have verbs that are only implied. These implied verbs must be added before a writer can determine the function of the pronoun in the sentence. Which pronoun is correct in the following sentence?

> George likes his hamster better than *I/me*.

For George's sake, fill in a verb at the end before you try to answer. Depending on your choice, this sentence can mean either

> George likes his hamster better than he likes *me*. (The pronoun is a direct object.)

or

> George likes his hamster better than *I* do. (The pronoun is a subject.)

Good writers complete such comparisons, not only because they don't want to fuss over the pronouns, but also because adding all or part of a verb gives balance to a sentence and often clarifies its meaning. Also

> Most of the women John dates are much taller than *he* is.

is much smoother and less stilted than

> Most of the women John dates are much taller than *he*.

However, both sentences are technically correct.

A sentence which has an appositive (a word or phrase usually appearing next to a noun which explains or identifies that noun) sometimes presents difficulties. A writer must determine whether the appositive represents the subject of a verb or the object of a verb in order to choose the correct pronoun. Pronouns must agree with the word or phrase— elsewhere in the sentence—that they represent.

> Everyone in the west stands, especially Marc and *I,* was blistered by the sun. (As an appositive to the subject *everyone, Marc and I* is the proper choice.)
>
> The sun blistered everyone in the west stands, especially Marc and *me.* (Here *Marc and me* is an appositive representing *everyone,* which is the direct object in this sentence.)

Normally the way to test an appositive for correct pronoun choice is to phrase the sentence without the word that the appositive identifies.

> Marc and *I* were blistered by the sun.
> The sun blistered Marc and *me.*

Sometimes an appositive is separated from the noun it is identified with. A recent television commercial had the following sentence with an appositive.

> When Bobby's sick, I don't know who feels worse, *him* or *me.*

The pronouns *him* and *me* are actually in apposition to the word *who,* which is the subject of the verb *feels,* so the correct choice of pronouns should be *he* and *I.* But it would be un-idiomatic to go by the rule and write

> When Bobby's sick, I don't know who feels worse, *he* or *I.*

When a writer faces a choice between what is "natural" and what is "correct," rephrasing the sentence is a good idea.

> When Bobby's sick, I don't know which of us feels worse.

or

> When Bobby's sick, I don't know whether he or I feel worse.

Pronouns as Predicate Nominatives Following the Verb *be*

As a rule, the nominative form of a pronoun should be used after a form of the verb *be* when the pronoun is a predicate nominative (a noun or phrase which follows the verb and identifies or renames the subject). This rule is disputed by many grammarians of English, who have two good reasons for opposing it: (1) it is based on Latin and not English and (2) *It's I* and *This is he* are stilted and many educated speakers say *It's me* and *This is him*. Other grammarians continue to insist that nominative forms should always be used after *is*, *was*, or any other form of *be*.

Practically speaking, sentences such as *This is me/I* rarely occur in writing; they can certainly be avoided entirely by expressing ideas in other ways. We were amused one day by a hotline caller who told us how many ways he could avoid saying *I am he* or *This is he* when answering the telephone or the doorbell: *He is speaking* (or more simply *Speaking*), *You're talking to him, I am John Doe* (or whoever). All of these alternatives are more direct and more natural answers than *It is he*.

But often, it is more satisfying to use the nominative-case form in writing when the pronoun does not stand alone after the verb.

> Hosts for the meeting are Frank Weinbaum, John Martini, and *I*.
>
> It was *I* who recommended that you be promoted.

As a predicate nominative in either of these sentences, *I* is preferable to *me*. Still, these sentences can be rephrased if a writer is uncomfortable with the sound of the pronouns.

> Frank Weinbaum, John Martini, and *I* are hosts for the meeting. (Since a predicate nominative is equivalent to the subject, the sentence can frequently be turned around easily.)
>
> I am the one who recommended that you be promoted.

or more simply

> I recommended that you be promoted.

Using Reflexive Pronouns

Reflexive pronouns are those ending in *self* and referring to the subject of a sentence or a clause. In writing, they should be used only when they refer to the subject.

> By the end of 1982 the Memphis State Athletic Department will be paying for *itself*.
>
> He, by his actions, brings credit upon *himself*.

but

> His actions bring credit upon *him*. (Not *himself*, because *actions* is the subject here.)

Some people tend to use reflexive pronouns in speech instead of nominative or objective pronouns because reflexive pronouns seem to express a more polite and a slightly less direct relationship between a speaker and a hearer than do objective or nominative pronouns. In writing, however, the reflexive pronouns should be avoided unless they refer to the subject of a clause.

> One of my friends and *I* (not *myself*) were asked to speak to you.
>
> Mrs. Jones and *I* (not *myself*) will be out of the office this afternoon.
>
> We are writing to confirm the agreement arrived at between *you* (not *yourself*) and the XYZ Company.

To decide if a reflexive is to be used, the writer should either isolate the pronoun to test its form (you would always write *I was asked to speak to you* and *I will be out of the office this afternoon*) or determine whether the pronoun refers back to the subject of the clause or sentence.

Many of the sentences in which hotline callers want to use reflexive pronouns have passive verbs and thus are often weak sentences. These sentences call for revision, usually by turning them around; the pronoun problem then often takes care of itself. In the following two sentences reflexive pronouns are erroneously used:

> Her talent was not taken seriously by *herself* or by her associates.

Here are a few examples collected by *myself*.

They can be improved by giving them active verbs:

Neither *she* nor her associates took her talent seriously.
Here are a few examples that *I* have collected.

Writers should be especially careful not to use reflexive pronouns after *than, as,* or *such as*.

Good students such as *you* (not *yourself*) are encouraged to apply for the scholarship.
On the exam my older brother did much better than *I* did (not *myself*).

Who and *whom*

Few dilemmas seem to make writers shudder more than the one between the two words *who* and *whom*. The hotline gets no more frequent question about usage (with the possible exception of *affect* and *effect*) than it does about these two words. It's easy to see why. Most users of English (and we include ourselves here) either are somewhat inconsistent in using these pronouns or use *who* universally in speech. In school we're drilled on the complicated rules for using *whom* and learn it is the preferred pronoun in many situations, but we wonder how the teachers can keep it all straight. What usually happens is that, when we're unsure which one to use, we use the objective form *whom,* often erroneously, as did the candidate who came in third in a primary election and said, "I will support *whomever* is elected." In such instances a rule which is mistakenly or only barely remembered is misapplied, and a poor sentence is the result.

Why do writers get worried about *who* and *whom*? One reason is that some readers, often the office grammarians, make a point to be fussy, sometimes to the point of pedantry, delighting in the splitting of grammatical hairs. Our business at the hotline is to enable callers to express themselves most clearly and appropriately. But because there are many hair-splitters and writers who insist on strict application of rules, we will explain both the formal and the general uses of *who* and *whom*. (For a discussion of the difference between formal and general usage, see the Introduction.)

Here are the facts about *who* and *whom*:

1. *Whom*, the objective form of the pronoun *who*, is slowly dying out in English. This does not mean that English is decaying or that it is losing a way of making an important distinction in meaning. After all, *thou* and *thee* were used in Shakespeare's day, and their subsequent disappearance did not lessen the ability of English speakers and writers to communicate. *Who* is gradually replacing *whom* and becoming both a nominative and an objective pronoun.

2. The usefulness of *whom* depends not on the meaning a writer wishes to convey (no one will misunderstand you if you use *who* exclusively) but on the style and tone a writer wishes to adopt. It is not "bad grammar" to use *who* for *whom*. The practice shows that a writer is not interested in adopting a formal style.

The choice between *who* and *whom* is one between the nominative- and objective-case forms. The rule for using *who* is basically the same as that governing the other nominative pronouns such as *I*, *we*, *they*, and *he*.

> Use the nominative pronoun *who* when the pronoun is the subject of a finite verb or the predicate nominative after the verb *be*.

A pronoun's function as subject or object must be determined first in its own clause. In almost all cases, this clause follows the pronoun rather than precedes it. In the following sentences, the pronouns seem to be the direct objects of preceding verbs (actually the entire clauses beginning with *who* are the direct objects), but they are subjects of following verbs. Therefore, *who* is used.

> Parents have an open avenue of communication and never wonder *who* should be contacted.
>
> They wanted to hire *whoever* was the best applicant.

Sometimes the pronoun is the subject of a following verb when it seems to be the object of a preceding preposition (the entire clause beginning with *who* is actually the object of the preposition). Again *who* is correct.

> I would appreciate your comments concerning *who* is eligible for the job.
>
> We would like to give credit to *whoever* deserves the recognition.

Remember that the correct choice is *who* if the pronoun is the subject of any verb. Occasionally a parenthetical clause (*we think, she mentioned*) comes between the verb and the subject, but *who* is still the correct choice.

> The commission wants to know *who* (we think) is responsible for the accident.
> The press asked *who* (the mayor thought) would be a candidate.
> *Who* (shall I say) is calling?

These sentences are deceptive. While the pronouns in them are in one sense direct objects of the verbs in the intervening phrases, they are subjects of the following verbs, and thus *who* is required.

Using *who* and *whom* in Questions

Modern usage favors, and even conservative authorities permit, the use of *who* to begin any question. According to the strict, formal rule, a sentence should be carefully analyzed to determine the pronoun's function before the case of the pronoun is chosen.

> *Who/Whom* do you take me to be?
> *Who/Whom* do you want me to believe?

Those of us who remember how to turn sentences around in order to diagram them recognize that *who* is strictly correct in the first sentence because it is the predicate nominative of *be* (*You do take me to be who?*), and *whom* in the second sentence (*You do want me to believe whom?*). From our experience, there is little point in writers analyzing their sentences so painstakingly in such cases. In general usage *who* is always used in questions, regardless of its function in the sentence. Following general usage produces questions that sound much more natural.

> Formal: *Whom* did you invite to the planning session?
> General: *Who* did you invite to the planning session?

The Use of *whom*

Formal and general usage have different rules for using *whom*. In general usage, *whom* is required only immediately after a preposition (except when the pronoun is the subject of a following verb). *Who* is used in all other instances. (This is the rule that most newspapers and many other publications follow.)

The rule in formal English, on the other hand, reflects the traditionally expected usage. A writer who always wants to be "safe" will never be wrong in using *whom* according to the formal rule.

> In formal usage, use *whom* when the pronoun is the direct object, the indirect object, the object of a preposition, or the subject of an infinitive.

According to the formal rule, *whom* is the preferred form in all cases except when the pronoun is the subject of a verb or the predicate nominative of *be*. A writer who wishes to use this rule should first follow the rule for using *who* (see page 65) and then use *whom* elsewhere. Writers should carefully and consistently follow whichever rule they choose, whether the formal or the general.

The greatest mistake a writer can make with *who* and *whom* is to overuse *whom*. Every instance in which a writer employs *whom* should be justified by a rule set forth in this section.

Avoiding *who* and *whom*

For the writers who do not enjoy choosing between *who* and *whom*, there are sometimes ways to avoid the choice altogether. Often the indefinite *the person* can be substituted for the pronoun.

> Give the book to *whomever* you have chosen.

and

> I would appreciate your comments concerning *who* this might be.

can be rephrased as

> Give the book to *the person* you have chosen.

and

> I would appreciate your comments concerning *the person* this might be.

When *who* or *whom* is used as a relative pronoun (see page 76), *that* can usually be substituted for either of them; also the relative pronoun can often be omitted without actually changing the sentence.

> It is the customer *that* is always right. (*That* is used for *who.*)
> It is the customer (*that*) we must please. (*That* is used for *whom,* but the pronoun is optional.)
> Is there a person over the age of twenty-one (*whom/that*) we could use as a reference? (The pronoun may be deleted if the writer wishes.)

A newspaper in Georgia once phoned the hotline to ask about a headline. Is *who* or *whom* correct: *The child who/whom no one wanted*? While the answer to the question is *whom* (it functions as the object of *wanted*), our advice was to leave the pronoun out entirely in order to avoid the choice and to save space as well.

Using Pronouns as Subjects of Infinitives

When a pronoun precedes and is the subject of an infinitive, the objective case is normally used. This rarely creates a problem with personal pronouns (*me, her, them,* and so on) but it does with *who* and *whom*. *Whom* is used in formal English before infinitives, but *who* is usually used in general writing because *whom* often sounds forced.

> The party has asked *her* to run for office.
> No one expected *them* to arrive on time.
> The report contained information about *whom* to contact.
> I don't know *whom* (or *who*) to ask for directions.

Pronoun Reference: Singular or Plural?

Pronouns should be singular or plural depending on the singularity or plurality of their antecedents (the words they refer to). Writers should carefully make all pronouns agree with their antecedents, no matter how far apart in a piece of writing the two may be. It is especially easy to lose track of an antecedent from one sentence to another. Here is an example of this problem.

> Another selling technique of the 60s was the jingle. These catchy tunes would linger in the head and force the audience to remember the product being offered.

The inconsistency represented in these two sentences (*jingle* is singular, but *tunes* is plural) sometimes occurs in speaking or writing about an indefinite number of a general class of objects (a jingle in this case). The writer has three ways to avoid the problem: (1) Make all instances of a noun and all pronouns referring to it consistently singular (by starting the second sentence above with *this catchy tune* or *it* or *this*); (2) Make all instances of a noun and all pronouns referring to it plural (by ending the first sentence with *jingles* rather than *the jingle*); or (3) Restructure sentences in some way to obviate the problem of agreement. The sentences above, for example, can be joined by using *which,* making the second sentence a relative clause:

> Another selling technique of the 60s was the jingle, which would linger in the head and force the audience to remember the product being offered.

Some pronouns refer to collective nouns (nouns that group together several like things and handle them as a unit, such as *team* and *committee*). Collective nouns may be treated as either singular or plural for the purposes of pronoun agreement, depending on the emphasis the writer wishes. In most situations, however, it is better to stick with the singular pronouns.

> The investigating committee handed in *its* resignation this morning.

The line of customers began forming at eight o'clock. By nine *it* stretched around the block.

Syracuse beat Rutgers last night. *It* (or *They*) played very well. (In such a case, *they* is as acceptable as *it* and probably more idiomatic because of the idea of the second sentence. The second sentence can be improved by replacing the pronoun with something like *the entire team.*)

Using the plural pronoun emphasizes the people who make up the group. This can sometimes be further shown by adding a phrase like *the members of* to the collective noun. Writers who find themselves in a quandary over whether to use a singular or a plural pronoun can often repeat the noun rather than use a pronoun.

Syracuse beat Rutgers last night. Syracuse played very well.

Companies and organizations often like to personalize themselves by using a plural pronoun to refer to themselves. Either the singular or plural pronoun is acceptable here, depending on whether the writer wants to emphasize the institution as a whole or the people who make it up.

General Motors stands behind every one of *their* (or *its*) cars.

Johnson Laboratories stakes *their* (or *its*) reputation on *their* (or *its*) products.

The membership annually awards a prize for the person *they* feel (or *it* feels) has done the best job.

Agreement with *everyone* and Other Indefinites

Writing problems involving pronoun agreement most often occur when the pronoun's antecedent is a singular indefinite noun or pronoun, such as *anyone, somebody, everyone, a person,* and *a student.* These indefinites do not have specific antecedents and refer potentially to any one member of a group. Because they are singular in form and take singular verbs (see pages 49–52), the conventional handbook rule is that a singular pronoun must always be used to refer back to them. There are two major problems with this rule. First, many of these pronouns contain an idea of plurality. Second, since English has no common-sex singular pronoun (that is, a pronoun whose only use is to refer to one person of unspecified sex), the writer is forced to make reference to a person of one sex or the other even when he or she does not care to. The traditional response to this problem has been to use masculine singular pronouns. Feminists and others object —with justice, we think—that this tends to reinforce many of the stereotypes of what has been a male-dominated political and economic structure. Another common response is the use of plural pronouns in most references, whether the antecedent is singular or plural. But too often this leads to unsatisfactory sentences such as *When a person exercises regularly, their heart stays healthy.* (The tendency to use *they, them,* or *their* in similar situations has been strong in English for many centuries.) We think it is better to write around these situations in one of the ways we present on pages 73–75.

Not all indefinite nouns and pronouns are singular. Most indefinite nouns can be made plural, and a plural verb form and a plural pronoun are then used.

> We must serve our customers; *their* needs are our business.
> People who think *they* have a complaint must be listened to.

And some indefinite pronouns, notably *both,* are always plural and always take plural pronouns as well as plural verbs:

> Both (children) are loved by *their* parents.

Some indefinite pronouns (e.g. *some, most, none,* and *all*), as we explained on pages 50–52, may be either singular or plural.

> Some (portion of the wine) loses *its* vitality while on the shelf.
> Some (kinds of wine) lose *their* sharpness on the shelf.

The pronoun then agrees with the number of the noun in the prepositional phrase—*wine* or *wines*—even when the prepositional phrase is only implied.

But sometimes the same subject can be either singular or plural, and the writer's choice of verb and pronoun may change the nuance of the sentence.

> None of the boys was willing to help *his* teacher.
> None of the boys were willing to help *their* teacher.

Everyone and *everybody* are special cases. They clearly refer to groups of people. Most usage guides and grammar books claim that after *everyone* and *everybody* the use of plural pronouns is less standard than the use of singular pronouns. But with regard to grammar and logic, as well as prevalent and historical usage, writers are free to choose either a singular or a plural pronoun to refer to these two indefinites.* In some cases, especially when *everyone* and the pronoun referring to it come in different clauses, the singular is difficult, and sometimes impossible, to use:

> I advise everybody to plant it, . . . but always charge *them* to also plant Delaware and Catawba . . . (cited in the *Oxford English Dictionary Supplement* under *every*).

There is simply no way that the *them* of the second part of this sentence can be changed to *him*. The *everybody* refers to a group, to all the people that the county agent quoted here advises. To handle the sentence in any other way is to falsify the thought. Even in less complex sentences, the same problem arises. Using the singular in the following sentence is forced, unidiomatic, and probably inaccurate.

> The supervisor gave credit to everyone because *he* had done *his* job well.

Changing the pronoun *he* to *each one*, although it rids the sentence of ambiguity, leaves a singular pronoun, *his*, which, in these days of mixed work crews, is likely to be inaccurate.

---

* The *Oxford English Dictionary* gives an interesting glimpse into the tension between the prescriptive point of view and actual language usage. In the entries for *everyone* (listed under *every*, Section 10.c.) and *everybody*, the editors have indicated that these words are often used with plural pronouns because of the absence in English of a singular common-gender pronoun. The editors comment in one place that "this violation of grammatical concord"— that is, the use of the plural pronoun—is necessary, yet in another place they say that this use of the plural pronoun is incorrect. But within these entries, in the illustrative sentences, the pronouns used to refer to *everyone* or *everybody* are invariably plural, not singular. The writers cited include such stylists as Samuel Johnson, Lord Byron, and John Ruskin. Bergen Evans and Cornelia Evans, in *A Dictionary of Contemporary American Usage*, cite Cardinal Newman: "[a gentleman strives] to make everyone at their ease."

Those of us who object to using masculine pronouns to refer to a person of unspecified sex also object to using masculine pronouns to refer to each member of a mixed group:

> The supervisor gave credit to everyone because *each one* had done *his* job well.

Using the plural pronouns creates a more accurate and more idiomatic sentence.

> The supervisor gave credit to everyone because *they* had done *their* jobs well.

But however justified by meaning, history, and prevalent, idiomatic usage, the use of plural pronouns with *everyone* and *everybody* has considerable prejudice against it. A writer who uses *their* in

> Everyone having a valid ticket will have *their* money refunded.

may be accused of being illogical and ungrammatical. But the writer who uses *his* in

> Everyone having a valid ticket will have *his* money refunded.

may be accused of being sexist. It may be a tempest in a teapot, but conscientious writers often feel damned if they do and damned if they don't. So the most sensible way to handle the matter of pronoun agreement and the *only* way to play it safe all the time is to write around the problem in one of the following ways.

Avoiding Pronoun Agreement Difficulties

To avoid clumsy pronoun agreement or pronouns which may be considered sexist, the writer may use any of four options.

1. Vary the use of singular male and female pronouns in a piece of writing. Use a feminine pronoun (*she, her,* or *hers*) as often as you use a masculine one (*he, him,* or *his*). This combats stereotypes which the constant use of masculine pronouns may create, but this solution calls attention to the pronoun-switching and has not won wide acceptance.

2. If you wish to use a singular pronoun, use *he/she, his or her*, or similar pairs of singular pronouns rather than *they, them,* or *their*. These usages can be stiff and become awkward if used often.

> Each employee should receive *his or her* paycheck by Friday noon.
>
> Everyone who has a valid ticket will have *his or her* money refunded.
>
> Whoever is appointed will find *his/her* job difficult.

3. Pluralize an indefinite noun or rephrase an indefinite pronoun so that a plural results.

> Employees should receive *their* paychecks by Friday noon. (better than *Each employee should receive his paycheck by Friday noon.*)
>
> Those who have a valid ticket will have *their* money refunded. (better than *Everyone who has a valid ticket will have his money refunded.*)

And sentences like

> If an applicant has no college experience, *he/she* will not be given first consideration.
>
> If a student does all *his* work, *he* will receive a passing grade.

can be revised by pluralizing their indefinite nouns:

> If applicants have no college experience, *they* will not be given first consideration.
>
> If students do all *their* work, *they* will receive passing grades.

The last sentence still indicates that each student must do his or her individual work to pass.

4. Revise a sentence so that there is no need to use a troublesome pronoun.

> Employees should receive paychecks by Friday noon.
>
> Money will be refunded to each person having a valid ticket.
>
> Everyone must pay social security tax before becoming eligible for benefits. (better than *Everyone must pay his/her social security tax before becoming eligible for benefits*)

Everyone on the committee resigned. (better than *Everyone on the committee submitted his or her resignation*)
Whoever is appointed will find the job difficult.

Insisting on the singular pronoun sometimes leads to a silly sentence, as this one quoted by H. W. Fowler in *Modern English Usage*:

There must be opportunity for the individual boy or girl to go as far as *his* keenness and ability will take *him*.

Adding the other pronouns (i.e. writing *as far as his/her keenness and ability will take him/her*) is hardly better, if it is better at all. But the sentence can be effectively recast:

There must be opportunity for individual boys and girls to go as far as *their* keenness and ability will take *them*.

or, in a fuller rephrasing:

Children must be given opportunities to develop as fully as *their* individual keenness and ability will allow.

Sometimes sentences can even be recast in the singular without the problem of pronoun agreement:

There must be opportunity for the individual boy or girl to go as far as *each one's* keenness and ability will allow.

Rephrasing can sometimes be inconvenient, but it is always possible.
Even the troublesome supervisor and workers can be rephrased in either the singular or plural:

The supervisor gave credit to everyone because *each worker* had done an excellent job.

and

The supervisor gave credit to her entire crew because *all the workers* had done *their* jobs well.

(What about the *her* in this sentence? It makes a specific reference. Don't get so carried away with writing around pronouns that you hesitate to use them to refer to a specific known person. Remember that we have been working with indefinite pronouns, the ones that refer potentially to any member of a mixed group.)

The Relative Pronouns:
that, which, who/whom, and *whose*

Relative pronouns relate one clause to the rest of a sentence by referring either to a noun or to the entire sentence.

> Dr. Blount is the physician *who performed the surgery.* (*Who performed the surgery* relates to and describes the physician.)
>
> The Vannattas took a sudden vacation to Puerto Rico, *which surprised us very much.* (*Which surprised us very much* relates to and describes the rest of the sentence.)

The meanings of the principal relative pronouns of English —*that, which, who/whom,* and *whose*—overlap considerably and so do their uses. Hotline callers usually want us to tell them which one is "correct" in a particular sentence or to make a sharp distinction between *who* and *that* or between *that* and *which.* But in many instances writers have two perfectly acceptable pronouns to choose from.

Both *who/whom* and *that* can be used to refer to people, *that* being slightly less formal. (Some writers use *that* whenever possible to avoid choosing between *who* and *whom.*)

> The man *who/that* was driving the red Toyota had no insurance.

While *who/whom* can refer only to humans, or to animals when they are individually named, *that* can refer to both humans and nonhumans. *Which* is not used to refer to people.

Some writers would rather use *who* in referring to corporations, as in

> Nelson's is the company who cares.

These writers argue that they are viewing the corporation as a collection of people. Be that as it may, it is better to use *that* or *which* in referring to corporations.

Some writers, following the lead of usage guides and some grammarians, want to make a rigid distinction between the use of the words *that* and *which,* limiting the use of *that* to defining (restrictive) clauses and the use of *which* to descriptive (nonrestrictive) clauses. (For a discussion of restrictive and nonrestrictive clauses, see pages 139–41.)

> The fruit that is on the table is ripe.
> The fruit, which is on the table, is ripe.

This recently formulated rule is partially based on usage. *That* is used almost exclusively in defining (restrictive) clauses. It seems to have an emphatic thrust to it that is inappropriate for descriptive (non-restrictive) clauses, whether spoken or written. But the other half of the rule, confining *which* to descriptive (nonrestrictive) clauses, is consistent with neither the usage nor the tradition of English. This is even admitted by thoughtful grammarians promoting the rule. H. W. Fowler in *Modern English Usage* says about this rule that "it would be idle to pretend that it is the practice either of most or of the best writers." In short, he admits that this distinction between *that* and *which* is artificial.

And where does the rule come from, since it originates in neither usage nor tradition? Quite simply, this "rule" was invented by grammarians and usage commentators wanting to "improve" the language by creating an either/or rule. The grammarians may succeed—they have before—but for now, as Fowler admits, this distinction is not general, educated usage.

Either *that* or *which* may be used with a defining clause. *That* is perhaps more often used, but the choice depends on personal preference. *That* may sound better to a writer at certain times, *which* at other times. Nor is *which* to be preferred as being more formal or more cultured than *that*.

> The materials *that* (or *which*) were ordered yesterday arrived this morning.

In summary—

Which is used with either defining or descriptive clauses. You may or may not need commas to set off a clause beginning with *which*. *Which* never refers to human beings.

That in modern-day usage is used only with defining clauses. Its use with descriptive clauses is literary and archaic. You never need commas to set off a clause beginning with *that*. *That* is acceptable to use for human beings but is less formal than *who/whom*.

Who/whom is used with either clauses:

The personnel manager notified those applicants *who would not be hired*. (defining relative clause)

The personnel manager, *who had conducted the interviews*, hired five of the applicants. (descriptive clause)

Writers thus have much latitude in choosing relative pronouns. But frequently, writers needn't use a relative pronoun at all; *who, that,* and *which* can often be deleted.

New York is a city (*that/which* is) nicknamed "The Big Apple."

The writers (*that/whom*) we want to buy this book are the conscientious ones.

Good writers ask themselves where they can get rid of unnecessary words, including relative pronouns.

Whose/of which

Handbooks of an earlier day stated that the relative pronoun *whose* should refer only to humans or to animals and not to inanimate nouns (cars, houses, or whatever). Contemporary usage allows it to be used with all nouns, however. It is always better to employ *whose* than a clumsy *of which* construction that is sometimes the only alternative.

New York is a city *whose* nickname is "The Big Apple."

is much superior to

New York is a city, the nickname *of which* is "The Big Apple."

and

The essay *whose* style well represents the period, is difficult reading for moderns.

is much superior to

The essay the style *of which* well represents the period, is difficult reading for moderns.

5

Adjectives and Adverbs:
Using Modifiers

Adjectives and adverbs are the descriptive words of English. They add color, detail, sharpness, exactness, and life to writing. Adjectives modify and give further information about nouns; adverbs modify and give further information about verbs, adjectives, other adverbs, and sometimes entire clauses and sentences. Adjectives and adverbs are often confused with one another because they are similar in function and it is sometimes difficult to tell whether a given word is one or the other. Some writing problems, such as how to make the comparative and superlative forms, involve both adjectives and adverbs.

Choosing Between Adjectives and Adverbs

While adverbs often differ from adjectives by ending in *ly,* we cannot depend on the *ly* suffix to identify an adverb. *Fatherly, lovely,* and *kindly* are normally adjectives. *Leisurely* and *early* are both adverbs and adjectives, as are *slow, deep,* and *quick* (this latter group has alternate forms with *ly*—*slowly, deeply,* and *quickly*). We discuss below the problem of keeping straight adjectives and adverbs in all these cases. A writer who is unsure of using a word ending in *ly* as an adverb should consult a dictionary.

The function, and not the form, of a word determines whether it is an adjective or an adverb. Adjectives modify nouns. Except for noun modifiers that immediately precede other nouns and except for the articles *a, an* and *the,* any modifier that is not an adjective is an adverb. As stated earlier, many words (for example, *well, fast, slow*) can function as either adjectives or adverbs, and to complicate matters further, some verbs (for example, *feel, look, turn, stay*), depending on their meaning, can take either kind of modifier.

Differences Between Writing and Speech

In casual speech, *good, sure, real*, and many other words are used as adverbs to modify verbs, but in writing they are acceptable only as adjectives. The proper adverbs for writing are *well, surely, really*, and so on.

> Mexican imports sold very *well* (not *good*) in Japan in 1978.
> She was shaken up very *badly* (not *bad*) by the incident.
> A strong tremor forced local geologists to take the volcano *seriously* (not *serious*).

Adjectives and Adverbs After Verbs

In English, some adjectives modify nouns by preceding them (for example, *a crucial decision*) but others modify nouns by following certain verbs (for example, *the decision was crucial*). These latter adjectives, sometimes called predicate adjectives, appear in the position within a sentence that is usually held by adverbs, so writers are often tempted to use an adverb where an adjective is needed. The verbs that express no action and only connect the subject with the adjective are called linking verbs. These include *be, appear, become, seem*, verbs of similar meaning, and the verbs associated with our five senses—*feel, look, taste, smell*, and *hear* when they express a state of being rather than an action. When the words following them modify the subject the verb, then an adjective is required. Compare the following

> The survivors of the mine explosion *felt* their way *carefully* along the blackened passage. (The adverb describes the action.)
> The starlet *looked nervously* at everyone at the party. (The adverb describes her activity.)

with

> The survivors of the mine explosion *felt wary* about going underground again. (There is no action; only a feeling is expressed.)

The starlet *looked nervous* to everyone at the party. (This is only a description of her appearance.)

In the first set of sentences, the verbs are action verbs, and they are followed by adverbs that modify that action. In the second set of sentences, the verbs are linking verbs; they are properly followed by adjectives. Linking verbs can be roughly equated with a form of the verb *be*. Such verbs do nothing more than connect a subject and an adjective. In the sentences above, the survivors *are* wary and the starlet *is* nervous.

A few other verbs are occasionally used as linking verbs:

arrive	grow	run
come	keep	sit
continue	lie	stand
get	prove	stay
go	remain	turn (meaning "become")

When these verbs convey only a state of being, they are followed by an adjective. A writer who carefully determines whether a modifier gives information about a noun or about a verb will rarely have much trouble using modifiers after these verbs, even though dictionaries do not indicate when, or which, verbs can take adjectives. Note that with linking verbs there is often an implied phrase *to be*, or the verb is equivalent to a form of *be*.

The weather continued (to be) *cold* through early April.
The tip may prove (to be) *lucky*.
The victims lay unconscious for three hours before help arrived. (*Lay* is equivalent to *were* here)

Several hotline callers have asked whether there is a difference between

The Atchleys arrived in Knoxville *safe*. (*Safe* describes the condition of the Atchleys when they arrived.)

and

The Atchleys arrived in Knoxville *safely*. (*Safely* explains the manner of their arrival.)

The difference is one of emphasis and not meaning. Use either one, but don't fuss over the choice.

Sometimes an implied *to be* follows an action verb and dictates the use of an adjective. Writers of English should have no trouble with these either.

> The judge considered the witness's remarks (to be) *thoughtful*.

but

> The judge considered the witness's remarks *thoughtfully* before instructing the jury.

Adjectives and Adverbs After *feel*

Feel may be either a linking verb or an action verb. As a linking verb, the question arises whether it should be followed by *good* or *well*, by *bad* or *badly*?

In general, *good* and *bad*, which should always be used as adjectives in writing, are required after *feel*. *Well* is most often an adverb, but it is also an adjective meaning "in good health" or expressing a state of well-being (as in *Ten o'clock and all is well*). Thus, *I feel well* differs in meaning from *I feel good*. The first means "I feel in good health" and the second "I feel in good spirits."

Badly, once only an adverb, is increasingly used in speech after *feel* to mean "sorry" or "regretful." Thus, some speakers distinguish between *I feel bad,* meaning "I feel ill" and *I feel badly about it,* meaning "I regret it" or "I am sorry about it." This usage of *badly* as an adjective, however, is not yet acceptable in writing. *I feel badly* should be rephrased. The same is true for *I feel poorly*.

Do not add *ly* to the modifier after *feel* unless the verb clearly conveys an action.

> I felt *different* (not *differently*) about her remark after hearing the full story.
>
> I felt *horrible* (not *horribly*) after having three large desserts.
>
> We felt *carefully* (not *careful*) along the ledge for our footing.

Adjectives and Adverbs That Look Alike

Usually adjectives and adverbs are distinct, with adverbs being formed by adding *ly* to adjectives. But many modifiers, especially short ones, can be used as either adjectives or as adverbs. The following modifiers are like this. All of them are acceptable as adverbs in certain cases.

bright	first	rough
cheap	hard	sharp
close	high	slow
deep	late	smooth
direct	loose	soft
early	loud	straight
even	low	tight
fair	quick	wrong
fast	right	

Compare

> The DC-10 was *high* above the turbulent weather below. (as an adjective)

with

> The DC-10 can cruise *high* above any turbulent weather. (as an adverb)

and compare the following two sentences:

> In the Mojave Desert, U.S. Highway 8 is perfectly *straight* for over a hundred miles. (as an adjective)

with

> The Porsche turned off the highway and headed *straight* into the woods. (as an adverb)

Adverbs with Two Forms

All of the words listed above can be used as adverbs, but most of them can have *ly* added to them also (the exceptions to this are *early, fast,* and *straight*). The two adverb forms may not be interchangeable because sometimes a specific meaning demands either one form or the other, as in

Simmons punted the ball *deep* (not *deeply*) into the end zone.

The kidnapping affected the entire community *deeply* (not *deep*).

The Rogues played *hard* (not *hardly*), but still lost 3–2.

The Rogues could *hardly* (not *hard*) play their best in the downpour.

More often, however, writers have two acceptable, interchangeable adverbs to choose between. The choice has nothing to do with grammar, but rather with the idiom and rhythm of the sentence and with how forceful a writer wishes to be. The shorter adverbs are more idiomatic in direct commands, but most writers prefer the longer ones in most other cases. Writers are safe to rely on their ear in choosing the adverbs that sound more natural.

Adverbs without *ly*	Adverbs with *ly*
Play *fair* (or *fairly*).	The Yankees lost the game *fairly*.
Come *quick* (or *quickly*).	The police came *quickly* to the rescue.
Go *slow* (or *slowly*).	The prisoner went *slowly* to the gallows.

Much controversy has been generated over the supposed "incorrect" use of *slow* as an adverb. In fact, zealous, self-appointed watchers of the language have even torn down traffic signs that say DRIVE SLOW and GO SLOW. Both *slow* and *slowly* have been adverbs for centuries, however, and there is no basis for considering *slow* incorrect.

By now, you can easily see that not all words ending in *ly* are adverbs and that adverbs do not necessarily end in *ly*. Still, the great majority of words ending in *ly* are adverbs formed by adding the suffix to adjectives. In choosing the form that an adverb should take, cautious writers sometimes assume that adding *ly* to a word will safely give them an adverb. Unfortunately, this often leads to unnecessary and unnatural adverbs such as *thusly, muchly, firstly*, and others. And rather than trying to add the suffix to an adjective already ending in *ly*, rephrase the sentence with a prepositional phrase ending with *manner* or *way*.

Professor Fisher treats all his students in a fatherly way.

Since there are so many exceptions in handling words with *ly*, we advise writers to be conservative in attaching the suffix to words and, when in doubt, to check the dictionary to see if a specific word is in current use.

Comparative and Superlative Forms

The guidelines for making adjectives and adverbs comparative and superlative are flexible, and writers have a good bit of discretion here. However, writers will normally be safe if they choose the comparatives and superlatives that sound best.

In English most adjectives and adverbs can be compared to express degrees of something. This is done with the endings *er* and *est* and with the words *more* and *most* (for upward comparisons) or *less* and *least* (for downward comparisons). The positive forms of adjectives and adverbs (*large, threateningly*) simply describe. The comparative forms (*larger, more threateningly*) compare whatever is described to one other thing. The superlative forms (*largest, most threateningly*) compare whatever is modified to at least two other things.

In general, add the endings *er* and *est* to all one-syllable modifiers

POSITIVE	COMPARATIVE	SUPERLATIVE
small	smaller	smallest
red	redder	reddest
close	closer	closest

The only exception to this occurs when a writer wants to be emphatic in a comparison. In this case, *more* and *most* can be used. For instance, a magazine recently asked in its pitch to new subscribers "Now what could be more fair?"

For modifiers of two syllables, using either *er/est* or *more/most* is permissible. Normally your ear will be the best guide.

POSITIVE	COMPARATIVE	SUPERLATIVE
lucky	luckier/more lucky	luckiest/most lucky
yellow	yellower/more yellow	yellowest/most yellow
scenic	more scenic	most scenic

(Comparison with *er/est* sounds unnatural in the last example.)

For words of three or more syllables, modifiers take *more* and *most* in comparisons. The only exceptions to this are adjectives not accented on the first syllable (*unhappy, unlucky,* and others), which may take *er/est* or *more/most.*

POSITIVE	COMPARATIVE	SUPERLATIVE
captivating	more captivating	most captivating
slovenly	more slovenly	most slovenly
exotic	more exotic	most exotic

A few modifiers have irregular comparative and superlative forms.

POSITIVE	COMPARATIVE	SUPERLATIVE
good	better	best
well	better	best
little	less	least
much, many	more	most
bad	worse	worst
badly	worse	worst

(The forms *worser* and *worsest* are not acceptable.)

Using Comparatives and Superlatives

A comparative form should be used when two things are being compared, the superlative when more than two things are being compared. Writers will sometimes use the superlative for a comparison of only two things, perhaps in an effort to make stronger and more cogent statements, but in general this should be avoided. It is acceptable only in certain set phrases, such as *May the best man win* when only two men are involved.

Avoid

Of the two leading shampoos on the market, Lavatel cleans carpets best.

Revised

> Lavatel cleans carpets better than the other leading shampoo on the market.

Of course, a sentence which makes such a comparison is always more effective if specifics are added to support the claim for superiority.

Obviously, writers owe it to their readers to write clear comparisons. A sentence that compares one thing with another or with others cannot be effective unless its comparison is complete, has a specific basis of comparison, and is logical.

First, writers may fail to complete comparisons by leaving part of them implied. Such elliptical comparisons are usually clear enough to be understood, but completing them prevents any possible ambiguity, shows which case of pronoun may be needed in the comparison, and provides smoother and better-sounding phrasing.

> Etheridge likes politics more than his wife.

This should be rephrased by adding a verb to complete the comparison. After all, this sentence can mean one of two things.

> Etheridge likes politics more than his wife does.

or

> Etheridge likes politics more than he likes his wife.

Second, writers may leave comparisons hanging by neglecting to say what the specific basis of comparison is (that is, what is being compared to what?). This kind of sentence is most typical of the hyperbole of advertisements that make exclusive claims without bothering to say what items are being compared. But this trap is easy for any writer to fall into.

> Midtown High prepares its graduates better for university demands. (better than for what else? better than who?)

Third, to clearly indicate what is being compared, and to be logical, writers often need to add *other* or *any other*.

Original

> Ace Hardware sells more color televisions than any store in the Mid-South. (This can be true only if Ace is not a store.)

Revised

> Ace Hardware sells more color televisions than any other store in the Mid-South.

Comparing Absolutes

Adjectives and adverbs like *infinite, perfect, impossible, exactly,* and *unique* refer to extreme degrees and qualities. It is often said that logically they cannot take comparative or superlative forms because they already refer to absolute, and therefore incomparable, qualities. Thus, it is said that the correct form is *more nearly infinite,* not *more infinite.* But this attempt to impose logic on language has not prevented these absolutes from often being compared in writing. It is clearly more idiomatic to write *more perfect* than *more nearly perfect* (as the writers of the Preamble to the Constitution were aware). Here's a list of the most common absolute adjectives; absolute adverbs are derived from these adjectives by adding *ly.*

absolute	fatal	round
correct	final	square
equal	impossible	ultimate
eternal	inevitable	unanimous
exact	infinite	unique
	perfect	

There are two basic problems here: whether comparative and superlative forms of absolutes are acceptable in writing and whether using these forms enables writers to describe items and events effectively and interestingly.

Writers should compare absolutes with great caution. Such comparisons are acceptable in writing only when no other way of phrasing an idea is available and when the idiom demands them. Formal written usage normally allows something to be *nearly impossible* and *quite unique* but not *more impossible* and *more unique* than something else.

Writers should also avoid comparing absolutes because such comparisons allow modifiers to be used as crutches for inexact and vague ideas. At the hotline, we have found that writers often rely on adjectives and adverbs to make strong points rather than write sentences with specific detail and with active verbs. Using compared absolutes is usually a way of avoiding being specific with readers. *Unique* and *uniquely* are the most abused absolutes in this regard. Even though *unique* has taken the meaning "very unusual" or "outstanding" in addition to its original meaning "one of a kind," it is greatly overused. Replace it by *remarkable, unusual, rare, singular,* or *one of a kind,* if possible.

Sentences containing compared absolute adjectives and adverbs can always be rephrased and improved by adding detail or choosing more precise words.

Original

> The Chagnon typewriter is the most unique machine currently on the market.

Revised

> The Chagnon typewriter has a special self-correcting key and typeface options that no other machine currently on the market has.

Original

> Hitler was a more absolute dictator than Mussolini.

Revised

> Hitler allowed less political dissent and persecuted minorities more than Mussolini did.

6

Possessives:
Apostrophes and Other Problems

Hotline callers are often bothered by apostrophes and possessives. Sometimes they wonder why a phrase like *yesterday's news* is possessive or whether *two-weeks' vacation* is possessive, possessive and plural, or simply plural. And sometimes callers simply want to know how to form the possessive of a word already ending in *s*, like *boss*. In this chapter we examine the various meanings of the possessive construction and how to form it, and we tell you when you don't need it. (For other uses of the apostrophe, see pages 166–167.)

Meaning of the Possessive

The term *possessive* is something of a misnomer because it refers to many more relationships between nouns or between a noun and a pronoun than mere ownership. In writing *tomorrow's stock-market report*, we are not saying that the report literally "belongs" to tomorrow. If we write *the President's critics were especially vocal last week*, we know that the critics don't "belong" to the President. Many grammarians use the broader term *genitive* to include ownership and several other types of close relationships, but we will stick to *possessive* here because it's the term hotline callers use.

The many uses of the possessive are not corruptions of one original use—that of ownership. All of the uses are very old and have been found in English for over a thousand years. The use of the apostrophe in addition to an *s* to indicate a possessive is not nearly so old, having been standard for only about three hundred years. Shakespeare sometimes used the apostrophe for possessives and sometimes only an *s*.

The Possessive of Ownership. A noun which indicates that one thing belongs to another.

the *investigator's* red Mercedes
Sue Ellen's picture (the one that belongs to her)

The Possessive of Measure. When one noun indicates the time, the space, or the value of another noun, the first noun is in the possessive case. No ownership is involved.

Time:	six *months'* profits
	a *moment's* notice
	yesterday's weather
Space:	a *mile's* walk
	an *acre's* crops
Value:	a *dollar's* worth

(These nouns may sometimes be expressed without the possessive: *six-month profits.*)

The Possessive of Origin. A noun which indicates the source or origin of something is in the possessive case.

the *vice-president's* ideas (They originated from, but do not belong to, the vice-president.)
Sue Ellen's picture (the one that she painted herself)

The Possessive of Description. Sometimes when one noun merely describes another, it should be put into the possessive case. At other times it is more idiomatic to juxtapose two nouns without making the first one possessive.

a *ladies'* man (This describes or tells what kind of man he is.)
women's shoes (This tells what kind of shoes they are.)
teachers college (This tells what kind of college it is.)

The Possessive of the Subject of an Act. When two nouns express an action, the doer of the action is in the possessive case.

the *prisoner's* escape
the *union's* decision

The Possessive of the Object of an Act. When two nouns express an action, the receiver of the action may also be in the possessive case.

the *President's* critics (In other words, people criticized the President; he was the object of their criticism.)
Sue Ellen's picture (the picture that is a likeness of her)

Forming the Possessive of Nouns

If a noun does not end in the letter *s*, its possessive is formed by adding *'s*. This is true whether the noun is singular or plural.

> A *child's* toys were scattered across the living-room floor.
> *Children's* toys are often sold out long before Christmas Day.

If a noun is plural and ends in the letter *s*, add only an apostrophe to form the possessive.

> *Workers'* insurance will be provided beginning July 1.
> The *Fords'* cabin is fifteen miles off U.S. Highway 241.
> The *stockholders'* petition was rejected by the board of directors.

But what about singular nouns ending in *s*? Here usage guides and handbooks are divided between adding only an apostrophe and adding *'s*. For words of one syllable, either practice is acceptable. So we tell callers to write either *Gus' Drug Store* or *Gus's Drug Store*. For words of more than one syllable, the apostrophe alone is more often recommended, but both *business's attitudes* and *business' attitudes* are acceptable. Neither practice can be termed incorrect.*

We tell callers who are uncomfortable with this diversity the following (adapted from the *United Press International Stylebook*):

---

* Good reasons have been cited for forming the possessive each way. Adding only the apostrophe after singular nouns ending in *s* is more economical, and it is consistent with the rule for forming the possessive of plurals ending in *s*. Grammarians who add only the apostrophe in these instances follow a simple rule for forming the possessive: "Add *'s* to nouns not ending in *s*, whether the nouns are singular or plural; add only the apostrophe to nouns already ending in *s*, whether the nouns are singular or plural." Other grammarians say that the *s* should be added to the apostrophe whenever it is pronounced, especially in one-syllable words, since the possessive creates an additional syllable. According to them, the spelling should reflect pronunciation whenever possible.

Add an apostrophe and an *s* to all singular nouns of one syllable that end in an *s* or *z* sound. Add only the apostrophe to singular nouns of more than one syllable ending in these sounds unless an extra syllable is clearly pronounced in the possessive form.

According to this rule, the *s* is added when it is heard at the end of the word. Thus *Bess's* and *Cass's* have two syllables when pronounced and the added *s* shows this. When an extra syllable is not pronounced, according to this rule, the *s* should not be added:

   Achilles' heel, *Jesus'* name, *goodness'* sake

Writers should consistently follow whichever practice they choose. They may choose to never add the *s*, always add the *s*, or add the *s* only when they hear it, but they must be consistent in their usage.

Note: Be sure to determine whether nouns ending in *s* are singular or plural before forming the possessive. *Happy Boss's Day* is a special occasion for one person, *Happy Bosses' Day* a special day for two or more. But notice that *Boss's* and *Bosses'* are pronounced alike.

   The *girls'* softball team won twelve straight games. (Many
      girls are on the team.)
   Both executives and secretaries call the *Writer's* Hot-
      line for help. (We've argued over this one ourselves.
      Is the hotline for *the writer* or for *writers*? We decided
      that our emphasis was on help for individual writers
      rather than for writers in general, so we determined it
      was a singular noun before making it possessive.)

Forming the Possessive of Pronouns

Unlike nouns, personal pronouns and the relative pronoun *who* never require an apostrophe when they are made possessive. An apostrophe with these pronouns can indicate only a contraction (*it's = it is, who's = who is, she's = she is*) and not a possessive form. Use the forms with an apostrophe only when a pronoun and a verb can substitute for them. The following chart lists the possessive pronouns that do not have apostrophes:

	SINGULAR	PLURAL
First person	my, mine	our, ours
Second Person	your, yours	your, yours
Third Person	his, her, hers, its	their, theirs
Relative Pronoun	whose	whose

Indefinite pronouns, such as *everyone* and *anyone*, form the possessive as nouns do, by adding *'s.*

> *Everyone's* approval was needed for the compromise.
> *Anyone's* help in moving the furniture would be appreciated.
> The applicant was erroneously assigned *someone else's* credit rating.

The Possessive of Compound Nouns

Compound nouns (nouns of more than one word) and word groups are all treated as units when being made possessive. When they are relatively short, an apostrophe or *'s* is normally used: *the golf coach's antics, the lab technician's report.* But using the apostrophe or *'s* to form the possessive of phrases of more than two words, or of two long words, can become clumsy, and writers should not hesitate to revise their wording and use a prepositional phrase beginning with *of.*

Original

> *The man who lives next to us'* apartment was broken into last night.

Better

> The apartment *of the man who lives next to us* was broken into last night.

Original

> *the President of the United States'* official limousine

Better

> the official limousine *of the President of the United States*

Sister-in-law, attorney general, and several other compound nouns (see pages 22–23) also add *'s* at the end. They are some of the very few nouns that do not add the *s* for plural and the *'s* for the possessive at the same point: *sisters-in-law* (plural), but *sister-in-law's* (possessive singular); *attorneys general* or *attorney generals* (plural), but *attorney general's* (possessive singular). Hotline callers have a habit of locating these unusual cases, and several have asked us how to form the possessive plural of a noun such as *attorney general.*

> the *attorneys general's cars* (awkward, but improved if a number is mentioned: *the three attorneys general's cars*)
> the cars *of the three attorneys general* (the better version)

Joint Possessives

When referring to an item or items jointly owned by more than one person, the apostrophe is added only after the name of the last one.

> *Ann and Andy's* books were arranged alphabetically by title.
> *Marilyn and Steve's* children are straight-A students.

If the item or items are individually owned, some by one person and some by another or others, each name or noun must have an apostrophe.

> *Ford's and Chrysler's* cars are competing better with imports this year.
> *Men's and women's* glasses are available in all sizes and designs.

If some of the items are individually owned and the rest jointly owned, expressing the possessive by using apostrophes alone is usually impossible. Some kind of parenthetical comment is required when it is necessary or desirable to specify all the details of ownership.

> *Ann's and Andy's* books (some of them his, some of them hers, and some of them belonging to both) were arranged alphabetically by title.

When one or more pronouns are used in a joint possessive, there does not seem to be a smooth and obvious way of phrasing. This problem exists whether the object or objects are jointly or individually owned. Writers may either place both possessives before the noun, as in

> *John and my* tax returns were both audited this year.
> Both *your and my* cars are in the shop for the weekend.
> (*Yours and my* is incorrect here.)

or put one before the noun and one after it.

> *John's* tax return and *mine* were both audited this year.
> Both *your* car and *mine* are in the shop for the weekend.

(*Our tax returns were audited this year* is ambiguous; the reader cannot tell from the sentence which returns belong to whom.)

But none of these sentences will win an award for having a natural sound about it. We advise writers either to repeat the noun being modified or to recast the entire sentence so that it has no possessives. This improves the sentence and avoids the problem of phrasing the possessives.

> *John's* tax return and *my* tax return were both audited this year.
> John and I both had our tax returns audited this year.
> Both you and I have our cars in the shop for the weekend.

Using *of* to Express Possession

Usually writers have the option of expressing a possessive by an apostrophe or by a prepositional phrase beginning with *of* (*Congress' privileges* or *the privileges of Congress*). The choice is a stylistic one, with the first being more economical and sometimes more straightforward, while the second is usually smoother and more idiomatic. They are not always interchangeable, however (would anyone want to rephrase *the luck of the Irish* as *the Irish's luck*?). Writers should feel free to form a possessive with a prepositional phrase if the result has a better rhythm to it. Using the *of* possessive normally leads to a sentence that sounds less cluttered.

Original

> Politicians rarely take into account the *man on the street's* views.

Much better

> Politicians rarely take into account the views *of the man on the street*.

The first sentence is shorter but is inferior to the second in every other way.

> The *Sumter Avenue bridge's* pylons gave way during the flood.

Better

> The pylons *of the Sumter Avenue bridge* gave way during the flood.

One day a hotline caller asked which was correct, *the President's committee's consultation recommendations* or *the President's consultation committee's recommendations*. The phrase had become so complicated by the writer's trying to put both possessives before the noun *recommendations* that it was no longer possible to tell what the intention was. Stacking possessives in front of a noun created the problem. The solution was to use an *of* possessive.

> the recommendations *of the President's consultation committee* (or the recommendations *of the consultation committee of the President*)
> the consultation recommendations *of the President's committee* (or the consultation recommendations *of the committee of the President*)

Note: Some writers, especially those who write newspaper headlines, take undue license in transforming possessives with *of* into possessives with apostrophes. Some grammarians object to the use of an inanimate noun as a possessor (there is no hard and fast rule against this, but it frequently involves poor phrasing).

Original

> The *maple tree's* leaves turn yellow, red, and brown in the fall.
>
> Officially, the *State Department's* policy was to remain neutral.
>
> The *cruise's* highlight was the stop in Bermuda.

Regardless of any grammatical issue, these sentences are awkward. Rephrasing them with *of* usually improves them (*the leaves of the maple tree, the policy of the State Department,* and *the highlight of the cruise*). Sometimes a writer can convert the possessives in these sentences to descriptive or attributive nouns (nouns that precede and modify other nouns without being possessive). But beware of overusing such nouns; they can make your writing look full of jargon.

Revised

> *Maple tree* leaves turn yellow, red, and brown in the fall.
>
> Officially, *State Department* policy was to remain neutral.
>
> The *cruise* highlight was the stop in Bermuda. (Not an improvement; rephrase with *of.*)

See pages 101–03 for other cases where possessives may be replaced.

The Possessive of a Gerund

In formal usage, a possessive noun or pronoun is required before a gerund. (A gerund is a word—such as *swimming* or *working*—ending in *ing* that looks like a verb but functions like a noun and is a subject, a direct object, or an object of a preposition.) In general usage, the possessive is preferred but not always required.

> We appreciate *your* taking time to respond to our questions. (*Taking time* is the direct object of *appreciate* and *your* modifies it.)

Clearly *your* is preferable to *you* in this sentence. But a proper noun may or may not so clearly require a possessive, depending on its sound. A possessive is optional in

We appreciate *Mr. Hundley* (or *Mr. Hundley's*) taking time to respond to our questions.

but required in

Mrs. Wright's (not *Mrs. Wright*) slipping on the ice led to a suit against the store. (*Slipping* is the subject of *led* and *Mrs. Wright* modifies it.)

Writers should be careful to use possessives only before gerunds and not before all words ending in *ing*. A possessive noun or pronoun should never precede a present participle (an *ing* word that functions as an adjective).

From our office we can hear the *policeman* (not *policeman's*) directing traffic during rush hour. (*Directing* is not the object of *hear;* what we hear is the *policeman*, not the *directing traffic*.)

At the airport one can always see *passengers* (not *passengers'*) rushing to catch their flights. (Using *passengers'* here would be incorrect. *Rushing* is a participle here, an adjective modifying *passengers*.)

These sentences sound unnatural if a possessive is used.

A simple test usually distinguishes a participle from a gerund: If the word *who* (or *that*) and a form of the verb *be* (*is, was, were, are*) can be added after the *ing* word, the *ing* word is a participle (*the passengers who are rushing* and *the policeman who is directing*). If they cannot be added, the *ing* word is a gerund.

Another problem arises when a writer uses an awkward gerund preceded by a possessive noun or pronoun and compounds the sentence's awkwardness. Some writers try to apply grammar rules at the expense of being clear and direct, and a rule can paint them into a syntactic corner, so to speak. Rather than sticking by a rule at all costs, however, a writer should rephrase the sentence to avoid having to apply a rule unwisely.

Original

In earlier centuries, diabetes was believed to result from the *body's tissues'* being wasted away. (Two possessives make this sentence impossibly clumsy.)

Better

> In earlier centuries, diabetes was believed to result from
> the *body's tissues* wasting away.

Better

> In earlier centuries, diabetes was believed to result from
> the wasting away of body tissue. (No possessive pre-
> cedes the gerund *wasting* here.)

The Double Possessive

An oddity that hotline callers occasionally ask about is a
phrase like *a friend of George's* or *a portrait of Sue Ellen's*,
expressions which have two possessive forms, one with the
apostrophe and *s* and the other with *of*. How can this be? As
we point out many times, English has idiomatic constructions
that are a part of the language, that everyone uses, but that
cannot be subjected to a logical analysis. This double possessive construction is one of them. Although its origin is obscure,
it has been a part of the language for many centuries.

The double possessive is required to clearly express a
possessive of ownership and is used to convey certain nuances
of this one kind of possessive relationship. *Sue Ellen's portrait*
may or may not be one she owns, but *a portrait of Sue Ellen's*
must be. We sometimes use the double possessive with *this* or
that to lend an informal flavor to our writing: *that child of
theirs, that gadget of Brenda's*. A double possessive is sometimes only a variant of an *of* possessive: *A friend of my wife*
and *a friend of my wife's* have the same meaning and are
equally acceptable.

Conventional Possessives

Some possessive proper names and other nouns have been
used so widely that, for one reason or another, their apostrophes have been dropped and the nouns have become
"frozen" in form. Here are a few instances.

citizens band (as in *citizens-band radio*)
Gerbers (as in *Gerbers baby food*)
menswear (as in the *menswear department*)
teachers college
Veterans Day, Veterans Administration

Except for the names of companies and organizations, conventional possessives can usually be found in any standard desk dictionary.

Possessive or Not? When It Doesn't Matter

Early in this chapter we showed the many relationships between nouns that require the use of a possessive, but this doesn't mean that all nouns in front of other nouns need to be in the possessive case. Callers have often asked the hotline such a question as "Which is correct, *a two-week vacation, a two-weeks vacation,* or *a two weeks' vacation?*" In these cases and others, the writer may use either a possessive noun or a descriptive noun (nouns can modify other nouns just as adjectives can). The difference between using a possessive and a descriptive noun is, at most, one of slight emphasis. Notice the difference in the following.

The exam will test the *student's* mastery of verbal skills.
(emphasis on the individual student)
The exam will test *student* mastery of verbal skills.
(emphasis on mastery)

Either usage is correct, so it is up to the writer to choose one or the other. At the hotline we have sometimes advised against using a possessive because it creates a little clutter and may be confusing. A florist from Los Angeles wanted to know whether she should write *a wedding flowers planning guide* or *a wedding flowers' planning guide.* In this and in other cases where there is no difference in meaning, it seems preferable to use a descriptive noun without the apostrophe.

On pages 102–103 we list a number of instances when either a possessive or a descriptive noun can be used.

The Possessive of Measure

With a noun measuring distance, time, quantity, or volume, a question arises whether to use a possessive (*a two-weeks' layoff*) or a descriptive (*a two-weeks layoff* or *a two-week layoff*) when the noun is a modifier preceding another noun. Either may be acceptable, depending on what kind of measure noun is involved, but the possessive form is never the only choice. A hyphen is always required.

With a noun that measures distance or area (*inch, mile, acre*) and that is not preceded by a numeral, either the possessive (*a mile's drive*) or the simple (*a mile drive*) form of the noun is acceptable if there is no numeral. With a numeral, the noun must be singular and cannot be possessive (*a twenty-mile race, a three-meter jump*).

With a noun that measures time and that is not preceded by a numeral, either a possessive (*a year's delay, an hour's walk*) or a simple (*a year delay, an hour walk*) form of the noun is acceptable. With a numeral, writers can choose either a singular or a possessive plural noun, whichever is more idiomatic. *An eight-hour day* requires the singular, but *six-months' pay* requires the plural. Either *a three-weeks' vacation* or *a three-week vacation* is idiomatic and permissible. If either a singular or a possessive plural can be used, the possessive plural is more often preferred by style guides and by the conventions of publishing and printing.

With a noun measuring quantity or volume (*bushel, gallon, ton*), only the singular, nonpossessive form can be used, whether or not a numeral is also used (*a ten-ton truck, a fifty-gallon drum*).

The Possessive of Description

Often when one noun comes before and describes another noun, the possessive form is not needed. Using a descriptive noun is smoother, especially when an inanimate noun is involved. (See pages 97–98 above.) There may be a slight difference in emphasis between the two forms.

the *government* policy (preferable to *the government's policy*)

a wedding *flowers* planning guide (preferable to *a wedding flowers' planning guide*)
technicians guide (preferable to *technicians' guide*)

The use of the apostrophe is not preferred here because these nouns are no longer considered possessive. Rather, they merely describe the nouns that follow. *Technicians* describes *guide* and tells what kind of guide is being discussed.

PART TWO

The Mechanics of Style

7

Punctuation:
More Than Just Avoiding Mistakes

Punctuation, that system of marks and signals for showing how written words are arranged, gives rise to as many questions as anything else the Writer's Hotline deals with. Is a comma needed after the date of the year? Does the period go inside or outside the quotation marks? How is a sentence within parentheses punctuated? The answers to these questions and most others about punctuation, for better or for worse, are governed primarily by rules and conventions that are invariable. Normally these rules and conventions have developed to prevent misreading and to show how sentences and words are organized. Some of the rules seem arbitrary and make little sense, but writers still know that readers expect the rules to be observed. So writers have questions.

Most of us were taught punctuation by the rules. We don't always remember the rules, but even when we want to put in a comma to match a breath pause, we try to find a rule to support it. Unfortunately, most of us last thought about the rules systematically in high-school or college composition. And usually the goal of such classes, for students and instructors, is survival. Students want to avoid mistakes and get a good grade. Instructors want to teach a few simple rules and have students follow them consistently. Surviving the semester is the goal, and the possibilities of the language are slighted. Punctuation is seen as the source of mistakes and is the enemy. But it should not be.

The goal of this chapter is to show the possibilities for punctuation that are slighted in most composition courses and in most style guides, as well as to review the basics needed for survival. The rules we present are the standard conventions. But we want to suggest, through discussion and examples (as well as through the "rules"), that effective punctuation involves more than avoiding mistakes and is more than adhering to rules and conventions. Effective punctuation is a set of tools for making writing clear and meaningful. It is a system of subtle choices a writer has to work with. In short, punctuation is the system of marks and signals that writers should learn to use as assets to their writing.

Paragraphs

Because we think of punctuation as the different marks found in and around sentences, we don't think of the paragraph as a kind of punctuation. Yet it is; with its indented first line and the white space following the last sentence, the paragraph is a tool writers use to show how their sentences are organized into units of thought. By paying careful attention to the form of each paragraph, usually during the editing stage, a writer can improve any piece of writing.

The following four basic principles should enable writers to compose effective paragraphs.

1. Have one idea or basic point for each paragraph, whether it is a major or a relatively minor idea. Be sure that each paragraph has one point to make, whether it is specifically stated or not.

2. Use paragraphing to point out and isolate ideas by devoting individual paragraphs to them. Too often paragraphs bury ideas rather than highlight and explain them.

3. Vary paragraph lengths. Paragraphs come in all lengths, from one-sentence transitions to page-long essays. But each paragraph should make a single point. Skillful writers will vary the length of paragraphs and so keep their reader's attention. (Even when a publication has a preferred paragraph length, some variation is acceptable and desirable.)

4. Begin each paragraph with the main idea or with an attention-getting or transitional device.

Finally, writers should simply ask themselves, "What is the purpose of each paragraph? How does each paragraph fit into the paper or article?" The main idea or topic sentence should answer both of these questions. The unified and focused paragraph is the basic rhetorical unit that writers have, regardless of what is being written. Individual punctuation marks will orchestrate these units of thought so that readers can follow them without difficulty.

Sentences

In an important way, this entire book is about nothing more and nothing less than writing sentences. Too often, however, writers give scant attention to their sentences. The words fall where they may, and punctuation is haphazard. Writers who punctuate only after they have finished writing often see punctuation as a matter of either/or rules. Sometimes a writer's choice is only whether or not to put in a comma, and if punctuation involved only such choices, then the usual listing of the uses of each mark would be satisfactory. But writers usually have greater choice. The skillful writer will *choose* one of several ways to combine independent clauses. The skillful writer will make use of the colon and the dash to highlight lists, will mark parenthetical material in a variety of ways to create different emphasis, and will choose how to emphasize words or phrases through sentence placement or with a mechanical marking. This section of this chapter reviews some of the fundamental choices writers have. Following this, we deal more traditionally, and in more detail, with the uses of the various punctuation marks, and there too we indicate some of the substitutions that can be made.

Independent and Dependent Clauses

Clauses contain subjects and complete predicates (a main verb and any helping verbs that are present). Clauses that can stand alone and that can be punctuated as complete sentences —whether or not they are so punctuated—are called "independent" clauses. Independent clauses do not need anything else to complete their grammatical construction.

Dependent clauses, however, are not complete by themselves. Some dependent clauses contain relative pronouns (e.g. *that, which,* or *who/whom*) as subjects; others are introduced by subordinating conjunctions (e.g. *although, because, after,* and *that*). Dependent clauses (also called subordinate clauses) can function in many ways in sentences—as nouns, adjectives, or adverbs—but they cannot stand by themselves.

The report was finished on time. (independent clause)
although the copy was received late (dependent clause)
which was a snap to produce (dependent relative clause)

A sentence made up of one or more dependent clauses and an independent clause is called a "complex" sentence.

Although the copy was received late, the report, which was a snap to produce, was finished on time.

Dependent clauses may function as nouns, adjectives, or adverbs; that is, they can be subjects, direct objects, or modifiers.

What he wanted was the report. (*What he wanted* is the subject of the sentence.)
She wants a copy of the report that was sent out yesterday. (*That was sent out yesterday* is an adjective.)

Joining Independent Clauses

Generally, independent clauses are punctuated as individual sentences, but they can be joined together in several ways to form compound sentences (sentences containing more than one independent clause).

Independent clauses can be joined with a comma and a coordinating conjunction (*and, but, or, nor, for* when the sense is "because," *so* when the sense is "therefore," and *yet* when the sense is "but").

The report was sent out Monday, for the deadline was noon Wednesday.
The report was sent out Monday, so you should receive your copy of it shortly.
The report was sent out Monday, yet you will receive your copy on time.

They can be joined with a semicolon when the two clauses are of equal importance.

The report was sent out Monday; copies of it should arrive during the week.

When the second clause explains or elaborates the first one, independent clauses can be joined with a colon.

> The annual report was, I admit, mailed late: the copy was received late, and the art department was slow.

Two short and closely related clauses are sometimes joined with only a coordinating conjunction. A series of three or more such clauses usually requires commas and a coordinating conjunction before the last clause.

> I left and the meeting began.
> The boy ran, the man followed, and the police drove slowly along behind.

If the independent clauses are short, closely related, and parallel in construction, they may be joined with only commas to give the sentence a rhythm. However, a coordinating conjunction generally accompanies the comma in joining independent clauses.

> The clock struck twelve, the fun began.
> I came, I saw, I conquered.

When the independent clauses are complex and punctuated with internal commas, it is permissible to use a semicolon and a coordinating conjunction.

> Sending out the annual reports, which were due a week ago and are unlikely to get out for another week, is becoming a nightmare; and now the mailroom clerks are threatening to walk off the job.

This sentence can be punctuated as two sentences, of course. Be careful of involved sentences like the one above unless you are trying for a specific impact. Here the writer (probably purposefully) tumbles over the words in exasperation. Write such a sentence by design, not by accident.

Other Combinations Involving Independent Clauses

A tag question—a question which follows directly after a statement and merely asks for the denial or affirmation of the statement—is generally treated as part of the statement and is set off with a comma. It can occasionally be separated as an independent sentence to give it greater emphasis.

> He was elected. Wasn't he?
> The mail is in, isn't it?

Words like *yes* and *no* may stand alone as one-word sentences, but they are usually included within a larger sentence and are set off with a comma.

> Yes, the bill was passed.

Using Conjunctive Adverbs

Some adverbs that seem like conjunctions (*thus, therefore, however,* and so on) are not true conjunctions; they can be moved around in a sentence without altering the grammar of the sentence. (Conjunctive adverbs are discussed on pages 136–37 and 337–38.) Independent clauses cannot be joined by a conjunctive adverb alone or by a conjunctive adverb and a comma.

Incorrectly joined

> The copy was mailed late, however, that should have made no difference.

Correctly joined

> The copy was mailed late; however, that should have made no difference.
> The copy was mailed late, and, therefore, it didn't reach Los Angeles until Wednesday.
> The copy was mailed late; therefore, it missed the deadline.

Independent Clauses Within Sentences

An independent clause included within another independent clause may be set off by parentheses or by dashes. Dashes are more emphatic. (For how to punctuate such sentences, see pages 149–50 and 153–54. For the use of capital letters with such sentences, see pages 173–76.)

Children's birthday games—too often they bore children —can be fun with a little creative effort by the supervising adults.

The skyhook itself cannot be attached to the axial drive until the axial sleeve coupling has been retracted (see illustration on page 12).

Sentence Fragments

Generally, writers work to avoid sentence fragments, just as they work to avoid other problems that diminish the effectiveness of their writing. Occasionally a sentence fragment may be useful. On rare occasion. (This fragment could have been as effectively attached to the sentence with a dash; it could also have been joined, but not so emphatically, with a comma.) Exclamations and answers to questions can be punctuated as fragments. Another permissible kind of fragment is the noun phrase that elaborates on a preceding sentence.

What a day!
Where did they find the painting? In the attic.
The university makes money on football. Lots of it.

(Noun fragments are often used as paragraph labels, almost as a newspaper or this book uses subheadings. These fragments can either be subheadings or can be run into the first sentence of a paragraph. If you begin a system of labeling with fragments—as in any other system of heading and subheading—be consistent.)

But be careful using fragments. Readers do not forgive a writer who ineptly uses sentence fragments. Another word of warning—the more formal the writing situation is, the less appropriate fragments are. Fragments, except as subheadings, are inappropriate in annual reports and scholarly works, but they are often effective, when not overused, in general writing.

Internal Sentence Punctuation

Commas are by far the most frequently used punctuation marks within sentences. The various uses of the comma are presented in the section on commas (pages 130–49). Occasionally writers choose to use dashes in place of commas, and this use is dealt with on page 151.

But many times writers have more choice than simply whether or not to use a comma. Particularly in the placement and punctuation of lists and series, in choosing how to mark parenthetical items, and in choosing how to emphasize particular words and phrases, writers have many possibilities. These possibilities are briefly outlined in the next few pages. The reader can then turn to the section of this chapter that deals specifically with the particular punctuation mark for further discussion and examples.

Lists

Commas often do not set lists off fully enough to be clear. Fortunately, there are other ways to incorporate and emphasize lists. A list at the beginning of a sentence may be set off with a dash but not with a colon:

> Faith, hope, and love—all three are crucial, but the greatest is love, according to St. Paul.
> Chemistry, physics, and calculus—I flunked them all.

A list at the end of a sentence may be set off with a colon or a dash:

> To avoid bankruptcy, we need some immediate help: additional short-term financing, an upturn in sales, and a price increase. (A dash may be substituted for the colon.)

A list in the middle of a sentence may be set off with dashes, parentheses, or commas:

> Only a few people—two parents, a schoolteacher, and three or four unidentified people—have called to protest the new rule. (Parentheses may be substituted for the dashes, but commas would be confusing.)
> Only two people, Jane Thomas and Mark Gage, showed up. (Parentheses may be substituted for the commas.)

One word of warning: Do not set off from your sentence a list that functions as part of the grammar of the sentence.

(This is particularly a problem for writers using colons; it is discussed on pages 126–27.)

Colon misplaced

> You will need: a pattern, cloth, a tape measure, pins, and shears.

Revised without colon

> You will need a pattern, cloth, a tape measure, pins, and shears.

Parenthetical Items

Parenthetical items, by definition, add nothing vital to the logic or the grammar of the sentence. Parenthetical elements are set off from a sentence with commas, dashes, or parentheses. Dashes call attention to the material being set off; parentheses deemphasize it. When parenthetical items contain commas, it is preferable to use dashes or parentheses to set them off.

> The most decisive battle of the War of 1812 (1812–1814) was the Battle of New Orleans, which was fought after the war had officially ended.
> The Battle of New Orleans—the most decisive battle of the War of 1812—was fought after the war had ended.
> The most decisive battle of the War of 1812, the Battle of New Orleans (January 8, 1815), was fought after the treaty ending the war had been signed (the Treaty of Ghent, signed December 24, 1814).

Emphasis

Words and phrases are sometimes emphasized through sentence position and word order, through the use of punctuation, and through one of three purely mechanical means—italics (indicated by underlining), quotation marks, and capital letters.

Emphatic word order often involves inverting sentences. The ordinary sentence

> There had never been such a summer.

turns into the much more emphatic

> Never had there been such a summer.

The ordinary sentence

> His life was guided by his thirst for honors, glory, and money.

can be turned into the much more emphatic

> The thirst for honors, glory, and money—this alone guided his life.

Obviously every sentence should not be inverted. But inversion is one way of highlighting an important thought or group of words.

Individual clauses, particularly subordinate clauses that function like adverbs and modify entire sentences, can be emphasized or deemphasized by the position they hold in the sentence. Whether one word or a full clause, these modifiers can usually be placed in front of the sentence, between the subject and verb when enclosed by commas, or after the verb. Consider the various arrangements of *Overnight, profits tumbled down.*

> Overnight, profits tumbled down.
> Profits tumbled down overnight.
> Profits, overnight, tumbled down.

Not one of the sentences is poor; not one is particularly memorable either. Now, look at the power the sentence generates when it is inverted and the sentence modifier is moved around again.

> Overnight, down profits tumbled.
> Down profits tumbled, overnight.

Now we have a sentence that is too strong for the middle of a paragraph. It belongs at the beginning or the end, because of its impact.

Punctuation also creates emphasis. A clause or prepositional phrase, particularly at the end of a sentence, is sometimes set off with a comma or dash to emphasize it.

Down profits tumbled—overnight.
The crops were lost, even though the heat abated.
We will be more than happy to assist you with your
design problems—after a contract is signed.

Emphasis can be created by using a colon or dash between
the sentence and an appositive or by using a dash before a
final prepositional phrase.

The goal of our company is simple: Success.
Yearly department reports are due at noon tomorrow—
not at 5 P.M.

Putting a modifying phrase into parentheses deemphasizes
it; this is a possible, but very unusual, sentence form.

The crops (even though the heat abated) were lost.

Three kinds of word marking—italics (indicated by underlining), capitals, and quotation marks can also emphasize
words and phrases, but their uses are not interchangeable. For
stressed words and phrases and for cited letters, words, and
phrases, use italics (see pages 164–65).

The word *that* has numerous grammatical functions.

To mark a special use of a word, usually an ironic or
sarcastic use, to mark a slang or coined word or phrase, or
to enclose the definition of a word, use quotation marks (see
page 160).

The word *for* when it means "because" is a coordinating
conjunction.

To mark common nouns as proper nouns, use capital
letters.

Let us look, not for what is true, but for Truth.

Names of books, ships, buildings, poems, and so on present
a variety of problems. Italics (underlining), capitals, and
quotation marks are each used in marking some of these
names. Titles and names of objects are discussed thoroughly in
Chapter 12, pages 240–47.

Quotations

Brief quotations are marked with quotation marks and introduced by commas, usually, or by colons. With fragmentary quotes that form part of a sentence, the comma or colon is generally omitted. Long quotations are set off by their typography: in typed, final copy, they are single-spaced and indented; in printed copy, they are often set in smaller type and indented. Both of these ways of marking quotations and the appropriate introductory punctuation are discussed on pages 157–62. Omissions in quotations are usually indicated by an ellipsis mark (see pages 162–64). For inserting parenthetical comments into quotations and for inserting changes so that a quotation reads smoothly as part of a text sentence, brackets are used (see pages 155–56).

The Period

The period has only one purely structural use: to mark the end of a declarative (statement) or imperative (command) sentence. All its other uses—including marking the numerals in lists, marking abbreviations, and separating items in bibliographies—are matters of convention and form.

Terminal Punctuation

Use a period at the end of a declarative sentence, an imperative sentence, or a sentence fragment that you are treating as a sentence. A period is the proper mark to end a sentence containing an indirect question or a polite request.

> The university makes money on football. Lots of it.
> Send the report immediately.
> She asked him why the report had not yet reached her desk.
> Will you please see that the order is filled at your convenience.

A sentence ending with an abbreviation containing periods does not require another period, unless a parenthesis intervenes.

> The session was scheduled for 10 A.M. (*not* A.M..)
> The trial was recessed for the weekend (and resumed the following Monday at 10 A.M.).

Internal Sentences

Do not use a period to punctuate a sentence within a sentence. Use parentheses or dashes to set off the sentence.

> The tea-drinking public—it seems to grow smaller each year—must be told the results of this year's tastings.

Abbreviations

Use a period with shortened word abbreviations and with some initialisms. See Chapter 10, pages 218–25, for a complete discussion.

> mi.
> Mr.
> B.C.
> etc.
> p.m.
> *or* P.M.

Initials in Proper Names

Use a period after an initial in a proper name, but not after initials used alone to identify a prominent person.

> John D. Rockefeller
> LBJ

Lists and Outlines

Use periods after the letters or numbers that enumerate a vertical list or outline. Use them after the items in a vertical

list or outline only when one or more of the items is a full
sentence.

    I. Punctuation
        A. Paragraphs
        B. Sentences
        C. Punctuation marks
            1. Period
            2. Exclamation point

Ellipsis Marks

The ellipsis mark is formed with three spaced periods and
indicates that something has been omitted from a quotation.
For its treatment, see pages 162–64.

Textual Citations

Use periods to separate act, scene, and line numbers in
plays, and to separate book and line numbers in references to
long poems. Biblical citations (chapter and verse) are traditionally punctuated with a colon, but a period may also be
used.

> *Much Ado About Nothing* III.v.15
> *Paradise Lost* II.105
> I Corinthians 13:3 (or I Corinthians 13.3)

Bibliographic and Footnote References

Periods are used in bibliographies, and to a lesser extent in
footnotes, to mark groups of information. Details vary with
individual style guides, however, and instead of listing various
styles here, we recommend that you consult the style guide
for your field. (A list of style guides and manuals is included
in Chapter 18.)

The Exclamation Point

The exclamation point is used to express very strong emotion, such as great shock, surprise, dismay, and sometimes even chagrin, contempt, or scorn. Statements ending with an exclamation point are generally short.

Call the police!
Who would have thought it!
Liar!

In expressing a strongly emotional question, an exclamation point overrides the question mark. On rare occasion, a question mark may be used along with an exclamation point.

How could you?!

With longer statements, the exclamation point by itself should not be expected to create irony or show outrage. The word choice and sentence structure must help do this. Especially in expository writing, the exclamation point should be used very sparingly. Its overuse is a sign of an inexperienced writer. A writer should generally not use it when another punctuation mark will serve.

Original

Our expert (!) guide led us in circles and finally stranded us in the middle of the swamp!!

Revised

Our guide, a self-proclaimed expert, led us around in circles and finally stranded us in the middle of the swamp.

Punctuation of Internal Sentences

Exclamation points are sometimes used in internal sentences. But again, be careful not to overuse them.

My father grew up in what Washington Irving (nobody reads him anymore!) called the Yankee Farmer's Shingle Palace.

The Question Mark

A question mark punctuates a direct question and, in parentheses or brackets, indicates doubt in biographical and bibliographical citations.

Direct Question

Use a question mark at the end of a direct question.

Can anyone fully explain the causes of the accident?
Who will be the party's nominee?

Some questions and requests have normal sentence word order. Use a question mark to show that these are questions.

The report will be ready in November?
Stop now?

Questions Within Sentences

A question quoted within another question requires only one question mark if both end together. A question elsewhere within a sentence is generally punctuated with a question mark. A series of questions is sometimes punctuated with one question mark and sometimes with questions marks following each question. (For a full discussion of the punctuation of a series of questions in a sentence, as well as a discussion of capital letters in questions within sentences, see pages 174–75.)

Who asked, "Why"?
Are more refugees to be allowed into the country? is the only question that needs to be answered.
We must now analyze the events of the past month: what happened? why? and how can a recurrence be prevented?

> What does his party say about rising crime rates? unequal taxation? inflation? and recession?

However, an indirect question embedded within a statement does not take a question mark.

> Judge Robinson asked the accused why he wouldn't defend himself.

Editorial Doubt

Question marks are used to indicate uncertainty, generally about biographical facts. (The abbreviations *c.* or *ca.*, standing for *circa* and meaning "about," can be used rather than the question mark.)

> Pancho Villa (1877?–1923)
> John Chapman (ca. 1774–1845)

To indicate doubt about the accuracy of a quoted source, use [*sic*] or make a comment in your text. Question marks as editorial comments are rude, belittling, and inappropriate.

Inappropriate

> The lecturer said, "Earth, Venus, and Mars, the third, fourth, and fifth [!?!] planets of the solar system. . . ."

Appropriate

> The lecturer said, "Earth, Venus, and Mars, the third, fourth, and fifth [sic] planets of the solar system. . . ."

The Semicolon

The semicolon links closely related independent clauses without a conjunction and separates items in a series containing commas. In punctuating independent clauses, the semicolon may be thought of as a light period. In punctuating a series, it can be thought of as a heavy comma.

Linking Independent Clauses

Use the semicolon to link closely related independent clauses. Do not use it with a coordinating conjunction—*and, but, or, nor, so, yet,* or *for*—unless the sentence contains commas in one or more of the independent clauses that might cause confusion.

> Enrollments will continue to decline; no end is in sight.
> The nude was removed from the exhibit; a picture of a barn with peeling paint was hung in its place.
> The heat generated by the fluorescent bulbs and ballasts warms the air, and when the lights go off, an equivalent amount of heat must be provided by the reheats in the air-supply ducts. (Between *air* and *and,* a comma is sufficient. The comma in the second independent clause does not cause confusion.)

With Conjunctive Adverbs

Remember that a comma and an adverb cannot join two independent clauses. The adverbs that seem like conjunctions —*thus, therefore, then, nevertheless, however,* and so on— are not true conjunctions; they can be moved around without altering the grammar of the sentence. Use a semicolon to join two independent clauses linked by such an adverb.

> The effective speaker often begins with a self-effacing story or joke; thus, the speaker captures the attention of the audience.

(Conjunctive adverbs are discussed on pages 136–37 and 338–39.)

With *namely, for example,* and So On

If an independent clause follows an introductory word or phrase such as *namely, for example,* or *that is,* a semicolon may precede the introductory phrase. The choice between a semicolon and a comma will depend on the desired emphasis, although a semicolon will normally be chosen because it reflects the independence of the following clause.

> The students maneuvered the instructor off the subject again; that is, they asked him about his ongoing battle with the electric company.

With Items in a Series

Use a semicolon in a series of items when one or more of the items contain internal commas. Use a semicolon after each item and before the final *and,* as you would use commas if the items did not contain commas.

> Several corporate vice-presidents attended, including Steve Smith, public relations; Catherine Plante, accounting; Elaine Rossi, quality control; and James Jefferson, experimental manufacturing.

The semicolons help readers track which explanations and appositives belong with which items.

Placement with Quotation Marks

The semicolon is always placed outside quotation marks. If quotation ends with a semicolon, replace the semicolon with a period.

Overuse of the Semicolon

The semicolon may be handy, but it can easily be overused. Use it only where a period could be used or in a heavily punctuated series. The semicolon, unlike the colon, doesn't indicate that a list will follow, and unlike the dash, it doesn't set off or emphasize an appositive or subordinate clause. Do not use a semicolon to introduce a quotation.

Original/Incorrect

> The council was aware of his position; that funds should not be made available to the protesters for any reason

or under any guise. (The semicolon is used incorrectly for a comma, a colon, or a dash. Change the punctuation or remove *that*.)

Revised

The council was aware of his position: that funds should not be made available to the protesters for any reason or under any guise.

Original/Incorrect

William Penn advised his children; "Much reading is an oppression of the mind, and extinguishes the natural candle." (The semicolon is used incorrectly in place of a colon or *that*.)

Revised

William Penn advised his children that "much reading is an oppression of the mind, and extinguishes the natural candle."

The Colon

The desire to reduce punctuation to a few unambiguous rules has almost done away with the colon. It survives primarily to introduce formal lists (where it is often misplaced), to introduce quotations, and in a number of conventional ways, such as in writing hours and minutes and in the salutations of formal letters.

In general, the colon introduces elaborations of the preceding sentences. Those elaborations may be single-word appositives, lists, or even independent clauses that further explain and amplify the sentence. The colon must *always* follow an independent clause. It never intrudes between the verb and its object (except when the object is a quotation), a preposition and its object, or between the word *that* and a following clause.

Misplaced between verb and objects

Participants will need: fishing gear, lunch, and a change of clothes.

Correctly written without colon

> Participants will need fishing gear, lunch, and a change of clothes.

Correctly written with colon

> Participants will need only a few things: fishing gear, lunch, and a change of clothes. (A dash may be substituted for the colon.)

Misplaced between preposition and objects

> We have sales representatives assigned to: Dallas–Fort Worth, Memphis, and Atlanta.

Correctly written without colon

> We have sales representatives assigned to Dallas–Fort Worth, Memphis, and Atlanta.

Correctly written with colon

> We have sales representatives assigned to three metropolitan areas: Dallas–Fort Worth, Memphis, and Atlanta. (A dash may be substituted for the colon.)

Misplaced between *that* and following clause

> Sherman said that: "war is hell."

Correctly written without colon

> Sherman said that "war is hell."

Correctly written with colon

> Sherman said: "War is hell."

Dash and Colon

Usually the dash can replace the colon, as indicated in some of the sample sentences above. The dash is more emphatic, less subtle, and less formal than the colon. But the dash can be substituted for the colon when an independent clause follows only with great caution; the following clause should be short and should elaborate or expand the first clause. Nor can a colon substitute for a dash whenever a dash appears;

the colon's uses are much more limited. The only place writers are tempted to use a colon incorrectly for a dash is following an introductory list. For instance, the sentence *Faith, hope, and charity—are these not model values?* requires a dash; a colon is incorrect. (See page 150 for further examples.)

Elaboration, Including Lists

The colon indicates that whatever follows will elaborate the preceding independent clause. The elaboration may be a list, a one-word appositive, or a full sentence.

> Participants will need a few things: fishing gear, lunch, and a change of clothes. (A dash may replace the colon.)
>
> The goal of our company is simple: Success. (A dash may also be used.)
>
> The students outmaneuvered their instructor at the beginning of each class: when the bell rang, they began asking "naïve" questions about tangential subjects. (A dash is inappropriate here; write this with a colon, semicolon, or as two sentences.)
>
> Positive identification is required: Neither a social security card nor an oil-company credit card will suffice. (A dash is inappropriate; write this with a colon, with a semicolon, or as two sentences.)
>
> We have sales representatives assigned to three metropolitan areas: Dallas–Fort Worth, Memphis, and Atlanta. (A dash may be used.)
>
> Sherman said simply: "War is hell." (A comma may also be used.)

Capital Letter Following Colon

A capital letter following a colon emphasizes the elaboration that follows. A capital letter may be used when an independent clause or a single item follows the colon; it is not as appropriate when a list of items follows the colon, unless a word that is ordinarily capitalized follows the colon. A full-sentence quotation following a colon should begin with a capital letter (*Sherman said simply: "War is hell."*). (For additional discussion and further examples, see pages 175–76.)

Groups of Sentences

While it is permissible to introduce a series of sentences with a colon, remember that unless the sentences are grouped together, as with quotation marks, the reader will see the colon only with the first sentence.

Introducing Quotations and Examples

Colons may follow a partial sentence when a quotation of one sentence or more is introduced or when an example that is being typographically set off is introduced. The partial sentences are, typically, adverbial phrases or clauses.

> As Sherman said: "War is hell."
> Thus spake Zarathustra: "No small art is it to sleep: it is necessary for that purpose to keep awake all day."
> Thus: (followed by a quotation of one or more sentences)
> As a result: (followed by a quotation of one or more sentences)

Colon Introducing Vertical Lists

In a vertical list, a colon is often used at the end of an introductory partial sentence. A dash is more appropriate and gives a greater sense of continuity.

> Sales are down—
> 1. because the economy is sluggish.
> 2. because coffee breaks are longer.

or

> Sales are down because—
> 1. the economy is sluggish.
> 2. coffee breaks are longer.

Biblical Citations

The colon is traditionally used between chapter and verse in Biblical references. (A period may also be used.)

> Psalm 143:1 (or Psalm 143.1)

Clock Time

Hours and minutes on a twelve-hour clock are separated by a colon.

(Time on a twenty-four-hour clock is customarily written without punctuation.)

6:05 P.M.	12:40 A.M.
1805 hours	0240 hours

Letter Salutations

Salutations in formal letters are usually followed by colons instead of the less formal comma.

Dear Sir:
Your Imperial Highness:

Publication Data

In footnote references, a title and subtitle have traditionally been joined by a colon, although a comma is common now and is acceptable. The place of publication and the name of the publisher are separated by a colon. A volume and page number may be separated by a colon whether the volume is written in roman or arabic numerals (commas are used in some styles).

A Distant Mirror: The Calamitous 14th Century
New York: New American Library
III:126 (*or* 3:126, *or* III—*for* volume 3, page 126)

Different disciplines follow different styles, however, and you should consult a style guide or follow the existing practice in your own field. (See Chapter 18 for style guides.)

The Comma

The comma, the most frequently used punctuation mark, has relatively few basic uses. But as soon as one tries to enumerate where writers should use commas, as well as where they may use them, their possible uses multiply beyond bounds.

There are two divergent schools of comma usage. One school says to put commas at breath pauses. Unfortunately, this leads to many superfluous commas. The other school reduces everything to rule. Unfortunately, the rules never cover everything, and by-the-rule writers often end up restricting themselves unnecessarily to the sentences they know they can punctuate rather than the sentences they want to write.

Commas set off parenthetical remarks and descriptive modifiers and appositives. They help coordinate parallel grammatical structures such as lists, coordinate adjectives, and compound predicates. They mark words omitted in repeated constructions. They set off introductory elements, interruptions, and words moved from their usual positions. Sometimes they are used, when no rules apply, to prevent misreading or to create emphasis. In addition to these uses, commas are used with numbers, addresses, and dates.

Despite these many uses, commas are not to be treated as a kind of tinsel for sprinkling over the page to brighten things up. A writer should have a reason for each comma used.

Commas in Series

Commas come between the items in a series when conjunctions are omitted. If the final item is joined to the series with a conjunction, use a comma in front of the conjunction also. This is traditional and is still recommended by most authorities, although newspapers and modern advertising often ignore it.*

* The arguments over this final comma are vociferous. The Logic First group argues that, except to prevent misreading, the comma is unnecessary since it is used in place of *and* or *or;* when the *and* or *or* is supplied, the comma is redundant. The Expectations First group argues that the reader expects the comma and that putting it in consistently allows the writer to add an appositive or a parenthetical element to the last item without confusing the reader. We at the Writer's Hotline tend to be of the second school; we put the

> The carpenter handed me six nails, a chisel, and a ball peen hammer.
>
> Whimsy, humor, curiosity, and insight—all these are developed in young children through play. (Omitting the comma after *curiosity* might cause readers to think that the writer regards curiosity and insight as the same.)

Phrases and clauses may also be put into series, of course.

> Through play, the child can participate in leadership, learn to appreciate the need for rules, discover the joy of winning, and learn to fail or lose gracefully.
>
> Dozens of people were injured, three were killed, and the building was utterly demolished.
>
> I came, I saw, I conquered.
>
> William Jennings Bryan—he spoke, he was nominated, he ran, he lost.

(But see pages 135-37 for a discussion of compound sentences and the problems of linking a series of independent clauses with commas.)

When items in a series are relatively simple and each is connected by a conjunction, commas may be omitted. (With one- or two-word items connected by conjunctions, commas should be omitted.)

> Which Caesar was it—Augustus or Julius or Tiberius?

When items in a series are long and complex, especially if one of the first items contains internal commas, separate the items by semicolons. (If only the last item contains internal commas, the use of semicolons is optional, since the individual items in the series usually remain well defined and distinct.)

> Several corporate vice-presidents attended, including Steve Smith, public relations; Catherine Plante, accounting; Elaine Rossi, quality control; and James Jefferson, experimental manufacturing.

---

comma in, although we also tell callers that many style guides and other authorities consider it optional, and often the comma isn't necessary to make the meaning clear. However, if you are inclined to leave out the comma, remember to put it in when there is the possibility of misreading.

Sometimes, in spite of all our counsel and advice, a writer will insist on using *etc.* as the final item in a series. If you must use *etc.*, place a comma before it. (See the Glossary of Usage for a fuller discussion.) A comma should also precede paraphrases of *etc.*, such as *and so forth* and *and so on*.

For example, that is, including, such as, and Other Introductory Expressions

Basically there are two groups of introductory expressions. Those like *like, such as,* and *including* are prepositions. They and their accompanying lists or examples remain attached to the clause or sentence. The prepositions are *not* followed by commas, although sometimes the entire prepositional phrase may be set off parenthetically.

> Many members of the committee—including Horowitz, MacDougal, and Greene—will oppose any attempt to alter the bill. (Parentheses or commas could be substituted for the dashes.)

The other group includes expressions like *that is, namely,* and *for example.* Normally a comma follows them. Punctuation preceding them depends on the break preceding them. The entire explanatory phrase may be set off parenthetically, or it may, when followed by an independent clause, form its own sentence.

> Unlike Costa Rica, most Central American countries (for example, Honduras, Nicaragua, and El Salvador) have reputations for political instability.
> Our student body remains heterogeneous. For example, city blacks, rural whites, and Vietnamese immigrants are likely to be sitting together in any given classroom.
> Enrollment seems to be declining throughout the district. Specifically, Forrest High expects a three percent decline, City High a five percent decline, and Oak Park a seven percent decline for this coming year.

(In sentences like these, the *for example, that is, specifically,* and so on function as conjunctive adverbs.)

The abbreviations *i.e.* ("that is") and *e.g.* ("for example") are punctuated like the phrases *that is* and *for example*—with a comma following and appropriate punctuation for the break preceding. However, the comma following *i.e.* and *e.g.* is optional when a list of words follows. The abbreviations, by nature of being abbreviations, are already set off.

> Oil-exporting countries that do not belong to OPEC (e.g. Mexico and Oman) follow OPEC pricing.

Coordinate Adjectives

When two or more adjectives precede a noun or noun group, it is sometimes difficult to determine whether the adjectives each modify the noun or whether one of the adjectives forms a grouping with the noun, as in *new jumbo jet*. At other times, nouns can function as adjectives, so that it may be hard to tell whether a phrase like *gray cotton hat* is a group of nouns or a noun preceded by adjectives. We can shortcut the need for grammatical analysis by a simple test and rule.

> When adjectives preceding a noun or noun group can be interchanged or when *and* can be inserted between them without altering the sense, place a comma between them.

If one of these tests works, the adjectives are coordinate. That is, each adjective modifies the noun or noun group in the same manner.

> She is a tireless, conscientious, reliable worker. (The adjectives may be interchanged without altering the sentence.)
>
> He is a hard-working, penny-pinching socialist. (*Hardworking* and *penny-pinching* can be correctly punctuated simply by seeing that they are reversible.)

If adjectives sound strained when being reversed or when having *and* inserted between them, they are not coordinate. Do not use a comma.

> One's first car can be an exciting, electrifying thrill, even if it is an old, beat-up Model T Ford. (*Exciting* and *electrifying* are separated by commas; *old* and *beat-up* are separated by commas. The adjectives are coordinate. There is no comma between *beat-up* and *Model T* because they are not coordinate.)

Traditional, established politics disgusted him, even though it was traditional, established political institutions that he was most fond of.

He wore his old cotton golf hat and his new brown wingtips. (*Old* and *cotton,* like *new* and *brown,* are awkward when *and* is placed between them; a comma is not required after *old* and after *new.*)

Compound Sentences

When independent clauses are joined by coordinating conjunctions, a comma precedes the conjunction. With short, parallel, closely related clauses the commas are sometimes omitted.

The book contains dozens of designs, and the reader should quickly learn to create his or her own designs.

Floyd ran the campaign and Jill ran Floyd.

A series of brief, simple, grammatically parallel, and closely related independent clauses may be joined with only commas whether or not the last pair of clauses is joined by a conjunction. (Some authorities say that the final pair must be joined by a conjunction, apparently as a way for the writer to demonstrate that the series is meant as a series. We disagree. But omit the conjunction only to achieve a rhythmic effect.)

Dozens of people were injured, three were killed, and the building was entirely demolished.

I came, I saw, I conquered.

William Jennings Bryan—he spoke, he was nominated, he ran, he lost.

The parallel nature of the clauses can be emphasized by omitting repeated verbs and including the final conjunction. Or semicolons can be placed between the clauses.

Dozens of people were injured, three killed, and the building entirely demolished.

I came; I saw; I conquered.

William Jennings Bryan—he spoke; he was nominated; he ran; he lost.

Comma Splices (Conjunctive Adverbs)

Joining together independent clauses with only a comma and without a coordinate conjunction is often called a "comma splice." Comma splices are roundly condemned; grammatical authorities allow an exception only with short parallel clauses, as discussed above. This condemnation involves more than grammatical snobbery, however. Comma splices often indicate a writer who refuses to exercise control over thoughts and sentences. The writer's thoughts are mixed together and tossed at the reader in a heap, with the hope that the reader cares enough to sort the thoughts out.

Comma splices are caused most frequently by writers mistaking conjunctive adverbs (e.g. *therefore, however, thus*) for coordinating conjunctions (e.g. *and, but, or*). Semicolons rather than commas are needed before *moreover* and *consequently* in the following sentence.

Comma splice

> He was the chairman of my dissertation committee, moreover, he was my stepfather's cousin, consequently, I expected an easy path to my degree.

Replacing the commas with semicolons, while eliminating the comma splices, doesn't create a good sentence: the sentence needs rewriting. This is why we say that comma splices often reveal writers who have not taken care with their thinking and writing.

Revised

> Since the chairman of my dissertation committee was my stepfather's cousin, I expected an easy path to my degree.

Conjunctive adverbs link one thought to another, but they cannot grammatically link independent clauses, as coordinating conjunctions do. Conjunctive adverbs are first and primarily adverbs, and like adverbs, they can appear in many places in a sentence. In fact, the easiest way to tell whether a conjunction-like word is a true conjunction or is an adverb is to try moving it around. For instance, in the sentence below the conjunctive adverb *consequently* can be easily placed in three positions. Coordinating conjunctions cannot be moved.

> (*Consequently*) the mailroom (*consequently*) did not mail the reports on time (*consequently*).

Shifting a conjunctive adverb around may shift the emphasis slightly, but it does not change the grammar.

Some words that function as conjunctive adverbs are also used as simple adverbs. These cause writers no problem. When there is no pause in the reading, no comma is needed.

> *However* it happened, the accident has been a disaster for the entire industry.
>
> I will stay *however* long it takes.
>
> Professor Jones put forward the most outrageous opinion on book censorship, *consequently* enraging his entire class.

Subordinate Clauses

Subordinate (or dependent) clauses are clauses that cannot stand alone as sentences. They are introduced by a subordinate conjunction and may appear in three places in a sentence: before the subject and verb, between the subject and verb, and following the subject and verb.

> *Although the mail was slow,* the packages arrived on time.
>
> The packages, *although the mail was slow,* arrived on time.
>
> The packages arrived on time, *although the mail was slow.*

If a subordinate clause precedes the subject and verb, place a comma after the clause. (This comma, which is almost never dropped in writing, represents a pause as we speak.)

> Although the copy was received a week late, the report will be ready on time.
>
> If you sign a contract during the next five working days, please notify this office immediately.

Subordinate clauses between the subject and the verb often modify the subject. These are called relative clauses and are of two different types. Descriptive or nonrestrictive modifiers are set off by commas; defining or restrictive modifiers are not punctuated. (See pages 139–41 for a fuller discussion of these clauses.) Clauses out of their normal position—usually adverbial clauses that modify the verb or the entire sentence—interrupt the sentence and are set off with a pair of commas.

Children's games, *which are usually fun for children,* often bore adults. (descriptive clause set off)

Games *that are fun for children* usually bore adults. (defining clause not set off)

The report, *although the copy was received in this office a week late,* will be ready Monday. (The clause interrupts and is set off by commas.)

Many people, *because they distrust themselves,* distrust other people. (The clause interrupts and is set off by commas.)

A subordinate clause that follows the subject and verb and modifies the verb or the entire sentence is normally not set off by a comma. The same clause coming before the subject or between the subject and verb is set off. Writers will do well to follow the usual rule that applies to clauses following a subject and verb: Do not put a comma in front of a final subordinate clause unless you wish to emphasize it—and a dash is often more effective—or unless it is clearly parenthetical. When the verb in the main clause is negative, the subordinate clause must sometimes be set off by a comma to prevent misreading.

Children's games bore adults because adults refuse to work at being children.

The report will be distributed Monday, if the mailroom clerks do not strike. (A dash could be used.)

The contract will be signed after its provisions are agreed to.

Usually, heated water is transferred to a well-insulated storage tank, particularly if overnight storage is desired. (a parenthetical addition)

He left because everyone he wanted to see had left. (no comma before *because*)

He did not leave because Jones had left. (He left for
some other reason.)

He did not leave, because Jones had left. (Jones left and
so he stayed.)

Personal financial disclosure is not required because of
the attorney general's opinion. (It is required for
another reason.)

Personal financial disclosure is not required, because of
the attorney general's opinion. (Disclosure is not required. The meaning is clearer if the subordinate clause
is moved to the front of the sentence: *Because of the
attorney general's opinion, personal financial disclosure
is not required.*)

Relative Clauses and Appositives

Relative clauses and appositives give information about the
nouns or noun substitutes they modify. Relative clauses are
subordinate clauses introduced by relative pronouns such as
that, which, who, whom, and *whose.* Relative clauses are
italicized in the following sentences.

The man *who is nominated* will win the election.
All the members *that were present* voted to increase the
penalty for being absent.
The Art Department, *which has never been very cooperative,* has been particularly slothful on this project.

An appositive is a noun phrase that follows a noun or noun
substitute and renames it. The appositive can be substituted
for the first noun without changing the grammar or the logic
of the sentence. In the following noun-appositive phrases, the
appositives are italicized.

the poet *Emily Dickinson*
Emily Dickinson, *the poet,*
Harry Truman, *the President,*
to him, *the leader of the group,*

Relative clauses and appositives are either descriptive (nonrestrictive) or defining (restrictive). A descriptive clause or
appositive adds information but does not alter or limit the

noun any further in the reader's mind. Defining clauses and appositives, on the other hand, further limit what is being talked about or point out which specific person or thing is being discussed. The punctuation rule is clear and unambiguous: Put commas around descriptive (nonrestrictive) clauses and appositives; they are a kind of parenthetical thought and are set off. Do not put commas around defining (restrictive) clauses and appositives; these are crucial to our understanding of the sentence.

The following clauses and appositives are descriptive; they are correctly punctuated with commas.

> Jefferson Jackson, president of Fiduciary Trust,
> Emily Dickinson, the poet,
> the report, which is on the table by the window,

The following clauses and appositives, slight variations of the ones above, are all defining or restrictive; they are correctly punctuated without commas.

> President of Fiduciary Trust Jefferson Jackson
> the poet Emily Dickinson
> the report that is on the table by the window

Notice that the handling of names and titles or descriptions, which sometimes causes problems for writers, follows the same punctuation rule. Titles and descriptions that follow names are considered descriptive or parenthetical and are set off with commas. Names following titles and descriptions tell the reader precisely who is meant; they are defining or restrictive. Do not set them off.

> His friend Shirley Jones has the flu.
> Shirley Jones, his friend, has the flu.

Sometimes the writer's understanding is conveyed to the reader by the presence or absence of commas.

> The financial report, which was due Monday, will be a week late.
> The financial report that was due Monday will be a week late.
> A flexible body, which takes much less energy to move than a stiff one, is a joy to behold.
> A flexible body that takes little energy to move is a joy to behold.

The motion, which was on the floor, was tabled indefinitely.

The motion that was on the floor was tabled indefinitely.

Adjective Phrases

Descriptive and defining adjective phrases that follow nouns are punctuated like other descriptive and defining phrases. Descriptive (nonrestrictive) phrases are set off with commas; defining (restrictive) ones are not set off.

The president, *warm and friendly as usual,* greeted the hostile delegation.

The tall, angry-looking man *at the front of the group* was not its leader, although he spoke frequently.

Introductory Prepositional and Other Phrases

Set off introductory phrases of all kinds: participial phrases, absolute constructions, prepositional phrases, and so on. There are two exceptions. The comma following a short prepositional phrase, when there is no danger of misreading, may be omitted. And an adverbial modifier that is part of the predicate in an inverted sentence should not be followed by a comma.

Having forgotten to notify the staff of the changes in accounting procedures, the comptroller was fired.

His heart on his sleeve, his head in his hands, he slumped down on the park bench.

On July 24, 1980, the company celebrated its anniversary.

Within hours after the attack on Pearl Harbor, the United States was mobilizing for war.

In December the company went bankrupt.

Down from the horse slid a small, freckle-faced girl.

Conjunctive Adverbs and Transitional Phrases

Conjunctive adverbs and transitional phrases are generally set off from the clause they modify whether they come at the beginning, in the middle, or at the end of the clause. But when these words do not represent a major break in continuity and there is no pause in the reading, do not set them off. Transitional phrases, simply because they are longer, almost always represent a break in continuity.

> *Moreover,* the opposition was in shambles.
> The witness, *consequently,* was hotly challenged by the defense.
> *Thus,* we had a situation on our hands in which we had only minutes, rather than hours, to respond.
> The drought was long-lasting and severe, *thus* giving us a chance to recommend the virtues of dry-land farming.
> The bank account was *indeed* empty.
> Leghorn had *in fact* become the chairman of the Committee on the Advancement of Poultry.
> All the welds were *therefore* reexamined.

Dependent Clauses and Introductory Phrases in Compound Sentences

Dependent clauses and introductory phrases in compound sentences are handled in the same way as they are in simple sentences. However, the comma that one is tempted to put between the coordinating conjunction and the following clause or phrase is omitted.

> The baby began crying, and while the mother tried to calm it, the father began to sob.
> The degree program has been adopted, and although the vote was unanimous, several reservations were raised about the program.

(No commas follow the *ands* although in each case the following dependent clause can be thought of as an interrupter.)

Correlative Conjunctions

Correlative conjunctions (*both . . . and, neither . . . nor,* and *not only . . . but* or *but also,* for example) link elements of equal grammatical rank. Commas are not used between the parts of the construction unless they are independent clauses.

(The temptation to use commas is greatest in correlatives that contain the word *but*.)

All roads lead *both* toward *and* away from Rome.
Not only the price *but* also the quality is unsatisfactory.
Not only is the cost unreasonable, *but* the workmanship is unsatisfactory. (two independent clauses)
Not only do they keep their children home from school, *but* they do so openly.

In joining clauses in general writing, the first portion of the correlative conjunction is sometimes placed where a simple *only* or *not* is often placed, and the second portion of the conjunction is dropped. The construction remains a correlative however. The thought will be more forcefully expressed if the correlative is completed.

Original

She was *not only* habitually late, she flaunted her lateness.

Revised

Not only was she habitually late, but she also flaunted her lateness.

Negative and Complementary Paired Phrases

Paired phrases, whether negative or positive, that refer to the same following word are separated by commas. Sometimes these paired phrases are parts of a complex subject; at other times they involve adverbial modifiers. In effect, the second of the paired phrases is treated as an interrupter. But remember that a comma should come between the end of the second partial phrase and the word that concludes both phrases.

The unfortunate, but obviously true, conclusion is that the children were not being cared for.
All roads lead away from, as well as toward, Rome.
The most titillating, but the least important, testimony was saved for the last day.
He would like, and apparently is trying, to believe in the equality of women.

A phrase beginning with *not* is usually set off unless its meaning is essential to the meaning of the larger clause.

> Simpson, not Adams, quickly became the candidate to beat.
> The delegation demanded to see the school superintendent, not her assistant.

Interdependent Clauses

Interdependent clauses are joined/separated by a comma. Short interdependent clauses are generally not punctuated.

> The higher the stock rose, the more excited they became.
> The more he read and heard about Watergate, the more he wanted to read about it.
> Monkey see, monkey do. (comma to prevent misreading)
> The more the merrier.

Omitted Words

Words that can be readily understood from the context but have been omitted from a sentence are sometimes marked with a comma. This often occurs in parallel constructions when a repeated verb or other phrase is dropped.

> Several states each have two dozen or more representatives: California has 43; New York, 39; Pennsylvania, 25; and Illinois and Texas, 24.
> Thousands acclaimed her in July; in November, no one.
> The preliminary report is due March 16, the final copy, April 2.

But the commas may, and often should, be omitted when the reading is clear without them.

> Although the copy was late, the art department sluggardly, and the printers inept, the report will be in the mail Monday, if the mailroom clerks don't strike.
> The public adored her, and she them.

Commas and Quotations

Commas separate a full-sentence quotation from surrounding comments such as *he said* and *the judge retorted*. Commas always go inside quotation marks. (For examples and discussion, see pages 157–59.)

Dates

Place a comma between the date of the month and the year when dates are written traditionally (*August 1, 1980*). In context, the year is traditionally followed by a comma (*August 1, 1980, is a day I will never forget*). This comma is disappearing, but it does reflect the natural breath pause at the end of a date. (For examples and illustrations of the various ways of handling dates, see page 234.)

Addresses

When addresses are written in copy, place commas after the street address, the city or town, and the state. (If the address includes a zip code, place a comma after the zip code but not between the state and zip code.) If a national name is needed, place a comma after it also. Like the final comma after the year of a date, the comma at the end of an address is disappearing, but it is still in general usage.

> Letters sent to 1600 Pennsylvania Ave., Washington, D.C. 20500, will. . . .
> The plane was forced to land at Gander, Newfoundland, in eastern Canada.

Direct Address

Commas are placed around names, titles, and even common noun references used in direct address. The entire direct address is set off. (*O*, which is always capitalized, is now used only as part of a direct address and is not set off separately.)

> Friends, Romans, countrymen, lend me your ears.
> Go west, young man, go west.
> My fellow Americans, let us move forward together.
> We pleaded for our freedom, "O most mighty and high. . . ."

Interjections

Punctuate interjections as interrupters. Treat *oh* as an interjection. Also set off the words *yes* and *no* with a comma when they begin sentences.

> Oh, did you receive many crank calls?
> Yes, we will make the loan.

Degrees and Name Designations

Use commas to set off abbreviated degrees that follow a name.

> Melissa Jones, Ph.D.,
> Howard Whittinghill, M.S.W.,

Use commas to set off name designations that are not part of the baptismal name. Do not set off numerical designations.

> Martin Luther King, Jr.,
> Raymond Miller Murphy, Esq.,
> John D. Rockefeller IV
> George III

Titles and Job Descriptions with Names

Place commas around titles and job descriptions that follow names. When they precede a name, commas are not required because the name acts like a defining or restrictive appositive.

> trial lawyer Joe Palooka
> Joe Palooka, trial lawyer,

Supreme Court Justice William O. Douglas
William O. Douglas, Supreme Court Justice,

Numbers

Use a comma to mark off numbers by thousands. Four-figure numbers are sometimes not marked off.

2,456,987
1,570 (or 1570)

Commas are generally not used in calendar years, serial numbers, identification numbers, addresses, and other special-use numbers. Commas are not used in decimal fractions.

Misreading

Use a comma, even in violation of a "rule," whenever necessary to prevent misreading.

If you want to, go to Mexico for Christmas.
The year after, the stock market fell precipitously.
To Josephine, Napoleon was never a mystery.
Alexander Pope wrote, "Whatever is, is right," and he meant it.
He looked carefully at the people who arrived, and left swiftly.
He looked carefully at the people, who arrived and left swiftly.

The Put-Commas-Where-You-Breathe Rule

Writers who put commas wherever they take a breath usually have little problem with correctly punctuating descriptive (nonrestrictive) clauses and interrupters. Unfortunately, they usually add commas in many other places as well. Paying attention to the stresses and intonation of a sentence often helps writers create natural and easy sentences. But commas do not belong everywhere a reader pauses in a sentence. To put a comma at each pause is to sprinkle so many commas through a sentence that the expected and necessary ones are lost.

Superfluous Commas

Superfluous commas annoy and confuse readers. The confusion seldom lasts long, of course, but readers who are distracted and annoyed begin to pay attention to their own discomfort instead of to the writer's words and ideas. The following sentences illustrate many common superfluous commas.

> The dogs, the cats, and the rats, chased each other through the house. (comma after series between the subject and the verb)
>
> The cat chased the dog, and worried the rat. (comma between parts of a compound verb)
>
> But, the sun's energy is the closest thing we have to an inexhaustible energy source. (comma following a coordinate conjunction)
>
> He is certain that, he is being treated unfairly while others are being rewarded, and promoted. (comma between *that* and its clause; comma between parts of complement)
>
> The board chairman is currently on a tour, of our proposed Bahamian operations. (comma for emphasis can perhaps be justified, but it is weak)
>
> The workers struck, for higher wages. (comma between verb and its prepositional phrase)
>
> The President has declared, war with the Soviet Union is unthinkable. (comma between verb and object; comma should be used in place of omitted *that* only with direct quote)

The commas above simply interrupt the expected flow of the sentence. Interrupting words, phrases, and clauses may appear in the middle of a sentence, of course, and then a *pair* of commas will set them off.

> The board chairman is currently on a tour, with his family and several friends, of our proposed Bahamian operations.

He is certain, without doubt or qualification, that he is being treated unfairly.

The When-in-Doubt-Leave-It-Out Rule

By-the-rule writers use a simple test to gauge the aptness of their punctuation: When in doubt, leave it out. When they are tempted to put a comma somewhere but cannot justify it with a specific rule, they omit it. The value of this rule is that it reminds writers not to sprinkle commas over the pages as they read along. However, this thinking may cause writers to shy away from unusual sentences for fear of mispunctuating them.

Rules are supposed to be, even if they are not always, based on good, educated practice. This implies that practice will change before the rules. But if a writer strays far from the rules, readers become confused, for the writer also strays from customary, expected practice. Rules reflect usage, not the eccentricities of a single, eccentric writer. So the when-in-doubt rule, applied judiciously, is a useful check, particularly for people who tend to overpunctuate.

The Dash

The dash, like the comma and parentheses, sets off parenthetical words and phrases. But while parentheses downplay what they set off and commas are generally neutral, dashes call attention to what is set off. The dash signals interruptions, changes of thought, and asides. It can function as a sort of supercomma, and it can replace a colon. Dashes can enliven sentences, but when overused and misused, they often reveal a writer whose thoughts are out of control.

Interruptions and Asides

Use a dash to set off a major interruption of a sentence, a parenthetical comment, an aside, or a response to the main part of the sentence. Dashes and parentheses are often interchangeable in these instances.

> The chancellor has requested—that is, she has required—that someone from each department volunteer to serve on the liaison committee.
>
> He pleaded innocent—he always does—and said that the charges were brought by political foes.
>
> If the bill fails—and we are working night and day for its passage—truck weights will remain woefully restricted.

Parenthetical Comments

Use a dash to set off a parenthetical comment that you want to emphasize or when it contains commas and so would be confusing if set off by additional commas. The dashes here act like highly visible supercommas.

> Several members of the staff—Mrs. Brown, Ms. Green, Mr. Black, and Dr. Jones—will be representing us at the meeting.
>
> Many states—including Texas, Arkansas, Oklahoma, and Missouri—are suffering severe crop losses.
>
> Many farmers—including many small poultry farmers—are being wiped out by this weather.

Introductory Lists

Use a dash after an introductory list when the following clause contains a pronoun that sums up the list. Usually this pronoun is the first word following the list. Such a list is actually an appositive that has been juxtaposed for rhetorical effect. Although many people are tempted to use colons in this position, dashes are alway preferred.

> Sanskrit, Hittite, and Greek—these three languages are among the many that have, along with English, descended from Proto-Indo-European.
>
> Einstein, Fermi, and Oppenheimer—each in his own way was the father of the atomic bomb.
>
> Coleridge, Poe, Longfellow, and Emerson—John Phoenix satirized them all.

Emphasis

The dash is always emphatic. It is sometimes used in place of a comma—and occasionally where no comma would ordinarily be put—to give emphasis to a clause, particularly the final clause of a sentence. As with all emphatic punctuation, this can be quickly overdone.

> We will be more than happy to assist you with your design problems—after we agree on contract terms.
> The streets were hot—steaming hot.
> Departmental annual reports are due tomorrow noon—not 5 P.M.
> We agreed that Margot's plan was bold and imaginative—bold and imaginative and completely unworkable.

Tangled Sentences

The dash is sometimes used to mark an extensive interruption, even allowing the writer to repeat the phrase preceding the dash. Sometimes this is effectively done for emphasis, as shown in the last example above. More often, it marks writers who are too lazy to straighten out the syntax of their own sentences.

Tangled syntax

> Sometimes the syntax of his sentences becomes so tangled —with parentheses here and there, with brackets inside one, and the whole thing set off by a dash or two, and with possibly a double or triple quote—the syntax becomes so tangled that the only response is to hack into it as Alexander once hacked into the Gordian Knot.

(And the only thing to do with a sentence like this one is to hack it to pieces and start again.)

In Place of Colon

Many writers prefer dashes to colons, and they substitute dashes for colons whenever possible. These writers consider dashes bolder and less formal. Structurally, dashes can substitute for colons with only one caution—don't overdo them. Dashes can even be used to join independent clauses without a conjunction, provided that the second clause is short and elaborates or explains the first. Be warned, however, that some readers have a prejudice against dashes, for dashes are often associated with gushing, overwhelmed writers, the sort who join random thoughts with a series of dashes.

> Participants will need a few things—fishing gear, lunch, and a change of clothes.
> We have assigned sales personnel to three metropolitan areas—Dallas–Fort Worth, Memphis, and Atlanta.
> Participants will need only a few things—these are available from the canteen. (semicolon or colon preferred)

Punctuation with Dashes

Question marks and exclamation points that are part of parenthetical comments set off by dashes are retained. If a comma and a dash logically come at the same point in a sentence, the comma is dropped. Periods in internal sentences set off by dashes are dropped, as periods in internal sentences always are. When a dash and a final period come together, the dash is normally dropped; when the dash indicates a broken or incomplete thought, drop the period.

Quotations

Use a dash following a quotation, in front of the author's name, when the quotation is set off by itself. (When the quotation is set off by itself, the quotation marks are usually dropped.)

> Politics has got so expensive that it takes lots of money to even get beat with.—Will Rogers

Vertical Lists

In a vertical list where each item of the column completes the sentence, the introductory portion of the sentence may be followed by a dash.

No matter how "busy" parents are, they should find time
every day—
1. to hug and hold each child.
2. to play or read with each child.
3. to talk with each child.

Omitted Letters, Dialogue

Use a dash to indicate omitted letters in words and to
indicate disruptions and interruptions in dialogue.

The book was given to Mr. A—.
"What the bloody h—l!" he shouted.

Parentheses

Parentheses, like dashes and commas, set off parenthetical
material, which explains, elaborates, or comments on what
has been said. The parentheses, more than dashes or commas,
suggest that this information is a minor aside, something that
could be put in a footnote. In addition to setting off parenthetical information, parentheses are used to enumerate items
in a series.

Parenthetical Information

Use parentheses to enclose minor, nonessential details, such
as specific dates of events, statistical figures, cross-referencing,
and brief comments.

The Pearl Poet (fl. 1370) is principally known for *Sir
Gawain and the Green Knight*.
The great English writers of the late fourteenth century
(Chaucer, Langland, the Pearl Poet, and the Wakefield
Master) apparently had no contact with each other.

Punctuation in Parentheses

A sentence enclosed entirely within parentheses is punctuated within the parentheses.

The vice-presidnt for sales promotions took up twenty minutes reading the sales figures for the past quarter. (He insisted upon doing that, even though we all had copies of the figures in our hands.)

A comment in parentheses that occurs as part of a sentence does not alter the punctuation of the sentence.

No children (not even yours) can behave well all the time.

Normally, punctuation will not appear in front of a parenthesis, but punctuation may follow the closing parenthesis.

When he goes fishing (and that is infrequently), he takes his Dictaphone, a briefcase full of mail, and several books that he has been waiting to read.

If the parenthetical material ends the sentence, final punctuation must follow the closing parenthesis, even when a complete sentence comes within the parentheses. The only exception to this occurs when an abbreviation ends the parenthetical material.

The Midwestern offices have surpassed by far their sales goals (Denver has almost doubled theirs). (no period after *theirs*)
The welcoming committee waited four hours at the airport (her plane arrived at 11 P.M.).

A question mark or an exclamation point (but not a period) that is part of the parenthetical material occurs inside the parenthesis. If the parenthetical material is at the end of the sentence, an additional mark of final punctuation occurs after the parenthesis has been closed.

Middle-class values (I will not call them virtues!) are responsible for much of the suffering in this country.
I could write twenty pages explaining the destructive consequences of following middle-class values (I will not call them virtues!).

Quotation marks will appear inside or outside parentheses to accurately reflect what is being quoted.

Paragraphs in Parentheses

If more than one paragraph appears in parentheses, the opening parenthesis is used at the beginning of each paragraph, but the closing parenthesis comes only at the end of the parenthetical material. Lengthy parenthetical comments usually belong in footnotes rather than in the text.

Enumerating Lists

Parentheses are often used around the numbers enumerating a list within the body of the text. (In a vertical list, follow each number or letter with a period instead of with a closing parenthesis.)

> Three offices have been particularly successful this month: (1) Denver, over $1,000,000 in new sales; (2) St. Louis. . . .
> Three offices have been particularly successful this month:
> 1. [not *1*)] Denver, over $1,000,000 in new sales
> 2. [not *2*)] Saint Louis. . . .

Brackets

Brackets have only two uses in general writing, both very restricted. They are used to insert editorial comments and changes into quoted material and for parenthetical comments within parentheses.

Editorial Comments

When you wish to comment on material you are quoting, place brackets around the comment within the quotation. This includes the word *sic*, which indicates that something you consider a mistake in fact or in form occurs in the original as you have presented it. *Sic* is Latin for "thus" and stands for "thus in the original." It is not an abbreviation, is not followed by a period, and is no longer put into italics or underlined. Beware of overusing it.

> The lecturer said, "Earth, Venus, and Mars, the third, fourth, and fifth [sic] planets of the solar system. . . ."

A writer's ridicule of or scorn for material being quoted is sometimes indicated by [!] or [?]. These are best avoided.

Editorial Changes and Alterations

Especially in a quotation being fused with a sentence in the text, it is sometimes desirable or necessary to make minor changes in the quotation, including replacing or altering a pronoun or changing the tense of a verb. This is done by putting the changed word into brackets and omitting the original. An ellipsis mark is not needed. You may want to replace a pronoun with its antecedent or to explain a pronoun or term. This may also be done in brackets.

> Othello said he would "a round [i.e. plain, honest] unvarnished tale deliver/Of [his] whole course of love."

Parenthesis Within Parentheses

Brackets are used for parenthetical comments within parentheses. Usually this happens with a parenthetical textual citation.

> Erich Fromm also departs from Freudian dream analysis (see *The Forgotten Language* [New York: Holt, Rinehart and Winston, 1951], particularly the sample dream analyses).

Quotation Marks

Quotation marks mark words quoted directly, give words special emphasis, and mark titles of shorter works.

Direct Quotations

The precise words from a book, a speaker, or any other quoted source, are put in quotation marks, whether the quoted words are a page long or simply a phrase or single word.

> James Thurber provided a unique definition of humor: "Humor is emotional chaos remembered in tranquility."
>
> Bill Stout said that his secret for designing airplanes was simply to "simplicate and add more lightness."

Be careful not to create a run-on sentence out of a two-sentence quotation. A two-sentence quotation interrupted by a phrase such as *he said* should be punctuated as two sentences. Normally, incorporate the interrupting phrase into the first sentence.

> "Wars are poor chisels for carving out peaceful tomorrows," said Martin Luther King. "We must pursue peaceful ends through peaceful means."

Of course, these sentences can be arranged in other ways.

> "Wars," said Martin Luther King, "are poor chisels for carving out peaceful tomorrows. We must pursue peaceful ends through peaceful means."

Omissions in Quotations

Omissions in quotations are generally marked with an ellipsis (three spaced periods), although an obviously incomplete quote, such as a phrase, does not need to be marked. (See pages 162–64.)

Quotes Within Quotes

Primary quotations are generally marked with double quotation marks. Secondary quotations, which are quotations within the primary quotation, are marked with single quotation marks. Quotations within the second quotation are marked with double quotation marks, and so on. In practice, however, readers cannot be expected to follow beyond a third-level quotation.

> Dad told me, "I always follow Aunt Madge's advice: 'Eat just enough to keep alert.' "

(British practice uses single quotation marks for the primary quotations and double quotation marks for the secondary quote.)

Punctuation with Quotation Marks

Hotline callers often ask about the placement of periods and commas with quotation marks. They vaguely remember the rule, but it seems illogical to them, so they call to ask. The answer is Always. Closing periods and commas *always* go inside the quotation marks even if only one word or letter is quoted. (Always in America, that is. British convention is the reverse.) Colons and semicolons always go outside the quotation marks. Question marks and exclamation points are handled more logically. If they are part of the quotation, they go inside the quotation marks. If they are part of the sentence, but not part of the quotation, they go after the quotation marks. If both the sentence and the quotation are a question or an exclamation, you will need one or two marks, depending on whether or not the quotation ends at the end of the sentence.

> "How much money will it cost?" is that all the senator asked?
> "Don't you scream 'Up the Establishment!' at me."
> Did he really tell you, "Go to hell!"?

When the sentence becomes a hodgepodge of marks, however, it is time to rewrite. In general, one question mark or one exclamation point should take care of a sentence.

> "Did the senator really ask how much money that will cost?" the governor asked.

If a period and either an exclamation point or a question mark are called for at one point—one to end the quotation and the other mark to end the sentence—only the stronger is used, and it is placed where logic demands.

> Did the senator really ask, "How much money will that cost"?
>
> The senator asked simply, "How much will this pork barrel cost?"

Indirect Quotations

Do not punctuate or set off with quotation marks indirect quotations (summaries of remarks or paraphrased remarks). Set off only the exact words a person has written or spoken. In the course of paraphrasing a person's thoughts, often a memorable phrase or clause from the original is retained; put it into quotation marks.

> He asked how one gets in to see the President.
>
> In his usual tone, he asked how one gets in to "have a sniff at the big cheese."

Yes, no and Other One-Word Summations

Unless they occur in the midst of a direct quote, treat the words *yes, no, maybe, never,* and other summary words as indirect quotes. Do not put them in quotation marks for emphasis. Capitalize them only when the sentence would be confusing without a capital letter or when you want dramatic emphasis.

> The bank told her yes, it would lend her the money.
>
> The best answer we can hope for is Maybe.

Mottos and Proverbial Expressions

In general, do not use quotation marks for proverbial expressions and the like when they are used figuratively in your text. When quoted and attributed to someone (to Poor Richard, for instance), they are handled as quotations.

> Even after his third speeding ticket, it is not possible to convince him that haste makes waste.
>
> Poor Richard's advice still holds true: "Early to bed, early to rise, /Makes a man healthy, wealthy, and wise."
>
> Arkansas is known as the Land of Opportunity.

Conventional Uses of Quotation Marks

Titles of Short Works

The use of quotation marks for some titles, particularly the titles of individual poems, songs, chapters of books, and magazine articles, is covered in Chapter 12.

Special Emphasis

Quotation marks can be used to call particular attention to words. They are used to indicate quoted words, of course, but they can also indicate a special use of a word or phrase.

> What does it mean to say that we should "treat clients with respect"?
>
> The president calls himself "a country lawyer" and does business like a "good ole boy."
>
> We experienced a "chill" today when the mercury finally stayed below 100°F.

Coined words and slang are sometimes put into quotation marks, especially in formal writing.

> After "sweating out" the border crossing, we had no trouble during our stay.
>
> The GNP (Gross National Product) is currently on a "downer."

The quotation marks are acceptable and should be used when writers are uncomfortable or think their readers may be uncomfortable with particular words. But the quotation marks do call attention to the slang and coined words. Slang and jargon, even for special "with it" effect, are quickly overused and, even within quotation marks, quickly dated.

Handling Long Quotations

Quotations of more than one paragraph not set off from the main text remain in quotation marks. Use a quotation mark at the beginning of each paragraph, but do not use closing quotation marks until the entire quotation is complete.

Generally, set off long quotations from your text instead of running them into the body of the text. Poetry quotations of more than two lines should generally be set off. If poetry is run into the text, separate the lines with a slash. Prose quotations longer than four typed lines (when final copy is to be typed rather than printed) or longer than eight typed lines (when final copy is to be typeset and printed) should be set off. These figures, however, are merely guides. Base your decision on appearance and readability.

The mechanics of setting off a long quotation vary with the format of the finished copy. In typewritten copy that is not to be typeset, the quote is typed single space and the left margin is indented as far as the usual paragraph indentation. In typeset copy, the quotation is indented or set in smaller type or both.

Quotation marks are not used for quotations that are indented and set off. The setting off by itself indicates the quotation. Editorial comments, discussions, and citations within the set-off quotation should be put in brackets.

Introductory Phrases and Punctuation

Long quotations are sometimes introduced with the same phrases and punctuation as short ones. But because the quotations are long, they are less often run into a sentence and are more often formally introduced with a phrase like *as follows* or *thus*. Such phrases are followed by colons.

Sometimes a partial sentence introduces a long quotation. A fragmented sentence should be followed by a comma if the quote is one sentence long and by a colon if the quote is longer than one sentence.

> Although Eisenhower contended, (to introduce a one-sentence quotation)

For example, as Churchill argued: (to introduce a quotation of more than one sentence)

His conclusion was as follows: (to introduce a quotation of more than one sentence)

The Ellipsis

The ellipsis is formed with three spaced periods. It indicates omission of material or breaks in thought and occasionally is used to suggest suspension and pause. (Asterisks have been used in the past to indicate ellipsis but are no longer used that way.)

Use three spaced periods to indicate material omitted from the middle of a sentence or the middle of a line of poetry, whether the omission is one word or twenty. (For how to alter material within a quotation, see page 156.)

> I returned and saw . . . that . . . time and chance happeneth to . . . all. (From the original, "I returned, and saw under the sun, that the race is not to the swift, nor the battle to the strong, neither yet bread to the wise, nor yet riches to men of understanding, nor yet favor to men of skill; but time and chance happeneth to them all.")

At the Beginning of a Quotation

Omissions at the beginning of a sentence may be indicated with an ellipsis, but when the quoted words are within a sentence of the text, as they usually are, the quote may begin with a small letter and the beginning ellipsis mark omitted.

> The writer of Ecclesiastes says that "the race is not to the swift, nor the battle to the strong. . . ."

At the End of a Quotation

If a sentence ends with a question mark or exclamation point and if the end of the sentence is being omitted, use three spaced periods followed by the question mark or exclamation point. If the sentence ends with a period, place a period immediately after the final word and follow this with the ellipsis. (This conventional usage is supported by printers, as it provides the most attractive spacing of periods.) A comma at the end of a phrase is dropped.

> I returned, and saw under the sun, that the race is not to the swift, nor the battle to the strong. . . .

Unneeded Ellipsis Marks

Generally, an ellipsis is not used to introduce or close an obviously incomplete quotation, such as a phrase or clause run into a sentence of the text. Nor is the ellipsis used when a word of the original has been replaced with another word enclosed in brackets.

> The office manager decided efficiency would be improved with "good old-fashioned competition" and suggested a Steno of the Month award.
> "The sun shines as hot [in Yuma] as it does on the planet Mercury," the old man said.

Long Omissions

The omission of several sentences within a single paragraph is shown with a single ellipsis. The omission of an entire paragraph or an entire line (or more) of poetry is generally indicated by a row of spaced periods.

> Hey diddle diddle
> . . . .
> And the dish ran away with the spoon.

Incomplete Thoughts

To indicate a broken-off statement or deliberately incomplete thought, an ellipsis, without the added period, is used.

> Once sung, even in jest, the words haunted him, "Be kind to your web-footed friends . . ."

Misuse of Ellipsis

The ellipsis is sometimes used in place of *etc.* to indicate that a list continues and sometimes in place of a dash or comma to indicate a pause. Both of these uses are easily abused. It is better not to use the ellipsis in these situations.

Original

> We went with our good friends: Sam, Joe, Sarah. . . .

Revised

> We went with our good friends, including Sam, Joe, and Sarah.

Original

> He worked at two speeds . . . slow and slower.

Revised

> He worked at two speeds—slow and slower. (A colon or comma could also be used in place of the dash.)

Italics (Underlining)

Italics (in typeset copy) or underlining (in typed or handwritten copy) is used for some titles and names (see Chapter 12), to mark cited words and letters, to indicate emphasis, and to mark some foreign words.

Cited Words and Letters

Put into italics words (including phrases) and letters of the alphabet being singled out. If the cited word or letter is made into a plural, the plural suffix is not italicized or underlined. (Quotation marks are sometimes used to single out words or letters, but italics or underlining is preferred.)

All the students received *A*'s.

Emphasis

Indicate a stressed word or a key word with italics (under-lining), but do not overuse italics. Emphasis is best achieved through word choice and sentence construction.

> Merit raises *must* be based on merit, not simply on seniority.
> Did Satchel Paige say, "Don't look back, some*one* might be gaining on you," or "some*thing* might be gaining on you"?

Often writers wish to emphasize a word or phrase within a quoted passage. Do this by italicizing or underlining, and add a note that the italics or underlining has been added to the original by the present author. This can be done with parentheses or in a footnote with a simple phrase such as *italics added, italics mine,* or *emphasis added.* If italics are in the original and you want to be certain that the reader knows you did not add them, a brief parenthetical note will suffice: *italics in original* or [name of author]*'s italics.* (The phrase *author's italics* is ambiguous.)

Foreign Words and Phrases

Italicize (underline) foreign words and phrases not yet part of the English language. Do not italicize words that have become Anglicized or that are common enough that they are recognized by most readers of English. This includes such abbreviations as *etc., e.g.,* and *i.e.* To decide whether the word or phrase needs to be italicized, consider whether you need to translate it for your reader. If you do, then it probably belongs in italics. But fewer foreign words are being italicized now than in the past. Overuse of italics or underlining is an affectation.

Hyphen

The use of the hyphen in English for compound nouns and adjectives, for numbers, and for dividing words at the end of a line is basically a matter of spelling in English. It is dealt with on pages 204–208.

Apostrophe

The apostrophe marks nouns and some pronouns in the possessive (or genitive) case (see Chapter 6), indicates omitted letters in contractions and sometimes omitted numbers in numerical contractions, and is used in forming some plurals.

Omitted Letters (Contractions)

Use the apostrophe to indicate omitted letters in a contracted word. The apostrophe is generally placed where the letters have been omitted. (A few contractions, such as *ain't* and *shan't* either do not correspond to recognized words or omit letters at more than one place. Spell these contractions in the accepted way, consulting a dictionary if you need to.)

> aren't
> can't
> jack-o'-lantern
> o'clock
> He OK'd the order. (very informal)
> won't

Recognized contractions are acceptable in general writings. Contractions are not often used in scholarly reports and other formal writing.

Omitted Numbers

Use an apostrophe to indicate when the first two numbers in a year have been omitted. Numbers are omitted only in informal contexts.

> the class of '23
> a '57 T-Bird

Overuse of Apostrophe

Do not use the apostrophe with clipped words that have become accepted words (e.g. *ad, phone, disco,* and *auto*). Form the plurals of such words without apostrophes. Do not use apostrophes in abbreviating words like *national* and *secretary*. These words are abbreviated by omitting internal letters. These abbreviations were once written with apostrophes but no longer are.

natl (*not* nat'l)
secy (*not* sec'y)

Apostrophe with Plurals

Along with an *s,* an apostrophe may be used to form the plural of letters, cited words and phrases, abbreviations, years, numerals, marks, and symbols. The apostrophe is preferred with lower-case letters (*p's and q's*) and abbreviations with periods (*Ph.D.'s, M.S.W.'s*). Elsewhere it has become optional.

Every child is taught the *ABCs* (or *ABC's*) in the first grade.
The baby boom lasted through the *1950s* (or *1950's*).
To the report's final sentence the manager added two *!s* and three *?s* (or *!'s* and *?'s*).

The Slash

The slash has a few well-defined, conventional uses.

Alternatives

The slash indicates alternatives like *and/or. And/or* is usually unnecessary and confusing and is best left for legal contexts (*thirty days and/or $500*). Replace it with *and* or *or* (usually *or*) or with the longer *. . . or . . . or both.*

Joined Dates

The date of a night and the year of a winter are difficult to express accurately. When referring to a night or a winter, and not just an hour or a month (either of which can be precisely written), use a slash to show the two dates.

the night of June 9/10
the winter of 1963/64
fiscal 1983/84

Writing dates with slashes (that is, *8/9/44* for *August 9, 1944*) is considered very informal and is appropriate only for notes and informal memos.

Lines of Poetry

Use a slash to separate lines of poetry that are being quoted in the body of the text.

Children learn to count with rhymes: "One, two, buckle my shoe./Three, four, shut the door."

Fractions

Use slashes between the numerator and denominator of a fraction in typewritten copy. Also use a slash between the measured units.

21 3/4 mi/gal
32 ft/sec^2

8

Capital Letters:
Many Ups and Downs

As Writer's Hotline callers have discovered, the logical and consistent use of capital letters, beyond a few universally observed conventions, is quite problematic. There are many gray areas where the simple rules and conventions do not apply unambiguously. There is often room for disagreement and interpretation. In capitalization, more than in most areas of punctuation and usage, the writer's taste and discretion, and the conventions within the writer's field, will be the guides. Capitalizing the first word following a colon, for example, is sometimes a matter of rule but sometimes a matter of how much emphasis the writer wants to give the situation. Capitalizing direction words is generally a matter of rule, but it too may reflect other considerations (e.g., *eastern Europe* refers to the geographical portion of the continent, but *Eastern Europe* designates a political division).

To make matters worse, a writer's ear, a guide through many problems of punctuation and usage, is of no help with capitalization. Capital letters almost never reflect anything in our speech; they are writing and printing conventions.

In this chapter we present the relatively clear agreed-on conventions. We also explain the flexibility that individual writers and editors retain within these conventions. The stylebook for a writer's particular field is the ultimate authority. (For a list of stylebooks, see Chapter 18.) The best advice we can give is to follow the well-established conventions for capitals that we set forth in this chapter and to refrain from capitalizing in other situations without a good reason. In other words, be able to justify every capital letter you use.

Being consistent in the use of capitals is as important as anything else. Inconsistency distracts and often confuses your readers.

For how to capitalize titles of printed works and other objects, see Chapter 12.

Capitalization Styles

The use of capitals has changed through the years. The first paragraph of the Declaration of Independence illustrates the heavy use of capitals that has at times been favored:

> When in the Course of human Events, it becomes necessary for one People to dissolve the Political Bands which have connected them with another, and to assume among the Powers of the Earth, the separate and equal Station to which the Laws of Nature and of Nature's God entitle them, a decent Respect to the Opinions of Mankind requires that they should declare the causes which impel them to the Separation.

This heavily capitalized example is typical of formal eighteenth-century writing.

Choosing whether to capitalize a particular word in a particular place and time will depend partially on how you view the guidelines that follow, but your choice may also depend on the formality of the occasion and even on how you view the politics of the situation. A "heavy" style (many capital letters) may be appropriate for a proclamation:

> Sam Jones, Representative from the Great State of Illinois

or

> Maxwell Smart, Founder and Chairman of the Board, whose Illustrious Career has enriched all Mankind

Yet such a style would seem labored in an office memo.

Not many of us write proclamations, but most of us do choose capitals based on the context of the situation. Hotline callers, for instance, often want to capitalize words such as *company* or *chairman of the board* when they refer to their company and their chairman of the board. Yet, these callers readily admit that a memo or letter from another company that is capitalized in the same fashion usually seems over-capitalized.

Still, within the guidelines that follow, one may easily choose a "heavy" or "up" (short for uppercase) style simply by choosing to capitalize whenever a choice is presented. A relatively "light" or "down" style will be developed by choosing not to capitalize at each of those points.*

Most of us, of course, find ourselves somewhere between the extremes. This handbook employs a light style of capitalization throughout.

First Letters of Sentences and Phrases

Everyone knows that the first letter of the first word of a sentence is capitalized. But beyond that, questions begin to arise. In this section we look at the use of capital letters at the beginnings of sentences, whether those sentences stand alone or are included within other sentences. This includes capitals in quotations and in a series of questions within a sentence. Very quickly it will become clear that writers have a great deal of choice, depending on their intended emphasis.

Sentences

Capitalize the first letter of a sentence. Also capitalize the first letter of a sentence fragment that you want to treat as a sentence.

The committee voted 10 to 1 against the proposal.
The university makes money on football. Lots of it.

But a tag question—a question which follows directly after a statement and merely asks for the denial or affirmation of the statement—is generally treated as part of the main sentence; it is not capitalized.

He was elected, wasn't he?

A tag question is occasionally separated to give it greater emphasis. It is then treated as a separate capitalized sentence.

He was elected. Wasn't he?

* The terms *upper case* and *lower case* refer respectively to capital letters and small letters. The terms derive from the days of handset type, when type was kept in trays or cases. Capital letters were kept in the upper case; small letters were kept in the lower case, closer at hand.

Quoted Sentences

Use a capital letter to begin a directly quoted sentence, even if the sentence is introduced by a clause equivalent to *she said*.

> Martha replied, "Not a word."
> The senator shouted, "This country needs more people like Davy Crockett."
> She clearly said, "We need to develop more alternative energy sources."

Compare this to the indirect quotation, which should be neither capitalized nor put into quotation marks.

> She said that the country needs to develop more alternative energy sources.

When a directly quoted sentence is interrupted by a clause such as *she said*, do not begin the second portion of the quoted sentence with a capital letter.

> "This country," he shouted, "needs more people like Davy Crockett."

Be careful not to run together two quoted sentences simply because the *she said* clause comes between the two sentences.

> "We need to develop more alternative energy sources," she told her audience. "Even solar energy should have its place in the sun."

There is a period, rather than a comma, after the word *audience*.

Fragmentary Quotes in Sentences

In general, do not capitalize the first letter of an incomplete or fragmentary quotation unless the word itself would normally be capitalized. A quoted phrase usually becomes a portion of your sentence and doesn't change the capitalization or the punctuation of the sentence, except for the quotation marks, of course.

She said that the country should develop more alternative
energy sources and that even solar energy has "its place
in the sun."

Churchill offered England "blood, toil, tears, and sweat,"
nothing else.

Yes, no, maybe, and Similar Words

Words like *yes, no, maybe, perhaps, definitely,* and *never*
may stand alone as one-word sentences, usually as answers to
questions, or they may be included within a larger sentence.
Within a larger sentence, they either modify the entire sentence
or serve as the direct object of the verb.

Yes, the bill was enacted.

The bank told her yes.

Capitalize these summary words only when the sentence
would be confusing without a capital letter or when you want
dramatic emphasis. Putting quotation marks around such
words or using italics or underlining adds clutter to the sentence without adding clarity.

Because of his credit record, we were forced to tell him
no.

The best answer we can hope for is an emphatic Perhaps.

Sentences Within Sentences

Between the capital letter that begins a sentence and the
period that ends it, we sometimes write several "sentences,"
that is, several independent clauses. When these clauses are
linked by commas or semicolons, the clauses do not begin
with capital letters unless they begin with words that would
ordinarily be capitalized.

Proxy statements have been mailed out; they will create
a commotion.

Generally a sentence within a parenthesis or between dashes
is not capitalized.

Proxy statements—they will create a commotion—have
been mailed out.

The tea-drinking public—it seems to grow smaller each
year—must be told the outcome of this year's tasting.
Now that the takeover bid has failed and tempers have
begun to cool (blood pressures are dropping and the
sale of antacids has declined precipitously), it is time
to analyze the events of the past six weeks.

Such internal sentences—generally they comment on the
main sentence—may be capitalized for dramatic emphasis
but only at the risk of having a reader lose sight of the structure and flow of the surrounding sentence. Capitals are permissible, but not advised.

For capitals following colons, see page 175–76.

Questions Within a Sentence

A single question acting as a comment on the sentence and
placed in parenthesis or between dashes should not be capitalized; it should be followed by a question mark.

The author of the book—can he be believed?—states that
the purchasing power of the dollar can be restored.

Questions may appear in many other places within a sentence: either as part of the basic grammar of the sentence or
as a comment or supplement to the sentence. In either case,
most handbooks state that the question should be capitalized
and punctuated as a unit within the sentence.

Are more refugees to be allowed into the country? is the
only question that needs to be answered.
We must now analyze the events of the past month: What
happened? Why? And how can a recurrence be prevented?
The editor expects that the facts—Who? What? When?
Where? and Why?—lead off every story, including
features.

But we at Writer's Hotline feel that this advice leads to
unnecessarily cluttered sentences. Particularly with a series of
questions, this punctuation and capitalization seems to destroy
the basic integrity of the sentence. We recommend either

reducing the amount of the capitalization and punctuation or rewriting sentences.

> Are more refugees to be allowed into this country? This is the only question that needs to be answered.
>
> Only one question needs to be answered: Are more refugees to be allowed into this country?
>
> We must now analyze the events of the past month: what happened? why? and how can a recurrence be prevented?
>
> The editor expects that the facts—who, what, when, where, and why—will lead off every story, including features.

In general, then, avoid using capitals with questions in a series. Use question marks if they seem necessary or appropriate. If, on rereading, the punctuation seems to undermine the unity of a sentence, then rewrite the sentence. We also advise against both capitals and question marks in a sentence such as the following, in which the questions are part of a request and the overriding nature of the sentence is the request, not the questions.

> Please tell us what happened, how it happened, and what is being done to prevent the recurrence of such an event.

Capital Letter Following a Colon

Usually a colon precedes an elaboration of the ideas of the basic sentence. This elaboration may involve a list of items, or it may involve a sentence expansion. If what follows the colon is merely a list, do not capitalize the first word following the colon, unless the first word is a word that would ordinarily be capitalized (a proper noun, for instance). Otherwise, capitalizing the first word is optional. The decision will be based on the desired emphasis. Generally, the further removed the second thought is, the more likely it is to be capitalized.

> Participants will need a few things: fishing gear, lunch, and a change of clothes.
>
> Caesar said he came and conquered: he never said he wanted to stay.

> The goal of our company is simple: Success.
> Positive identification is required: Neither a social security card nor an oil-company credit card will suffice.

When a colon introduces a quotation of a full sentence or more, the quotation always begins with a capital letter.

> Sherman summed up his feelings about war succinctly and eloquently: "Its glory is all moonshine. It is only those who have neither fired a shot nor heard the shrieks and groans of the wounded who cry aloud for blood, more vengeance, more desolation. War is hell."

Capitals in Phrases: Outlines and Lists

The first word of each item in a formal outline is normally capitalized, even though the outline may be made of noun phrases rather than complete sentences.

> I. First-letter capitals
>   A. Independent sentences
>   B. Sentences within sentences

In an enumerated series or outline, particularly one set up in outline form, the first letter of each item, whether a phrase or a sentence, is often capitalized.

> He quickly learned the steps in baking a cake:
>   1. Get out a bowl.
>   2. Open the box.

> We need to consider the loading and unloading of several kinds of household effects—
>   Furniture
>   Kitchenware
>   Personal effects

Letter Salutations and Closings

Capitalize the first word of the salutation and of the complimentary closing. (Also capitalize names and titles, or the substitutes for them, in the salutation.)

Dear Sir or Madam
Dear Customer Complaint Department
Yours truly

Capitals in Quoted Materials

In quoting written materials, follow the capitalization of the original. Most poetry written before World War II, for instance, uses a capital at the beginning of each line. Much poetry written since does not.

(In general writing, quoted materials written before the nineteenth century may be put into modern spelling, punctuation, and capitalization without making note. In scholarly writing, this modernizing should be noted. Of course, always retain the original spelling, punctuation, and capitalization if they are pertinent.)

Single Letter Words

The Words *I* and *O*

The pronoun *I* and the interjection *O* are always capitalized. The interjection *oh* is capitalized only when it is the first word of a sentence or of a quoted sentence.

Letters Used As Words

Generally capitalize letters used by themselves as words or in hyphenated compounds.

The B vitamins include vitamins B-6 and B-12.

Similarly

A-bomb
A-frame
G-string
I-beam
U-joint
X-ray
X-shaped

Cited Letters and Parts of Words

Cited letters and parts of words are generally in lower case and in italics (underlined).

> The *i* in *hit* is pronounced like the *i* in *pit*.
> the letter *z*
> the suffix *ful*
> Cross your *t*'s and dot your *i*'s.

The italics (underlining) is sometimes ignored in proverbial expressions.

> Mind your p's and q's.

Proper Nouns

In school we were told simply to capitalize proper nouns and adjectives made from proper nouns. A proper noun was neatly and unambiguously defined as the name of a specific person, place, or thing, real or imaginary; thus, a proper noun referred to a unique item, not to one of a category. A proper adjective was an adjective made from a proper noun, the word *American* made from the noun *America*, for example. Any remaining problems could, we were told, be resolved by the dictionary. Life was simple.

Except for two problems, the rules are fine. First, we don't capitalize all proper nouns and certainly not all adjectives made from proper nouns. The word *Monday* and the word *summer* make equally unique references. Yet we capitalize days of the week but not seasons of the year. (A season may be capitalized when it is personified, but this is seldom done.) We capitalize map features like *Tropic of Cancer* and *North Pole*, but *equator* is usually not capitalized. Proper adjectives are even less consistently treated.

The second problem area involves an abbreviated reference to a name. When, in a later and partial reference, *St. Martin's Hospital* is shortened to *hospital*, is the word capitalized? What about the *chairman of the board* or the *chairman*? When are these capitalized and when not? Again, the handy rules we were once given don't help.

Of course, hotline callers focus on these problem areas. After all, they know most of the rules. Because of the difficulty in determining what a proper noun is and when it is capitalized, we will try to enumerate most kinds of words that the writer is likely to question.

The problem of whether or not to capitalize an adjective made from a proper noun is dealt with at various places throughout the chapter and, in summary, on pages 200–201. The handling of incomplete and abridged references to proper nouns is also illustrated throughout the chapter and summarized on pages 201–202.

Personal Names and Titles

Capitalize personal names and initials, nicknames, and epithets linked directly to a name and used in place of a name. Capitalize fictitious names as you would real ones.

> Abraham ("Honest Abe") Lincoln; Honest Abe
> Thomas ("Stonewall") Jackson; Stonewall Jackson
> Andrew Jackson, Old Hickory
> JFK
> Alexander the Great
> Richard the Lion-Hearted
> Catherine the Great
> George III
> Uncle Sam
> Jack Frost
> John Q. Public

And capitalize most adjectives made from given names. (For exceptions, see pages 200–201.)

> Shakespearean sonnet
> Jacksonian Democracy

Capitalize names in sayings but not in most other common expressions.

> Let George do it.
> For Pete's sake.
> every Tom, Dick, and Harry

but

> jackplane
> jack-o'-lantern
> every man jack
> tomfoolery

Names in Direct Address

Capitalize the words used in place of a name to address someone directly. In general, do not capitalize words that are only descriptive. (For titles, ranks, and job descriptions, see immediately below. For mother, father, and kinship terms, see page 181.)

> Dear Sir or Madam
> Dear Mr. President
> Good morning, Madam Senator.
> Hi, Mom.
> Forgive me, Father. (*But* My father hasn't forgiven me.)

Titles, Ranks, and Job Descriptions

When they precede a name, capitalize political, religious, professional, and all other titles, including titles of nobility and courtesy titles. When a title follows a name and is set off by commas, or when it stands alone, do not capitalize it unless it represents a preeminent rank such as the president or prime minister of a country or the head of a major religion. There is no need to capitalize job descriptions. (Courtesy titles, such as *Mr.* and *Mrs.*, never stand alone or follow the name.)

> President William Henry Harrison; the President
> Senator Daniel Webster; Daniel Webster, senator from Massachusetts
> Secretary of State William Jennings Bryan; Secretary Bryan; William Jennings Bryan, secretary of state; the secretary
> Pope John Paul II; the Pope
> Stephen Cardinal Wyszynski, archbishop of Warsaw; the archbishop
> Chancellor G. Robert Ross; Bob Ross, the chancellor of the university; Chancellor Ross
> Governor Frank White; the governor of Arkansas

Winston Churchill, Prime Minister of England during World War II

President Henry Ford; the president of Ford Motor Co.

Juvenile Court Judge William C. Fields; Judge Fields; William C. Fields, juvenile court judge

Associate Professor Mel Blanc; Mel Blanc, associate professor of drama

Senior Chemist Joseph Schlitz; Joe Schlitz, the senior chemist; the chemist in charge of this project; the head of the chemical laboratory

Chairman of the Board Roger Easson; Roger Easson, chairman of the board; the office of the chairman; the office of Chairman Easson

the Reverend Terence Harris, rector; Reverend Harris; the Rev. Terry Harris

Dr. Marcia Leppert; Marcia Leppert, M.D.

(Courtesy titles are never used with academic degrees. For details on using courtesy titles, see page 182.)

Descriptive Titles and Coined Titles Preceding Names

Do not capitalize descriptive or coined titles preceding names. Such descriptions, in spite of prevalent journalistic practice, are better placed after the name.

Acceptable

> former corporate lawyer Michael Drayton
> convicted bookie Joe Palooka

Better

> Michael Drayton, former corporate lawyer
> Joe Palooka, convicted bookie

Mother, Father, *and Other Kinship Terms*

There is a powerful tendency to capitalize words like *mother, father,* and their diminutives (e.g. *mom, dad*) out of respect. On the capitalization of these and other kinship terms, guidebooks differ, but our advice is to capitalize such words only when they are substitutes for a name or are used as titles immediately preceding a name. If the name can substitute for the term without altering the structure of the sentence, the word is a name substitute and may be capitalized.

> Give the book to Mother. (The name can be substituted without altering the sentence.)

but

> Give the book to my mother. (The word *my* must be omitted before the name can be substituted.)
> Give the book to Uncle Jake.
> Give the book to Pop Jones. (The kinship term is a title. Preceding the name, as here, it is capitalized, as is any other title.)

Courtesy Titles

Courtesy titles—*Mr., Mrs., Ms., Dr.,* and other abbreviations of rank or courtesy—never stand alone. (When words such as *doctor* or *professor* are used alone, they are, of course, spelled out. They are capitalized only in direct address.) Courtesy titles are not used when an academic degree or indication of rank follows a name. Spell out courtesy titles other than *Mr., Mrs.,* and *Ms.* when only the last name is given.

> Dr. Sarah Jones; Doctor Jones; Sarah Jones, M.D.
> Dr. Deirdre LaPin; Deirdre LaPin, Ph.D.; Professor LaPin
> the Rev. John Frederick Schell; the Reverend Schell
> Sen. Dale Bumpers; Senator Bumpers

Names of Companies and Agencies

Company and Organization Names

Whether or not it seems logical or correct, capitalize and spell company and organization names as the company or organization does; the final *Inc.,* however, is usually dropped in the text copy and the word *the,* even when part of the name, is almost never capitalized. Key words used as shortened references are capitalized, but common nouns (e.g. *hospital, university,* and *company*) by themselves, even though they refer to the specific company or organization, are not capitalized.

> J. C. Penney Company; Penney's; a department store; the store
>
> Sears, Roebuck and Company; Sears; the store management
>
> St. Vincent's Infirmary; St. Vincent's; the hospital staff
>
> Nelson's Old Fashioned Potato Chips; the food producer
>
> the University of Arkansas at Little Rock; UALR; the university
>
> the American Bar Association; the ABA; a member of the bar association
>
> Daughters of the American Revolution; the DAR
>
> the Benevolent and Protective Order of the Elks; the Elks; the Elks Club
>
> American Cancer Society; the society
>
> Girl Scouts of America; the Girl Scouts; the Scouts

Branches and Agencies of Government

Capitalize the full names of divisions of governments and their agencies. Capitalize their abbreviations and key words of incomplete references. Common-noun references are usually *not* capitalized except in referring to the highest federal levels. (For instance, the word *court* is capitalized in an incomplete reference only when it refers to the United States Supreme Court.) Paraphrased references (for example, a reference to the *upper chamber,* meaning the United States Senate or a particular state senate) are not capitalized. The word *federal* is capitalized only when it is part of a proper name.

> the United States government; the federal government
>
> the executive branch; the Presidency; the vice-presidency
>
> the Treasury of the United States; the National Treasury; the Treasury (national); Treasury notes
>
> The U.S. Supreme Court; the Court
>
> the Eighth Circuit Court of Appeals; the court of appeals at St. Louis; circuit court
>
> the Illinois State Supreme Court; the state supreme court
> juvenile court

the Congress; the Eighty-Sixth Congress; congressional
actions

the United States House of Representatives; the House;
the lower chamber

the Arkansas General Assembly; the state legislature; the
state assembly

Federal Trade Commission regulations; FTC regulations;
Trade Commission regulations; federal regulations

the Office of Consumer Affairs; Consumer Affairs; the
agency

Capitalize *United Nations* and terms involving the United
Nations and other world organizations in a similar fashion.

the United Nations; the UN

the UN Secretariat; the Secretariat

World Health Organization; WHO; a World Health
Organization spokesman

Trademarks and Generic Terms

Capitalize trademarks but not generic terms. Especially in
more formal writing, avoid using trademarks for generic terms.

Kleenex; a tissue

Coca-Cola; Coke; a cola; a soft drink

Styrofoam; plastic foam

Xerox; a photocopier

Some former trademarks have become generic terms. These
words have passed into the language and have lost their initial
capitals.

mimeograph

mason jar

thermos

A listing of current trademarks, as well as former trademarks that have become generic terms, can be found in the
Trade Names Dictionary by Gale Research Company. The
work seems exhaustive, but the publisher clearly specifies that
its listing "is not, and is not intended to be, a source of legal

authority." It does, however, carry a great deal of practical authority.

Other Generic Terms

A number of place-names have become generic terms. These are never capitalized (unless, of course, they refer to their location on the map):

> burgundy (originally from the Burgundy region of France, but now simply a type of red wine)
> champagne
> china (porcelain)
> delft

Names of Places, Regions, and Map Features

Shared Common Nouns

Capitalize a common noun (such as *lake, mount, river, avenue,* and *street*) that is part of two or more capitalized names and precedes or follows them.

> Lakes Erie and Huron
> Mounts McKinley and Whitney
> Niagara and Yosemite Falls
> the Pacific and Atlantic Oceans
> the Missouri and Mississippi Rivers
> San Bernardino and Riverside Counties
> the corner of 14th and Merced Avenues

(Not all authorities agree on this. All do agree that the shared noun preceding two proper nouns should be capitalized, as in the first two examples, but some—notably *Chicago Manual of Style*—say that the shared noun following two proper nouns should be in lower case. We at the Writer's Hotline feel that the natural and logical inclination is to capitalize the shared nouns in both places, and we have given up trying to rationalize why a shared common noun preceding should be capitalized and not the one following. Consequently, we have come to agree with those who capitalize both, and we recommend doing that.)

Geographical Names

Capitalize the names of recognized geophysical features: mountain ranges, oceans, rivers, lakes, valleys, fault lines, and so on. Spellings can be checked in *Webster's New Geographical Dictionary*, an atlas, or a gazetteer, but a gazetteer may not capitalize the common nouns such as *river* that are part of the name. Also, be careful not to duplicate part of a foreign name with its English equivalent. *Rio Grande*, not *Rio Grande River*; *Sierra Madres*, not *Sierra Madre Mountains*; *Fujiyama* or *Mount Fuji*, not *Mount Fujiyama*.

> the Pacific Ocean; the Pacific
> the Dead Sea
> the North Slope (Alaska)
> the Gulf Stream
> the Continental Shelf
> the San Andreas Fault
> Lake Tahoe; Tahoe; the lake; the lake area
> the Mississippi River
> the Mississippi-Missouri River Basin
> the basin of the Missouri and Mississippi Rivers
> the flyway of the Mississippi River Valley

Geopolitical Names

Capitalize the recognized names of continents, portions of continents, nations, states, counties, and political subdivisions. Capitalize recognized names whether or not they have autonomy and whether or not they still exist. Imaginary and legendary names are treated in the same way as actual ones. Common nouns, such as *state*, *county*, and *city*, following the name are occasionally taken as part of the name and capitalized (e.g. New York City); those preceding the name are almost never capitalized (e.g. the city of New York). (For a discussion of regional names and terms involving compass headings, see pages 188–91.)

> the Southern Hemisphere
> Europe
> Asia Minor
> Atlantis
> the Augustan Empire; *but* the empire under Augustus

Albania
Camelot
Transylvania
More's Utopia; *but* a utopia, utopias, utopian daydreams
New York; the state of New York (except in proclama-
    tions and the like where the *Great State of New York*
    may be desired); the Empire State
San Bernardino County
Queens; the Borough of Queens; a borough of New York
the Midwest
the North
Greater Dallas; the Dallas area
the Los Angeles Basin
Watts
Greenwich Village; the Village
The Hague (one of very few names with a capitalized
    article in the name); *but* the Second Hague Peace
    Conference
Birmingham; the Pittsburgh of the South

Groups of Countries

Groupings of countries—usually the groupings are political
—are generally capitalized. These groupings sometimes change
with the historical era being discussed.

the Allies (World War II); the Big Four
the Axis Powers
the Balkan States
Central America
Central Europe (World War I)
NATO Powers

Nicknames and National Symbols

Capitalize the nicknames for places and countries if the
actual names would be capitalized, and capitalize the names of
national symbols.

the Golden State (California)
the Land of Enchantment (New Mexico)
the Dust Bowl

the Golden Triangle (Pittsburgh)
the Big Four Powers (in World War II)

Capitalize the names of unique national symbols.

Old Glory; the Stars and Stripes; *but* the flag
the Liberty Bell
the Stone of Scone

Regions

Capitalize the names of generally recognized regions whether or not they have ever been political units.

A region is more than an area, a type of vegetation, or a climate. A region generally has an identifiable geography or history or culture, sometimes all of these. Thus, when the word *highlands* refers simply to a type of geography, it is not capitalized, but when it refers to the *Scottish Highlands,* which is a recognized cultural and historical area, as well as being a geographical region, *Highlands* should be capitalized.

the Highlands; Highlands speech (referring to the Scottish Highlands)
the Ozarks; Ozark cooking
the Maritimes (referring to the Maritime provinces of Canada)

Using a capital letter to begin the name of a region indicates that the region has more significance than merely being a contiguous area of the earth's surface. In deciding whether or not to capitalize the *m* of *Middle Tennessee,* for example, ask whether the region has some particular identity or is just the central portion of the state. Employees in a Tennessee tourist bureau may feel differently about this than employees of a travel agency in New York City. But for that *m* to be capitalized, *Middle Tennessee* should be an area of land with discernible boundaries and more than the area recognized as Greater Nashville.

Compass Headings

Compass headings—words like *north, south,* and *southwest* —indicate directions of travel and locations.

Capitalize compass headings only when they indicate specific regions. Do not capitalize directions of travel or generalized locations.

The usual rule—capitalize locations, but not directions—is not as helpful as it should be, for in actual practice, writers distinguish between generalized locations (such as *the south of France*) and recognized regions (such as *Southern California*). Since this rule is a continuing problem for many writers, we illustrate it in some detail.

Do not capitalize compass headings when they represent directions or movement. The following sentences are correct:

> Drive south for three miles.
> The accident occurred a mile south of town.
> Go west, young man, go west.

In these cases, the compass heading represents a direction of travel. The last example might be a problem for a writer, but the statement says that a young man should travel toward the west, westwardly. This is similar to the statement:

> Throughout the history of the United States, people have been moving west.

If these two statements were phrased with *into the West,* with a capital *w,* then a specific region would be named. This is true even though the word *West* has referred to different regions during the nation's history. Even though the geographical concept of the West has changed, the word has always referred to a specific region, identified by customs, manners, and myths.

Capitalize compass headings when they refer to a recognized region.

> We live in the South. (of the United States)
> The migration from the rural South to the urban North has slowed and perhaps been reversed.

Each of these compass headings specifies a region of the United States. Without additional modifying or explanatory words, the regions are recognized by both writer and reader. But consider two other sentences:

> Gray whales are often seen frolicking along the west coast.
> Our west coast representative will call on you shortly.

In both these sentences, *west coast* is better left in lower case. In the first sentence, the writer does not mean the region known as the West Coast (of the United States) but means the literal coastline. In the second sentence, the west coast is a company territorial division, which may or may not coincide with the region. (Many companies do capitalize the names of company regions. If it is company style, do so. It may also be company style to capitalize the entire phrase *west coast representative*. However, this phrase is clearly a job description or title that stands alone. There is no need to capitalize it.)

COMPASS HEADINGS IN CITIES

Locations within cities are handled in the same way. One may live in the north side of town or one may live in a locality that is identified as the North Side. If a phrase, such as *north side*, needs to be modified or explained, do not capitalize it. These locations should have as much identity (at least locally) as a named region like Watts or Hollywood.

> the East End (London)
> the South Side (Chicago)

COMPASS HEADINGS FOR FOREIGN COUNTRIES AND CONTINENTS

Regions of foreign countries are more accurately and less ambiguously identified by regional names than by compass headings. Use the regional names; do not capitalize compass headings in foreign countries.

> Cornwall (rather than southwest England)
> Sinaloa (rather than west Mexico)

Some countries contain compass headings in their names. These are always capitalized even though these names are sometimes paraphrases of official names.

> East Germany (the German Democratic Republic)
> Bangladesh (formerly East Pakistan)

In considering regions of continents, be guided by the same rules and traditional usage. Capitalize compass headings that indicate defined regions, not generalized locations or directions.

> Southeast Asia
> the Eastern Hemisphere, the East (the Orient)

Political considerations may also enter into choosing whether or not to capitalize a compass heading. Since World War II, for instance, the words *Eastern Europe* have had a meaning very different from *the eastern portions of the European continent*. And the terms *East* and *West* in Cold War politics are capitalized.

ADJECTIVES FROM COMPASS HEADINGS

Adjectives formed from compass headings are generally capitalized.

> Southern cooking
> Western fashions
> Eastern manners

Not everyone would capitalize each of these phrases, and writers will need to decide for themselves whether or not the phrases refer to specifically regional cooking, fashions, and manners.

We usually advise against capitalizing the compass headings in phrases such as *eastern longshoremen, northern lumbermen,* and *west coast fishermen*. These compass headings denote little more than generalized locations. Admittedly, there is a fine line here, and if you feel strongly that there is something unique about the *longshoremen of the East* or the *lumbermen of the North*, then capitalize the heading.

Map Features

There is amazingly little agreement in rule or usage about capitalizing imaginary and conventional map lines and regions. All authorities capitalize *Arctic Circle*, for instance, but very few capitalize *equator*. *Arctic Zone* is spelled with a capital *a* and *z*, with only a capital *a*, and without any capitals. And how does one explain one standard authority's capitalizing only the *n* and the *p* of *North Polar ice cap*. (Obviously it is meant to suggest that this is a specific ice cap, but why are *ice* and *cap* not capitalized?)

This lack of agreement is all the more frustrating since the various style manuals and dictionaries normally assert their preferences without explanation, except for an occasional "We recommend a down style." In light of this, what we give here are only recommendations.

Capitalize the names of unique map features and the names of specific areas defined by them.

> Equator
> Arctic Circle
> the Arctic; the Arctic Zone; the North Frigid Zone; the North Polar Ice Cap
> the Tropic of Cancer; the Tropics; the Torrid Zone; the North Temperate Zone
> the International Date Line

In general, capitalize words like *equatorial, tropical, temperate,* and *arctic* only in proper names. Do not capitalize them in generic uses or in the names of animals.

> arctic fox
> equatorial crops; the Equatorial Current (the name of a specific current); equatorial currents
> polar bear
> the polar regions
> temperate climate
> tropical conditions

And do not capitalize the words *latitude, longitude,* and *meridian*—with the exception of *Prime Meridian.*

Parts of the Calendar, Times

Capitalize days of the week, months of the year, and holidays, both religious and secular. Do not capitalize descriptive names or seasons (unless they are being personified).

> Monday
> February
> Christmas
> Hanukkah; Chanukah
> July Fourth; July the Fourth; the Fourth of July; Independence Day
> Dominion Day (Canada)
> Labor Day

but

> spring; springtime; *but* Old Man Winter
> Indian summer

leap year
the summer solstice
election day

Capitalize the names of time zones and their abbreviations. (Some style guides recommend capitalizing only the proper nouns in the name; the abbreviations remain capitalized.)

Central Daylight Time; CDT
Greenwich Mean Time; GMT

but

New York is in the eastern time zone.

Races, Nationalities, Ethnic Groups, and Languages

Capitalize the names of races and nationalities, the names of ethnic groups formed from a racial or national name, and the names of their languages. With the possible exception of *black* and *white* (see note below), do not capitalize descriptive terms or the names of groupings based on color or on social or economic social criteria.

Afro-American
Caucasian
Chicano
East Indian
English
Gullah
Italian
Mongoloid
Native American
Serbo-Croatian
Swahili

but

black
the bourgeoisie
the middle class; middle-class values
the red man
redneck
white

Note: Some publications primarily concerned with black/ white relations do capitalize both *black* and *white*, but in general usage both are still in lower case and only the anthropological racial terms—Negro and Caucasian—are capitalized. Especially in articles dealing with racial relations where a writer is likely to have a phrase like *black and white storeowners*, consistency is important. In common usage, writers do capitalize *black* in *Black English,* however. Here, as elsewhere involving choices in capitalizing, be consistent.

Religious Names and Terms

Capitalize the names of religions and the followers of religions, the names of deities and sacred persons, the names used to refer to a supreme being, the names of sacred events, unique objects, and sacred books.

RELIGIONS AND THEIR FOLLOWERS
>Buddhism
>Zen Buddhists
>Christianity
>Catholics; *but* the charismatic movement

DEITIES AND SACRED PEOPLE
>God; the One; the All
>Krishna
>Christ; King of Kings
>the Trinity; the Third Person (of the Trinity)

SACRED EVENTS, OBJECTS, AND BOOKS
>the Last Supper
>the Crucifixion (referring to Jesus)
>the Enlightenment; the Awakening (both referring to the Buddha)
>the Cross (of the Crucifixion)
>the Tabernacle (of Moses)
>the Talmud; Talmudic
>the Upanishads; the Bhagavad Gita; the Song Celestial
>the Book of the Dead
>the Bible; the Gospels; the Gospel of John; Biblical

The names of services and sacraments are generally in lower case.

> baptism
> bar mitzvah
> confirmation
> communion; eucharist; *but often* Holy Communion; the
>   Lord's Supper

Do not capitalize figurative or generalized uses of words such as *god, bible,* or *gospel.*

> the gods of Olympus
> Roman gods
> ungodly
> godson
> The *Blue Book* is the used-car salesman's bible.
> a gospel singer
> the gospel truth

Capitalization of pronouns referring to the supreme deity of a religion is a matter of choice and context. In the past, writers often capitalized pronouns, except *who, whom,* and *whose,* when referring to the Deity.

> We know His love is everlasting.

But in keeping with the modern tendency to avoid capitals, many writers now capitalize these pronouns only when there is danger of ambiguity.

> The preacher spoke of His love for mankind.

Of course, if you begin capitalizing pronouns, you will need to continue using the capitals throughout a passage to avoid confusing your readers.

Names of Historical Events, Documents, and Ages

Historical Events, Documents, Ages, and Movements

Capitalize the names of events, wars, councils, documents, and historical ages and movements. In general, do not use italics (underlining) or quotation marks for these items.

EVENTS, WARS, AND COUNCILS
> Fall of Rome
> South Sea Bubble
> Great Depression; a depression
> Dust Bowl
> New Deal
> Great Society
> American Revolution; the War of Independence
> Battle of Bunker Hill; the battle fought on Breed's Hill
> World Wars I and II
> Cold War; *but* a cold war; a hot war; a shooting war
> Council of Nicaea
> Glassboro Summit; the summit conference at Glassboro

DOCUMENTS
> Magna Carta
> Constitution of the United States; the Constitution
> Constitution of Arizona; the state constitution
> NATO Pact; the pact

HISTORICAL AGES AND MOVEMENTS
> Middle Ages; the late Middle Ages
> Renaissance
> Age of Elizabeth; the Elizabethan Age; *but* an Elizabethan sonnet
> Age of Enlightenment
> Jazz Age
> Roaring Twenties; *but* the twenties, thirties, and forties; the early twentieth century; the nuclear age; the computer age (see below)
> Romantic Movement

A list such as this cannot answer every specific question that arises. A dictionary may tell whether or not a name or term is "traditionally capitalized." If a term isn't in one dictionary, it may be in a second. The practice of other people who write in a given field also serves as a guide.

Here are a few other guidelines.

For cultural and historical periods, capitalize well-defined periods—*Dark Ages, Middle Ages, Age of Revolution*—as long as the terms are used with their traditional meanings. Avoid capitalizing vague appellations—*antiquity, ancient, modern, movement,* and *avant garde.* Thus, one might capitalize *Romantic Movement, Age of Romanticism,* and *Romantic poet,* when these refer to the artistic movement in early nineteenth-century England. When *romantic* refers simply to a type of personality or art, even though the personality and work are being compared with those of the Romantic Movement, use lower case.

She is a romantic poet, in the finest tradition.

Generally avoid capitalizing the descriptive terms for contemporary society, even though these terms are modeled on historical models you might capitalize: *nuclear age, space age, computer age,* and *electronic age.*

Archeological, Geological, and Prehistoric Ages and Eras

The names of archeological and anthropological periods and eras are capitalized. These designations are widely agreed on and can be checked in a dictionary.

Bronze Age
Stone Age
Neolithic man

In geological designations, only the name of the era or epoch is capitalized. (Words such as *era, period,* and *epoch* are not.)

Upper Carboniferous period
Pliocene epoch

Descriptive modifiers, such as *early, middle,* and *late,* unless they designate a conventionally agreed on era or age, are not capitalized.

early Bronze Age
late Stone Age
late Pliocene

Common and Scientific Names of Animals and Scientific Names and Terms

Common and Popular Names of Animals and Plants

Capitalize the names of pets. Do not capitalize popular names, common names, or the names of breeds of animals or plants except for proper adjectives and patented names.

> Our dog is named Oliver T.
> calla lilly
> red fox
> tufted titmouse
> African violet
> American Beauty rose
> Arabian
> Clydesdale
> German shepherd

Scientific Names

In scientific names, capitalize the genus name (and the names of the larger biological divisions), but put species and subspecies names in lower case even if they are proper adjectives. (The genus and species names are in italics or are underlined; larger divisions are in regular roman type.)

> Chordata (phylum)
> Vertebrata (subphylum)
> Mammalia (class)
> Primates (order)
> Hominidae (family)
> *Homo* (genus)
> *sapiens* (species)
> *Felis catus; Felis catus cheshire* (or *F. catus cheshire*);
>   the Cheshire cat

Do not capitalize English derivatives of scientific names, even when the scientific name and its derivative are identical.

> *Amoeba*

but

Several types of amoebas are found in man's digestive
tract.

Mastodon

but

a mastodon

Planets and Astronomical Bodies

Capitalize the names of planets and astronomical bodies
but do not capitalize general references to them. Capitalize
sun, moon, and *earth* only in astronomical contexts when the
words are used as the scientific names.

Cassioppeia
the Crab Nebula
Earth; *but* We must protect our planet earth.
Halley's Comet; a new comet
Jupiter
Mars
the Milky Way; the Galaxy (in reference to the Milky
Way); a spiral galaxy
the moons and rings of Saturn
white dwarfs

Scientific Terms, Names, and Laws

Scientific terms—the names of laws, diseases, and medical
conditions—are not capitalized although the proper nouns
included in them are capitalized.

chicken pox
Down's syndrome
the first law of thermodynamics
German measles
Kepler's law
Pap smear

Chemical Symbols and Names

Capitalize chemical symbols and the symbols for the elements, but do not capitalize the full name, even if the
name is formed from a proper noun.

benzine ring
carbon-14; C-14; ^{14}C (*but in recent scientific writing* ^{14}C)
Es; einsteinium
Na; sodium
NaCl; sodium chloride; table salt

Proper Adjectives

A proper adjective is an adjective made from a proper noun, as *American* is formed from *America,* for instance. Capitalization of proper adjectives follows the peculiarities of proper nouns and adds some other ones. (For words such as *southern* and *eastern,* see page 191.)

In general, capitalize adjectives made from proper nouns whether or not the noun they modify is capitalized.

American cooking
Brahma bull, a Brahma
British English
Carolina parakeet
Geiger counter
German shepherd
Jacksonian Democrat; *but* anti-Republican feelings
Jersey cow, Jersey
Renaissance beliefs
Siamese cat

But when adjectives lose the modifying force they had as nouns and act only to distinguish a type of window, salad dressing, or other object, the capital letter should be made lower case. (Dictionaries, by the way, are much slower to drop these capital letters than writers and editors. To test your own sense of a word, ask whether or not the adjective carries its original modifying force; that is, is a *french fry* something we identify as being fried in the manner of French cooking? For most of us, *french fry* has nothing to do with France; *French pastry,* however, does. The major exception to this rule is animal breeds, which continue to capitalize the proper adjective. A Jersey cow has nothing to do with the Isle of Jersey for most people, but the capital *J* is retained.)

china (porcelain)
diesel engine
french door
french fries; *but* French pastry
india ink
italic type
jersey (the fabric); *but* Jersey cow
klieg light
manila envelope
platonic love; *but* Platonic ideals; Neo-Platonic thought
quixotic
roman type; *but* Roman numerals
russian dressing
swiss cheese; *but* a Swiss watch
venetian blind

Verbs from Proper Nouns

When verbs made from proper nouns lose their original force, the capital letter is dropped.

boycott
gerrymander
lynch
maverick
pasteurize
vulcanize

Second, Abridged, and Incomplete References

The handling of many second references has been illustrated through examples in this chapter, but a couple of general notes and a few examples may be useful here by way of review.

The general rule regarding second and incomplete references is straightforward. In a second reference made from key words or from proper nouns, only the key words or proper nouns are capitalized. Common nouns appearing with the key words and second references made from common nouns are not capitalized.

> St. Vincent's Infirmary; St. Vincent's; the hospital staff; the hospital board
>
> the Federal Bureau of Investigation; the FBI; the bureau; agency regulations and procedures; bureau standards
>
> Montgomery Ward & Co.; Ward's; Ward's sales personnel; the store management; the company

Many writers tend to capitalize common-noun references to their own companies and their own committees. There is also a tendency to capitalize incomplete references and references to job descriptions when they represent high executive positions, as the *president* or the *board of directors* of one's company. A page can become cluttered with capitals, and it may seem, to a reader outside the company, that the writer is being pushy or grandiose. We recommend a down style, a style with relatively few capitals. But if your office's in-house practice is clear and reasonable, by all means follow it.

> the Board of Directors; the chairman of the board
> the Board of Regents; the board; the regents

More Information

A good desk dictionary will give you reasonable answers to many remaining questions, particularly on the capitalization of events, terms, treaties, and the like. In addition, you may want to consult the Government Printing Office (GPO) *Style Manual* and the Chicago *Manual of Style*, both of which were consulted extensively during the compilation of this section, and both of which are more extensive than this chapter. One word of caution is needed, however. The GPO *Style Manual* overcapitalizes, as far as we are concerned, terms dealing with the United States government, its agencies and its employees, even capitalizing such terms as *Federal Government* and *Military Establishment*. (See Chapter 18 for a list of reference works.)

9

Spelling:
Beyond the Dictionary

For some writers, accurate spelling seems to be an inborn talent. It comes to them naturally, and they have to spend little of their writing time on it. Others are not so lucky; they find themselves interrupting their work to make sure their spelling is correct. Yet the burden of correct spelling is on all writers because, for better or for worse, readers will often judge a writer on spelling if nothing else. They will consider a bad speller careless or ignorant or worse.

The best advice the Writer's Hotline can give writers about correct spelling is to keep a good dictionary handy when writing and to look up any word whose spelling they are unsure of. We also advise writers to keep a list or file of words they occasionally misspell and to review it frequently (this is a good idea for new vocabulary that a writer learns, too).

The authority for spelling is any standard or unabridged dictionary. The most widely consulted dictionary in the United States is *Webster's Third New International Dictionary of the English Language* and its abridged version, *Webster's New Collegiate Dictionary*. (For a list of spelling guides and dictionaries, see Chapter 18.)

But a dictionary doesn't provide all the answers writers need. New terms, especially in technical fields, appear every year, and years pass before they are included in a dictionary. In order to spell new words, writers need to know the basic processes of English spelling (and not just the inconsistencies of spelling that English has inherited). How are compound words spelled? How are prefixes and suffixes added? Which member of a pair of suffixes should be used (one is still "alive" and is still added to words; the other is "dead" and is no longer added)?

The spelling questions the Writer's Hotline usually receives concern problems not covered in dictionaries or not readily findable in them. For this reason, we cover here spelling principles that will be a useful supplement to a dictionary, especially in spelling new words. We do not provide a review of the spelling "demons," because such words are easily found in the dictionary.

For how to spell and use plurals, see Chapter 2.
For how to spell and use abbreviations, see Chapter 10.
For how and when to spell out numbers and fractions, see Chapter 11.

Compound Words

Half of the hotline's spelling questions concern how and whether to use spaces and hyphens in spelling compounds (two or more distinct words or figures treated as a unit— *mother wit, mother-in-law, motherland*). Compound words are so plentiful and so easily created in English that many of them are not in a standard dictionary. Many are known only in a specialized field, and often their correct spelling, with a space, a hyphen, or neither, depends on prevailing practice within the field, not on a rule.

Many compounds have gone, or are going, through an evolution from being spelled as two words (*foot ball*) to being spelled with a hyphen (*foot-ball*) to being spelled together with neither (*football*). The hyphen's basic function in English is to mark the closeness of words or parts of words. When it is necessary to show that two or more words are related to one another to prevent confusion or misreading, the hyphen is used (*a long-standing policy*). However, it is not used between words that communicate clearly just as well if left standing separately (*a widely circulating rumor*).

We provide here the general principles governing the spelling of most compounds in English. These are guidelines for spelling compounds, not rules without exception. Especially with noun compounds, prevailing practice determines correct spelling. Consult a standard dictionary first (and an appropriate specialized dictionary, if possible), and then follow the guidelines below.

Compound Adjectives

Hyphenate two or more words that function as a unit and modify a noun when they immediately precede a noun. Do not hyphenate them when they follow a form of the verb *be* and are used as predicate adjectives (She is *quick tempered*) or if they are an adverb ending in *ly* and an adjective together modifying a noun (*a quickly passing thunderstorm*).

a two-ounce igniter	(*but* an igniter that weighs two ounces)
a well-behaved child	(*but* a child who is well behaved)
far-reaching implications	(*but* implications that are far reaching)
a ten-year-old boy	(*but* a boy who is ten years old)
follow-up examinations	(*but* examinations that follow up)
face-to-face discussions	(*but* discussions that are face to face)
a twelve-by-fourteen den	(*but* a den that is twelve by fourteen)

Some adjectives, formed from two or more words, are closed (written without hyphens or space).

the dropout rate
firstborn son

Compound Nouns

Compound nouns are the most inconsistently spelled compounds in English. Many compound nouns are first spelled as two words and gradually evolve into being spelled as one, but there are many exceptions to this. Consult a dictionary or other source for the spelling of any compound noun in question.

fatherland	father-in-law	father confessor
paperweight	paper work	
salesperson	sales slip	

However, the compound nouns that are derived from other structures are usually hyphenated.

sit-in   (an occasion when people "sit in"; derived from a verb and a preposition)

has-been   (someone or something that "has been" but is no longer popular; derived from a helping verb and a verb)

put-on   (an act of "putting on" someone else; derived from a verb and an adverb)

Improvised Compounds

When two or more words functioning as a unit are used in an improvised manner, hyphenate them to show they are a unit.

an Alice-in-Wonderland approach
bad-mouth (as a verb)
a not-soon-to-be-forgotten insult
a now-you-see-it-now-you-don't accountant

Suspended Compounds

When two or more compounds have an identical element, the nonidentical elements can be suspended with hyphens and the identical element placed at the end.

low- and medium-income families (*or* low-income and medium-income families)

a butane- and electric-powered forklift (*or* a butane-powered and electric-powered forklift)

a classroom full of six-, seven-, and eight-year-olds (*or* a classroom full of six-year-olds, seven-year-olds, and eight-year-olds)

Other Compounds

Hyphenate a single capital letter forming a compound with a word.

A-bomb
G-flat
X-shaped

Use a hyphen with two-word numbers under one hundred even when they are part of a larger number.

twenty-one
twenty-one hundred
four thousand twenty-one

Use a hyphen between the numerator and the denominator of a fraction unless one or both already contain a hyphen.

one-half
three and one-third
thirty-one ten-thousandths

Hyphenate a number and a unit of measurement when used as an adjective.

a 10-yard loss
a 3-foot fence
a 4-day layoff
a 40-hour week

Word Division

At the end of a line, a word of two or more syllables may be divided with a hyphen at a syllable boundary and then continued on the next line. (One-syllable words are never divided, no matter how long—e.g. *strength, straight, scruffed, smirked, stumped*). Any dictionary shows with dots the syllable boundaries of a word and is a guide to correct syllabication. Since syllable boundaries are sometimes based on a word's pronunciation and sometimes based on its etymology, do not hesitate to consult a dictionary.

A word should never be divided between two or three consonants pronounced as one.

leath-ery (*not* leat-hery)
cush-ion (*not* cus-hion)
catch-ing (*not* cat-ching)

Do not divide a word contrary to its etymology or between double consonants when both consonants are part of the original word.

> pains-taking (not *pain-staking*; the word means that pains are taken)
> hiss-ing (not *his-sing*; the original word is *hiss,* to which *ing* is added)
> scoff-law (not *scof-flaw*; the word refers to one who scoffs at the law)

Divide a hyphenated compound only at a hyphen.

> person-to-person (not *per-son-to-person*)
> brother-in-law (not *bro-ther-in-law*)

Do not isolate one or two letters of a word on either line; the following are incorrect.

> a-fraid   hiss-er   flaunt-ed

Dividing Names and Other Units

Divide dates only between the day of the month and the year.

> May 15, / 1982   (*not* May / 15, 1982)

Do not divide units of time, money, temperature, or anything else measurable.

> 12:40 p.m.   (*not* 12:40 / p.m.)
> $1,808,767   (*not* $1,808, / 767)
> 118.3° F.   (*not* 118.3° / F.)

Do not divide contractions and abbreviations.

> shouldn't   (*not* should-n't)
> L.L.D.   (*not* L.L.-D.)

Do not divide proper names (including given names and surnames) and company names. Do not divide titles unless they are unusually long.

> Francis Christianson   (*not* Fran-cis Chris-tianson
>
> Sears, Roebuck & Company   (*not* Sears, Roe-buck & Company)

Administrator Jim Free   (Adminis-trator Jim Free
                                   is acceptable)

If a given or a surname must be separated from one line
to another, initials belong on the same line as the given name;
degrees and name designations (e.g. *Jr., Sr., III*) belong with
the surname.

Roy G. / Biv, Sr.   (*not* Roy / G. Biv, Sr. *and
                           not* Roy G. Biv, / Sr.)

Spelling Words with Prefixes

A prefix added to a word normally becomes a part of the
word and is written without a space or hyphen following it.
This is so regular that dictionaries omit many combinations
of prefixes and base words. However, the prefixes *self, ex,* and
quasi nearly always require a hyphen (*self-indulgent, self-
respect, ex-wife, ex-serviceman, quasi-legal*), and a few other
prefixes such as *anti* and *non* often require a hyphen. A writer
should consult a dictionary to be sure. If the word is not in a
dictionary, spell it without a hyphen, unless it uses one of the
prefixes above or is one of the four instances below. In
general, the hyphen is used with prefixes only in four cases:

1. When a prefix is added to a capitalized word.
   anti-American   pro-Soviet
   trans-Asiatic   post-World War I
2. When a prefix is added to a number.
   pre-1945   post-1918
3. When a writer wants to show clearly the base word to
which the prefix is added, to prevent ambiguity or misreading.
   re-cover ("to cover again," distinct from *recover,*
   "to reacquire")
   un-ionized (distinct from *unionized*)
4. When a double vowel results, the hyphen is sometimes used. The hyphen is required with double "*i*" (e.g.
anti-inflation), usually optional with double "*o*" (e.g. cooper-
ate or co-operate), and usually omitted with double "*e*" (e.g.
preeminent, reenter).

Adding Suffixes to Words Ending in a Consonant

Many words ending in a consonant double the final consonant before a suffix beginning with a vowel. Words ending in a consonant remain unchanged before a suffix beginning with a consonant.

Suffixes Beginning with Vowels

Most suffixes beginning with a vowel (e.g. *ed, er, est, ent, able, ant*, and *al*) require the doubling of a final consonant. The suffixes *ing* and *ish* follow the same pattern, but all other suffixes beginning with *i* (such as *ive* and *ize*) do not.

When adding a suffix beginning with a vowel to a one-syllable word, double the final consonant if the word ends in a single vowel and a single consonant.

> put, putting
> rid, ridding, ridded, riddance
> bid, bidding, biddable
> sneak, sneaked (two vowels precede the final consonant)
> kick, kicking (two consonants end the word)

This rule is invariable, so follow it even if the result looks a little unusual. Thus, *bussed* and *bussing* are correct spellings, although *bused* and *busing* are also correct. The plural of *gas* is *gasses* (although *gases* is also correct).

When adding a suffix beginning with a vowel to a word having two syllables or more, double the final consonant if the word ends in a single vowel and a single consonant and if the stress is on the last syllable and stays there after the suffix is added.

> prefer, preferred, preferring; *but* preference (stress doesn't remain on *fer*)
> occur, occurred, occurring, occurrence (stress remains on *cur*)
> appear, appeared, appearing, appearance (two vowels precede the final consonant)
> benefit, benefited, benefiting (stress not on the final syllable)

British spelling makes several exceptions to this rule, among them

BRITISH	AMERICAN
travelling	traveling
labelled	labeling
programming	programing (*also* programming)
worshipped	worshiped

The American exceptions to this rule (e.g. *excellent*) are very few.

The spelling of compound verbs (verbs formed from more than one word) is variable. Thus, the past tense of *kidnap* (derived from the verb *nap*) has two spellings, *kidnapped* and *kidnaped*. *Handicapped* is the only correct spelling of the word derived from *handicap*. The past tense of the computer term *input* (and of other new verbs derived from one-syllable verbs) may be spelled *inputed* or *inputted*.

Suffixes Beginning with Consonants

When adding a suffix beginning with a consonant (e.g. *ment*, *ness*, *ly*, and *ful*) to a word ending in a consonant, never double or change the final consonant.

contain	containment
even	evenness
sudden	suddenly
mirth	mirthful

The suffix is added directly to the word in all but a few cases involving *ly*. *Ly* cannot be added directly to a word ending in *c* without first adding *al*.

	basic	basically
	fanatic	fanatically
	maniac	maniacally
Exception:	public	publicly

Adding Suffixes to Words Ending in Vowels

Of the words in English ending in a vowel, words ending in *a, i, o,* and *u* are not very common. They remain unchanged when a suffix is added and give writers no problems.

hero	heroic, heroism
ski	skiing, skied, skier

The difficulties arise in adding suffixes beginning with vowels to words ending in *e* and *y.*

Words Ending in *e*

Final, silent *e* is usually dropped when a suffix beginning with a vowel is added.

mature	maturing	maturation
release	releasing	releasable
make	making	makable
state	stating	stative
base	basal	basic

The exceptions to this are few but of several different types. Keep the *e* with words ending in *ce* and *ge* when the suffix begins with *a* or *o.* This is to reflect the pronunciation accurately.

notice	noticeable	(*but* noticing)
replace	replaceable	(*but* replacing)
enlarge	enlargeable	(*but* enlarging)
courage	courageous	(*but* encouraging)

Keep the *e* with words ending in *ye* or in *oe.*

eyeing (eying *also* acceptable) dyeing hoeing shoeing

Keep the *e* in some words to show their base words.

acre	acreage
line	lineal, lineage
mile	mileage

singe	singeing, singeable
tinge	tingeing (*tinging* also correct)

Final *e* Before a Consonant

The final, silent *e* is kept when a suffix beginning with a consonant is added.

base	basement
hate	hateful
late	lateness

There are several limited exceptions to this rule. Drop the *e* in most cases if the word ends in *ue*.

argue	argument
due	duly
true	truly (*but* trueness)

but

rueful
vagueness

In American English, drop the *e* if the word ends in *dge* (British usage retains it).

abridgment
acknowledgment
judgment
lodgment

Drop the *e* in *wholly* (*whole* + *ly*), *awful* (*awe* + *ful*), and *ninth* (*nine* + *th*).

Words Ending in *y*

As a rule, words ending in *y* change to *i* before all suffixes, whether beginning with a vowel or with a consonant.

uneasy	uneasily	uneasiness
likely	likelihood	likeliest
holy	holiness	holier
fancy	fanciful	fancier	fancies

There are three major and two minor exceptions to this. Keep the *y* if it is preceded by a vowel.

payment	joyful	enjoyment
attorneys	grayness	monkeys

But change the *y* to *i* in some one-syllable words when a vowel precedes *y*.

daily	paid	said	laid

Keep the *y* if *ing* or any other suffix beginning with *i* is added (except for the suffix *ize*). This is to prevent two successive *i*'s from coming together.

studying	fancying	flying	worrying
thirtyish	eightyish		

but

theorize
agonize

Keep the *y* of a proper name when making it plural.

Murphys	Kennedys	McNallys	Kathys

Keep the final *y* in some one-syllable words ending in *y*.

fly	flier or flyer	fliable or flyable
gay	gaily or gayly	(*but* gaiety)
spry	spryly	spryness
dry	dryer or drier	dryness

Troublesome Pairs of Suffixes

English has several pairs of suffixes that sound alike and mean the same thing but that are added to different words seemingly without any rule. Actually, only one member (e.g. *able*) of each pair is still "alive" in English and can still be added to form new words. The other member (e.g. *ible*) is "dead" and is not added to new words. If you are unsure of the spelling of any word ending in one of the ten suffixes dealt with below, consult a dictionary first. If the word isn't there, you are safe to use that suffix that is still alive.

Able and *ible*

The two suffixes *able* and *ible* sound alike and have the same several meanings, such as "capable of being" and "worthy of being." Both are added to verbs and to nouns to form adjectives.

irritable (capable of being irritated)
permissible (worthy of being permitted)
navigable (capable of being navigated)
divisible (capable of being divided)
lovable (worthy of being loved)
durable (capable of enduring)
comfortable (having qualities of comfort)

The hotline is often asked how a writer can know when to add one and when to add the other. There is a rule that usually determines the choice, but it's a rule most writers can't use. Only if you know the etymology of the base word can you usually make the correct choice. If the base word is English or comes ultimately from the first verb conjugation in Latin, *able* is the correct suffix. If it is from any other conjugation in Latin, add *ible*.

All English words to which the suffix is added, and all new words created by adding the suffix (whether they are in the dictionary yet or not), take *able* and not *ible*. If the word you want to spell correctly is not in the dictionary, it is spelled with *able*.

A handy rule works for many *able/ible* words: When you can form a related word ending in *ation*, *able* is the correct suffix. When you can form a related word ending in *ion* or *ive*, *ible* is correct.

durable (duration)   repressible (repression, repressive)
irritable (irritation)   permissible (permission, permissive)
commendable (commendation)

When *able* is added to a verb ending in *e*, the final *e* is dropped unless preceded by *c* or *g*.

desirable   noticeable
excusable   knowledgeable
lovable   salvageable

Ant and *ent, ance* and *ence*

Ant and *ent* sound alike, as do *ance* and *ence,* and all four suffixes change verbs to nouns and adjectives.

attend	attendant	attendance
ignore	ignorant	ignorance
insist	insistent	insistence
recur	recurrent	recurrence

There is no rule for knowing when to use one and when to use the other; as with *able* and *ible,* the choice often depends on which Latin conjugation the base verb goes back to. However, *ant* and *ance* are the "alive" members of these suffix pairs. If the word you want to spell is not in the dictionary, spell it with *ant* or *ance.*

Er and *or*

Er and *or* sound the same and both mean "one who _____."

    actor (one who acts)
    speaker (one who speaks)
    dancer (one who dances)
    visitor (one who visits)

Er is much more common and is the suffix added to all new words in English. *Or* occurs chiefly with Latin root words, especially legal terms, and is no longer added to verbs in English. Some words have alternate spellings (*advisor, adviser; grantor, granter*).

If a word with one of these suffixes cannot be found in the dictionary, spell it with *er.*

Ize and *ise*

Many words in English are spelled with only *ise.*

| advise | chastise | enterprise |
| exercise | disguise | |

Many more have variant spellings with either *ize* or *ise* (e.g. *mesmerise, mesmerize*). These two suffixes are added to adjectives and nouns to make verbs.

legal	legalize
apology	apologize
custom	customize
critic	criticize

The *ize* is the American version, the *ise* spelling the British version. If a word with one of these suffixes is not in a dictionary, spell it with *ize*.

10

Abbreviations:
More Than Capitals and Periods

Abbreviations are useful shortcuts, if they are not overused and if writers don't make up their own. Writers should use abbreviations only when certain their readers will understand them as effortlessly as the words they stand for. We still remember the caller who wanted to know the correct abbreviation for *environmental engineer*. We replied that an abbreviation for this term probably would not be understood by the reader. An indication of that, we said, was that the caller herself didn't know the abbreviation. But she insisted. With the aid of a dictionary, she finally decided to use *env. eng.* Perhaps in context—was it part of a classified ad?—it would be understood. But if it is possible that an abbreviation will not be immediately understood, the writer should spell it out on first reference.

> The ALA (American Library Association) convention was held in the city last week.

or

> The American Library Association (ALA) convention was held in the city last week.

Most hotline callers want to know either the proper abbreviation of a term or whether or not an abbreviation is written with periods. Many abbreviations gradually evolve from being written with periods to being written without. *Collect on delivery*, once universally abbreviated *c.o.d.*, is now commonly abbreviated *COD* or *C.O.D.* Because of such changes, dictionaries may vary in the abbreviations they provide, but any standard desk dictionary can be considered authoritative in the forms of abbreviations it cites.

Finding an accepted abbreviation for a particular word or phrase can be a problem. Of the major desk dictionaries only the *American Heritage Dictionary* makes a practice of listing abbreviations within the entry for a word or phrase, thus allowing readers to find an abbreviation by looking up the word they want to abbreviate. The most extensive list of this sort is the *Reverse Acronyms, Initialisms, and Abbreviations Dictionary,* published by the Gale Research Company. (This is volume three of their *Acronyms, Initialisms, and Abbreviations Dictionary.*)

Abbreviations seem to fall into three groups based on the way we pronounce the abbreviation on the printed page. Shortened word abbreviations (*Co.* and *St.*) are always pronounced as if the entire word or phrase were present. Initialisms are abbreviations that are pronounced as a series of letters (*FBI* and *NAACP*). They are usually written without periods. Acronyms are abbreviations that have come to be pronounced as words (*NATO, SALT, UNESCO*). In this chapter we'll examine these three forms of abbreviations and the general guidelines for writing each one, and we'll look at some of the exceptions.

Shortened Word Abbreviations: Titles, Places, and Units of Measurement

Abbreviations that are shortened forms of words and phrases are pronounced as if the entire word or phrase were present. For instance, when we see the abbreviation *Mr.*, we pronounce it *mister*; similarly, we pronounce *saint* or *street* for the abbreviation *St.*, depending on the context. *Cal.* or *Calif.* is *California*, *Jan.* is *January*, *p.* is *page*, *pt.* is *part*, and *c.* is not *cee* but *copyright* or *circa*.

Shortened word abbreviations are usually written with periods. The exceptions are two-letter post-office abbreviations for states (*NY, MA, TN*) and some chemical and other scientific symbols—*Na* (sodium), *Cl* (chlorine). Units of measurement (*mi* for *mile*, *h* for *hour*) are sometimes abbreviated and written without periods in tabulated material when preceded by numerals. Shortened word abbreviations are generally capitalized if the words being abbreviated are capitalized.

Don't overuse these abbreviations. Except as titles appearing with people's names and occasional Latin abbreviations (see below) in a parenthetical comment, these abbreviations should not appear in the body of your text. Abbreviations for measurements may appear in tables or columns of material, in calculations, and in footnotes. And abbreviations for parts of books, pages, and line numbers, as well as bibliographic abbreviations, will appear in footnotes and in parenthetical documentation. But, in general, abbreviations such as *Jan.*, *Tues.*, *Dr.* (unless it is a title preceding a name) *Mass.*, and *Blvd.* do not belong in the body of anything except perhaps a note to a friend.

Professional and Courtesy Titles, Degrees and Titles

Common personal titles are always abbreviated when they immediately precede a name.

>   Ms. Ledbetter   Mr. Brumley   Mrs. Keys   Dr. Eberly

Certain honorary and professional titles are abbreviated only if a person's name is included.

>   the Rev. James C. O'Donnell *or* Reverend O'Donnell (*but not* Rev. O'Donnell)
>   Sen. Edward M. Dirksen *or* Senator Dirksen (*but not* Sen. Dirksen)

(Further information on forms of address is provided in Chapter 15.)

Degrees and titles that immediately follow a name should be abbreviated, but do not use *Mr.*, *Mrs.*, *Ms.*, or *Dr.* when a degree follows the name.

>   Sam Jones, Jr., M.S.W. (*but not* Mr. Sam Jones, Jr., M.S.W.)
>   Marylyn Parins, Ph.D.
>   Dr. Margaret Taylor, supervisor of the chemists

(Unlike a title, a job description such as *supervisor of . . .* should be neither capitalized nor abbreviated.)

Academic degrees may be abbreviated in an informal text.

>   The applicant received her Ph.D. from Stanford.

But in formal contexts, use the appropriate noun.

>   She received her doctorate from Stanford.

Abbreviations of titles cannot be made plural; titles must be pluralized and then abbreviated.

> Drs. Johnson and Johnson (*not* Dr.s Johnson and Johnson *and not* Dr.'s Johnson and Johnson)

Ms. has no established plural; the plural of *Mr.* is *Messrs.*, of *Mrs.* is *Mmes*, of *Miss* is *Misses*.

Units of Measurement

In the body of a report, units of measurement (miles, years, gallons) are always spelled out, even when they are preceded by a numeral. The only exceptions are multiword units that are pronounced letter by letter and spelled without periods, such as *Btu* (British thermal unit) and *rpm* (revolutions per minute), and the units for temperature, *C.* for Celsius and *F.* for Fahrenheit. When placed in columns, tables, or in computations, all units of measurement are generally abbreviated (*ft., lb., yr.*). Abbreviations for units of measurement are the same for the singular or the plural (1 *gal.*, 20 *gal.*).

The only rule we can discern about capitalizing abbreviations of units of measure is this: Single-letter abbreviations of units of measurement are sometimes capitalized (*N.* rather than *n.* for *newton*, *F.* rather then *f.* for *fahrenheit*). Writers should consult a desk dictionary or a specialized dictionary or style manual in the field in which they are writing.

Initialisms: Abbreviations of Institutions, Countries, Phrases, and Time Zones

The names of companies (*IBM*, *NBC*), organizations (*NCAA*, *AMA*), and especially government agencies (*TVA*, *FBI*, *FCC*) are often known by their initials. When these initials are pronounced as a series of individual letters, we have a second kind of abbreviation, an initialism. As an initialism becomes widely used and recognized, its periods become superfluous and are dropped. Thus, the abbreviation *A.F.L.-C.I.O.* of an earlier day has now become *AFL-CIO*. Generally, initialisms do not require periods. Writers may freely use initialisms, unlike shortened word abbreviations, in the body of their copy if they are sure readers will recognize them.

The national abbreviations *USA, US, USSR,* and *UK* are the widely known initialisms for countries (*USA* and *USSR* may be written with or without periods). Most national abbreviations are shortened forms of the words: *Can., Brit., Ger., Mex.*

Initialisms sometimes develop from well-known words or phrases. These too have dropped the periods: *mpg, PDQ, R&R, EKG.* The most common exceptions to this are B.C. and A.D., A.M. and P.M., always written with periods. Some abbreviations, especially of chemical terms, are being treated as initialisms (*DDT, LSD, DNA*). Remember to consult a dictionary if in doubt for the proper form.

Abbreviations for time zones are always written without periods, but usage is divided between writing them with capital and lower-case letters. The use of capital letters seems more widespread, however, and we recommend it. *PST* (*Pacific Standard Time*) and *CDT* (*Central Daylight Time*). The abbreviations should be used only in connection with figures. By themselves, they should be spelled out. Terms such as *Central Time* and *Pacific Time*, which make no reference to standard or daylight savings time, must be spelled out.

> The Writer's Hotline is open from 9 A.M. to noon Central Time.

Acronyms

The third kind of abbreviation consists of the true acronyms. An acronym is a group of letters made up of the first letter or letters of words and is pronounced as if the letters themselves form a word. Many recent organizations attempt to create catchy acronyms to enhance their causes: *NOW* (*National Organization of Women*) and *SANE* (*Society Against Nuclear Energy*). Eventually an acronym may become so well known that people forget that each of its letters actually stands for something. Two acronyms that have passed into the language are *radar* (*radio detection and ranging*) and *scuba* (*self-contained underwater breathing apparatus*). Acronyms such as *UNESCO* and *WAC*, however, continue to recall the original words they stand for.

Acronyms are usually, but not always, written without periods. Occasionally one sees *U.N.E.S.C.O.* or *S.A.L.T.*, but not often. You will be safe writing acronyms without periods, but capitalize only acronyms made from words already capitalized. Acronyms, unlike shortened word abbreviations, may be used freely. However, if your writing begins to look like alphabet soup, avoid using some of the abbreviations. If the acronym is not well known, be sure to introduce and define it.

Latin Abbreviations

Latin abbreviations are generally being dropped in favor of their English equivalents. They continue to be appropriate, however, in parenthetical references. Many guides (including the Chicago *Manual of Style*) no longer put these abbreviations into italics (i.e., underline them). Again, be consistent throughout your text. That is, don't write *e.g.* in roman type on one page and underline or write *i.e.* in italics on the next.

The traditional footnote using Latin abbreviations is being replaced by a form of footnote that consists of the author's last name and a shortened, unambiguous title for the second reference to a work. However, if the Latin abbreviations are used, they should be placed in italics (underlined) when, as they usually do, they stand for the name of a book or periodical. *Ibid.*, however, according to some style manuals, is always put in roman type.

The most commonly used and recognized Latin abbreviations include:

ABBREVIATION	LATIN MEANING	ENGLISH MEANING AND EQUIVALENT
i.e.	*id est*	that is
e.g.	*exempli gratia*	for example
etc.	*et cetera*	and so on (see Glossary)
vs.	*versus*	versus

The following abbreviations are now less well known and should be used with more caution. In general, these will be found only in parenthetical references and in footnotes or bibliographies.

viz.	*videlicet*	that is; namely
N.B.	*nota bene*	note well
q.v.	*quod vide*	which see (reserved for cross-references)
cf.	*confer*	compare
et al.	*et alia*	and others (only in footnotes and bibliographies)
ca. (*and sometimes* c.)	*circa*	about (in reference to dates)

The following abbreviations are best replaced by shortened footnote references.

ibid.	*ibidem*	in the same place as the preceding footnote reference
loc. cit.	*loco citato*	in the place cited (follows an author's name)
op. cit.	*opere citato*	in the work cited (follows an author's name)

A.M., P.M., A.D., B.C.

In printing, small capitals are usually used for A.M., P.M., A.D. and B.C. In typewriting, these abbreviations are generally typed as capitals with periods although A.M. and P.M. may be typed in lowercase, again with periods.

A.M. and P.M. are used only with figures; they should not be used with *o'clock* or with another designation of morning or afternoon.

> 10:30 P.M. (*or* 10:30 p.m.)
> ten-thirty o'clock
> half-past ten in the evening

Is 12:00 A.M. noon or midnight? It makes a difference, and the ambiguity is not always resolved by the context. Is noon the last instant of the morning or the first instant of the afternoon? One can find knowledgeable and rational people firmly entrenched on each side of the issue. Our own survey suggests that "morning" people believe noon to be 12 A.M., the last moment of the morning, while "night" people consider noon the beginning of the afternoon, 12 P.M.

To people comfortable with the Latin meaning of A.M. (*ante meridiem*) and P.M. (*post meridiem*) and who know that the sun crosses the meridian or the zenith at noon, it seems logical enough to avoid the issue by writing 12 M.

And this is the accepted convention. But many people do not know the meanings of these abbreviations, and these people are certain that 12 M. is midnight.

The only sure way to resolve the issue is to write *noon*. Midnight can be dealt with equally well by writing *midnight*. But another question arises with midnight. To what day does midnight belong? The UPI *Stylebook* says that it "is part of the day that is ending." And that is the generally recognized convention.

> Tax returns are due midnight April 15.

We know that this refers to the end of April 15, not the beginning.

A.D. and B.C. are used either with year figures or with spelled-out designations for centuries: B.C. (before Christ) follows figures and spelled-out designations; A.D. (*anno Domini*, "in the year of the Lord") precedes a figure but follows spelled-out century designations. (This placement reflects the way the full words were originally read into the sentences: "three hundred seventeen years before Christ" and "in the year of the Lord four hundred and fifty-six.")

> 317 B.C.
> the fourth century B.C.
> A.D. 456
> the fifth century A.D.

Punctuation Following Abbreviations

An abbreviation written without periods (*UN, FBI*) does not affect the punctuation of the sentence in any way.

Abbreviations written with periods sometimes present a puzzle. Never add a sentence period to an abbreviation period, but let all other punctuation marks fall as they are needed.

> Did he send the package to Washington, D.C.?
> He sent many things, e.g. twelve lords aleaping, five gold rings, and a partridge in a pear tree.

Symbols and Abbreviations

The symbols $, %, &, ¢, @, #, +, =, and others are appropriate only in tables in the writing of certain technical fields. Generally, they do not belong in the body of your writing. The primary exceptions are $, &, and %. The dollar sign ($) may be used to avoid a lengthy, cumbersome phrasing. The ampersand (&) often appears as part of a company name.

> The Girl Scouts collected $137.79 at the bazaar.
> The down payment on the house was $1,792.
> Adcock Lighting & Supply Co.

The percent sign (%) is used only with figures. It is appropriate in business, statistical, and more general writing. The word *percent* may be used with figures or with spelled-out numbers. The percent sign is not a substitute for the word *percentage*.

> A large percentage are going.
> Sixty percent are going.
> Almost 60% (*or* 60 percent) are going.

Clipped Words

Words like *phone* (short for *telephone*) and *disco* (short for *discothèque*) are called "clipped words." Clipping is one of the ways English acquires new words. But the clipped words are words, not abbreviations, so don't put periods after them.

Many clipped words are popular for a time and then disappear. Most clipped words that were voguish a generation ago are now perfectly acceptable in all levels of writing.

> ad (advertisement)
> flu (influenza)
> gym (gymnasium)
> co-op (co-operative association)

Making Abbreviations Plural

Most abbreviations are names referring to single objects and cannot be pluralized. When you need to form the plural of an abbreviation, however, you may add either *s* or *'s*. Both are acceptable, but be consistent in your practice.

> Thousands of *Ph.D.s* (or *Ph.D.'s*) are granted in the United States every year.
> During election year, politicians collect their *IOUs* (or *IOU's*).

The more traditional practice is to add *'s*, but it becomes more common each year to add only *s*, especially with acronyms (*MIRVs, SAMs*).

Abbreviations of titles cannot be pluralized without first making the words they stand for plural. Thus the plural of *Dr.* is not *Dr.s* or *Dr.'s*; it is *Drs.*, the abbreviation of *Doctors*. There seems to be no plausible way to make the title *Ms.* plural, as we have had to tell several hotline callers. Of course, *Ms.* is an artificial term (and a useful one), and it is not an abbreviation of an actual word. Our best guess is that *Mses.* will become the accepted plural form, but custom has yet to determine this. For now, we advise writers to write around the problem of pluralizing *Ms.*, if possible, by repeating the title.

> Ms. Chandler and Ms. Boyd have practiced law together since 1962.

The plural forms of abbreviations of units of measurement are the same as the singular forms: 1 *mi.*, 26 *mi.*; 1 *in.*, 12 *in.*

Making Abbreviations Possessive

The possessive of an acronym or an initialism is formed by adding *'s,* but it is unacceptable to make a shortened word abbreviation (especially a title or geographical name) into a possessive.

Acceptable

> *NATO's* first line of defense is Central Europe.
> The *FCC's* ruling about equal time has many station managers worried.

Unacceptable

> One of Fla.'s primary exports is citrus fruit.

Florida should not be abbreviated in this sentence. (When the state name is spelled out, there is no problem forming the possessive.) A better sentence often results if a cumbersome possessive form is converted to a descriptive noun such as *FCC* and *television station* below.

> The *FCC* ruling about equal time has many station managers worried.

More Information

A good desk dictionary will clear up remaining questions about the form of a particular abbreviation. Even though dictionaries will not all agree, you can at least cite a reasonably reputable authority for your own choice. A desk dictionary may list abbreviations alphabetically or in a special table. Most specialized fields also have dictionaries of abbreviations for their own fields. Two comprehensive listings of abbreviations are *The Complete Dictionary of Abbreviations* by Robert J. Schwartz and the three-volume *Acronyms, Initialisms, and Abbreviations Dictionary* published by the Gale Research Company. Remember to be kind to the reader, however. Use only those abbreviations readers are likely to understand. A style guide (see Chapter 18) will answer questions about abbreviations in footnotes and bibliographies.

11

Numbers:
Using Words and Figures

From time to time our hotline callers have questions about how to handle numbers, the most common question being whether or not to spell out a particular number. We tell callers that different publications and types of writing have different styles and conventions and that spelling out numbers is usually a matter of style. But many callers don't have an office style guide, so they call us.

In this chapter, we provide general guidelines for when to use figures and when to spell out numbers. We also examine the spelling of number words and the use of hyphens, the problems of writing dates and inclusive numbers, and some usage problems writers encounter when they want to use numbers.

Figures or Words

The handling of numbers is very much a matter of style. Journalists, for instance, spell out very few numbers. Book editors, writers, and most of the rest of us spell out many numbers. If there is a generally accepted style manual for your field or company, use it, of course. If there isn't such a style manual, the guidelines we give our callers will lead you through most problems.

In deciding whether or not to write out numbers, we are concerned with the ease of reading. It is easier to read *1,213* than *one thousand two hundred thirteen* or *twelve hundred thirteen*. However, it is easier to read *three million* or *3 million* than *3,000,000* and easier to read *3.6 million* than either *3,600,000* or *three million six hundred thousand*.

In general, spell out numbers below one hundred and

numbers that can be expressed in two words, including approximate numbers and references to decades and centuries.

> ninety-nine men
> fourteen hundred complaints
> twenty-five hundred acres (a hyphenated number is considered one word)
> thousands of customers
> a million-dollar deal
> as many as fifteen hundred geese
> during the twenties
> the fourth century
> the 1980s (*more recognizable than* the nineteen eighties)

Use figures for dates (including years standing by themselves), for street numbers, for page and line numbers, and in referring to parts of books and to times (written with A.M. or P.M.).

> your January 24, 1982, memo
> 24 January 1982
> 1980 (*not* nineteen eighty)
> 400 Springwood Drive
> 1760 Fifth Avenue (*preferable to* 1760 5th Avenue)
> pages 6–12, pp. 6–12
> Chapter 23
> figure 7b
> table 2.3
> 12:30 A.M., twelve-thirty in the morning

Especially in business and scientific writing, use figures for numbers written with decimals (including specific dollar amounts and percentages), for numbers with units of measurement and with abbreviations, and for tabulated data. Here as elsewhere approximate numbers are usually spelled out.

> 0.0003 inch (*or, in a general discussion*, three ten-thousandths of an inch)
> $14.58
> 3.68 billion dollars or $3.68 billion (the dollar sign is used in technical, statistical, or financial copy where it would need to be spelled out several times)

but

> a billion and a half dollars (*or* $1.5 billion)
> a hundred customers
> 17 percent
> a 125% (*or* 125 percent) increase in sales
> 25 rpm
> 12.5 mpg

Do not begin a sentence with figures. Spell out the figures or recast the sentence. Change *1,750 customers attended the grand opening* to

> The grand opening attracted 1,750 customers.

or

> There were 1,750 customers at the grand opening.

or

> Seventeen hundred fifty customers attended the grand opening.

Do not mix figures and spelled-out numbers for similar items in the same sentence or paragraph. Spell out all the numbers or use figures throughout, whichever seems more readable.

> He saw 423 blackbirds, but only 2 cardinals and 6 sparrows.
> One hundred ten people signed up for the trip, but only forty-seven went.

but

> The three new parking lots will provide spaces for 1,238 more cars. (Dissimilar items are being enumerated.)

Plurals of Numbers and Figures

Spelled-out numbers form their plurals according to the usual rules.

> The students scored in the eighties.
> The residents are in their seventies and eighties.

We are at sixes and sevens with each other.
The Depression of the thirties intensified the problems
    of the dust-bowl farmer.

Numbers written as figures form plurals by adding *s* or *'s*.
(Either is correct, accurate, and adequate. Omitting the
apostrophe is the more modern fashion.)

The temperature was in the 80s (*or* 80's).
The Depression of the 1930s (*or* the 1930's) intensified
    the problems of the dust-bowl farmer.

Hyphens

Use a hyphen with two-word numbers under one hundred,
even when they are part of a larger number.

twenty-one
twenty-one hundred
thirty-five million
four thousand thirty-one

In fractions, including decimal fractions, use a hyphen
between the numerator and the denominator unless one of
them already contains a hyphen. (A hyphen belongs in numbers under one hundred and in decimal denominators, e.g.
ten-thousandths, hundred-thousandths.)

one-half
three and one-third
three-tenths
thirty-one ten-thousandths

Use a hyphen with a number and a unit of measurement
preceding a noun. (This number-measurement combination
acts as an adjective group.) Use a hyphen in a compound such
as *twenty-odd*.

ten-foot pole
90-meter jump
three-meter platform
one-inch margin
100-odd performances
twenty-plus nights
a hundred-plus students

Writing Dates

Dates may be written in several ways. In the sentence *Your memo of April 9, 1944, has recently come to our attention,* the date may be written in the following ways:

> memo of April 9, 1944, (The final comma, present only by convention, is disappearing.)
> your April 9, 1944, memo (final comma even less likely here)
> your memo of 9 April 1944 (no commas)

and if the year is clear,

> your April 9 memo
> your memo of April 9
> your April ninth memo
> your April 9th memo (Ordinal numbers in dates are very informal and seldom appropriate.)

A problem arises when writing dates with the words *night* and *winter.* When is the night of April 15 or the winter of 1981? Recast such references to eliminate the ambiguity. If that is not possible, then make the date clear by giving both dates and a slash.

> in the early-morning hours of April 15
> in the late-night hours of April 14
> during the night of April 14/15
> in December 1980
> the winter of 1980/81

Inclusive Numbers

Inclusive numbers *include* both the first and the last number given. They are primarily used with dates and with textual citations: page numbers, line numbers, chapter and verse numbers, and other numbers.

In writing inclusive numbers, it is never wrong to give the beginning and ending numbers in full.

the 1914–1918 war
the Great Depression (1929–1939)
pages 64–71

But inclusive numbers are usually written more succinctly. In writing citations, write all digits in numbers below one hundred. In other numbers always write at least two digits, and include all numbers that change.

pages 25–33
pages 106–09
pages 124–33
pages 516–19
pages 1013–2020
Genesis 1:26–27

Note: Do not combine *from-to* or *between-and* dates and numbers with hyphens. When writing *from-to* or *between-and*, full figures must be cited.

from 1914 to 1918 (*not* from 1914–1918)
between 1914 and 1918
from January 1941 to August 1942
from 126 to 130 pounds
between 17 and 23 mpg

Inclusive Dates

In writing dates, write the two final digits if both years are in the same century: otherwise write all digits. Write all digits in years containing three or less digits.

Sir Richard Burton (1821–90)
Pancho Villa (ca. 1877–1923)
Julius Caesar (ca. 102–44 B.C.)
Augustus (63 B.C.–A.D. 14)

Handling Numbers and Statistics

A handbook of grammar and usage hardly seems like the place to discuss the ways we use numbers and statistics. But our society thinks numbers are important. We respond to numbers—tallies, percentages, averages, and medians—with greater emotion than we do to verbal statements. When writers use numbers, we take notice, we give them credence, we think that they know what they are talking about. Perhaps they do.

But numbers can be confusing, (at least interpreting them can be confusing and contradictory) and the interpretations of a set of statistics can vary radically during an election year. In 1968 the federal government, wishing to reduce the percentage of the national budget being spent on defense, began to include social security trust funds and the highway trust funds in the annual budget. Immediately, without a dollar change in amounts, there was an enormous reduction in defense spending and a corresponding increase in spending for human needs. Of course, the government said that this presented a clearer picture of national priorities and spending. Perhaps it does. But the point is that without changing a dollar of income or outlay, the appearance of the budget was radically altered.

Majority/Plurality

Apart from problems arising from questionable motives, there are a number of ways that writers may inadvertently mislead readers with statistics. For instance, many readers, and apparently some writers, do not know the difference between a majority and plurality; you can, however, be certain that the candidate knows the difference between a two-to-one *majority* and a plurality in which one candidate leads the next by a two-to-one *margin*. (A majority of votes is at least one over half of the number cast; a plurality is one more than the second highest number of votes. Of one hundred votes, fifty-one is a majority, but a plurality, if there are five candidates, might be twenty-one.)

Increase and Decrease

Units of increase and decrease (in prices or profits, for instance) are always measured against a base. The base is 100 percent. A twofold increase in profits is a 200 percent increase, a profit three times the earlier profit. That's pretty straightforward.

Now suppose that last year, a company made a profit of $5 a share, and this year, it made $6 a share. The increase is $1, an increase of one-fifth, a 20 percent increase, or a profit that amounts to 120 percent of last year's profit. This is a 20 percent increase, *not* a 120 percent increase.

Items that are less than 100 percent cause more problems. If a furniture store slashes prices by 50 percent, everyone understands what's going on: prices have been cut in half, a 50 percent decrease, a reduction of one-half.

That seems straightforward, and it is. But then someone writes a sentence like this one taken from a recent newspaper: *The findings . . . indicate the concentration of elements in these ancient stars are five times lower than previously predicted.*

If you expect a profit of $5 and you receive a profit of $1, have your profits fallen five times lower than expected? Of course not. They are *one-fifth* as high as expected. Clearly the intent of the newspaper writer was to express the idea that concentrations are one-fifth the level predicted. (At least we guess that was the intention.)

"Significant" Zeros

You should be aware too that zeros sometimes have meaning. When using tabulated material or figures of any kind, do not add zeros simply to have all the numbers look the same. Statistically, a zero, even a zero that comes after a decimal point with no number following it, is a significant number, for it reflects the accuracy of the figures. A hole that is thirty ten-thousandths (0.0030) of an inch in diameter may or may not be the same size as a hole that is three-thousandths (0.003) of an inch in diameter. They may in fact be the same size, or the second may be slightly larger or smaller. The first measurement indicates the hole is neither twenty-nine nor thirty-one ten-thousandths of an inch in diameter. The second figure indicates the hole is neither two-thousandths nor four-thousandths of an inch in diameter. Similarly, a construction cost of $3.60 million should have been more accurately figured than a cost of $3.6 million. (But it may not have been.)

Inflated Number Rhetoric

The words around numbers are often exaggerated until there is no meaning left. What, for instance, does this sale claim mean?

Savings of up to 50% and more.

This says that there are savings of less than 50 percent, of 50 percent, and of more than 50 percent. It actually means only that there is a sale going on and that the store owner wants prospective customers to get excited. What about this one, another typical advertisement?

Savings average 50% and more.

Again, the writer has not said anything except that the store is having a sale. The sentence makes no sense. Savings may average 50 percent or more than 50 percent, but not both.

Averages, Means, Medians

Some quick, unambiguous definitions may be useful.

Average has a number of general meanings and is used in a number of very specific phrases usually meaning "typical." With a figure, the word *average* should mean the amount that each member of a group would have if the highs and lows were balanced out. (To find an average, add up the quantities —scores, amounts, sales, whatever—and divide the total by the number you are averaging among. Tom, Dick, and Harry have a total of $27 among them. They have an average of $9 each, even though Tom has $15; Dick, $12; and Harry has nothing. That is, $15 + $12 + $0 ÷ 3 = $9.)

Mean—average. Mean is the mathematical term for the value obtained by the formula above. While it is a more precise term, it is not used much in general writing.

Median is the middle value in a set of quantities. This is not an average, although sometimes the average and the median are near each other. In the example above, the median (or middle) amount is Dick's $12. One person in the group has more than Dick does, one has less. The median amount is the amount in the middle.

Percentage, coming from the Latin *per centum* ("by the hundred") is simply a fraction with the denominator of *one hundred*; that is, a percent is the number of parts in a hundred. Three-quarters of the students passed the test. Three-quarters is .75, or 75 percent; that is, seventy-five parts out of a hundred. But .75 percent (using both the decimal point and the word *percent*) indicates not three-quarters of the whole but three-quarters of one part of the whole, three-quarters of one percent.

12

Titles: Capitals, Italics, and Quotation Marks

The titles of publications, compositions, paintings, and many man-made objects are capitalized and then either set in italics (underlined) or placed in quotation marks. A few titles (e.g., names of buildings and documents) are only capitalized. And while there is some reason and a little rhyme to the general outlines of what is done, much of it seems to be done because it is conventional and expected. Instead of scattering the rules and examples of titles through discussions of capitalization, italics, and quotation marks, we will treat them here by category, considering first the capitalization of titles and then considering whether names of particular objects are put into italic type (underlined), quotation marks, or left in regular type.

The rules given here are for general usage. They correspond to specific usage in several academic areas, particularly in the humanities, but they may not be appropriate in all details for writing in specific technical fields, especially in citations, footnotes and bibliographies, and so on. If you have a particular style guide for your field, use that. However, these rules and guidelines will be sufficient for most writing.

Capital Letters in Titles and Names

Capitalization of the titles of all items discussed in the following sections is handled the same way. Capitalize the first letter of the first word, the last word, and all other words of the title except an article (*a, an,* or *the*), conjunction, or preposition less than five letters long. Capitalize the initial article if the article is part of the title or name.

Knowing whether the title or name includes the initial article is sometimes a problem, but unfortunately, there is no easy way around it. Sometimes a dictionary, encyclopedia, or other reference work that is known for its careful editing can help. Sometimes a call to a library reference department will yield the answer. But often a writer is left guessing. We advise writers to assume that the article is not part of the title.

> *The Christian Science Monitor*
> the Empire State Building
> *The New York Times*
> *Time* magazine
> the aircraft carrier *Kitty Hawk*; the U.S.S. *Kitty Hawk*

A title does not include the descriptive common nouns, such as the words *magazine* and *aircraft carrier* above, that may precede or follow the actual words of the title.

When blending a title into a sentence, initial articles that are part of the title may be dropped.

> in Eliot's *Waste Land*

or

> in Eliot's poem *The Waste Land*

Second Reference to Titles and Names

On second reference, when the title is generally shortened, key words will still be capitalized and treated in the same fashion as the first reference. But an initial article will no longer be in capitals. Common nouns, such as *paper* and *play* below, that refer to the item will be in lower case and should not be given special treatment.

> *The Christian Science Monitor*; the *Monitor*; the paper
> *A Midsummer Night's Dream*; *Dream*; the play
> "Arkansas Traveler"; the "Traveler"; the popular fiddle tune
> "Ode to Joy"; the "Ode" in Beethoven's Ninth

Newspapers, Magazines

Capitalize and italicize (underline) names of newspapers as they appear in the masthead. Sometimes this includes the name of the city, sometimes not. Place titles of articles and headlines in quotation marks. Names of magazines should be italicized (underlined), but names of articles, columns, or other parts of magazines should be put in quotation marks.

> *The Times* (London); the London *Times*
> *The New York Times*
> the *Arkansas Gazette* in an editorial headlined "Measures Against Inflation"; an editorial in the *Gazette*
> *Newsweek*
> "Who's Taking Care of the Children?" a survey published in *Family Circle*

When a copy of the periodical is not at hand, it is sometimes difficult to determine whether or not an initial article and the name of the city should be treated as part of the title. In such cases, do not treat the article as part of the title, and the name of the city is probably best omitted from the italicized title. Do be consistent from one mention of any title to the next, however.

> *Los Angeles Times* (Los Angeles *Times* is also permissible.)

Books, Essays, Unpublished Manuscripts, Sacred Works

Separate Publications

Italicize (underline) the names of books and pamphlets published by themselves. This includes novels, full-length plays, and most long poems.

> *One Flew over the Cuckoo's Nest*
> *Waiting for Godot*
> *The Waste Land*
> *Instructions for Form 1065*

Chapters of Books, Sections of Poems, Essays

Titles of portions of books, sections of long poems, and essays or articles included in periodicals or in a collection are not placed in italics (underlined) but are enclosed in quotation marks.

> "A Game of Chess" in *The Waste Land*
> "The Individual Structural Marks" in George Summey's *American Punctuation*
> "Progress and Change" from *One Man's Meat* by E. B. White

Parts of Books

The names for parts of books are capitalized when they refer to specific parts of a given book; they are not italicized (underlined) or placed in quotation marks.

> in his Foreword
> Chapter 23
> Preface
> Index

but

> He thinks prefaces are usually irrelevant.

Unpublished Works

The names of unpublished manuscripts of any length—diaries, journals, novels, poems, dissertations—are placed in quotation marks.

> "A Structural Analysis of the Plays of the King's Men's Repertory," an unpublished dissertation

Sacred Texts

The books of the Bible, the word *Bible,* and the names of other sacred scriptures are capitalized but are not put in italics or quotation marks.

Revelation
King James translation of the Bible
the Koran
the Talmud
the Bhagavad Gita
the Gospels

Documents, Treaties, Councils, Legislation, and Similar Items

Documents, treaties, and agreements with specific titles are capitalized but not set in italics (underlined) or placed in quotation marks. Simplified references are generally in lower case, as are references to pending legislation.

Magna Carta
Declaration of Independence
the Constitution of the United States; the Constitution
the Arkansas Constitution; the state constitution
Council of Nicaea
a gun-control bill
the windfall profits tax bill

Visual Compositions

Place the names of paintings, prints, lithographs, and statues in italics (underlined).

Michelangelo's *David*
The Last Supper
Arrangement in Grey and Black, No. 1: The Artist's Mother, better known as *Whistler's Mother*

In scholarly or formal writing, only the original name of the work is placed in italics (underlined); coined or descriptive names are placed in quotation marks:

La Gioconda, the "Mona Lisa"

Musical Compositions

Titles of long musical works—such as operas and symphonies—and titles of collections—whether of dances, songs, or sonatas, and including record albums—are set in italics (underlined).

> *Carmen*
> *The Nutcracker Ballet*
> *The Well-Tempered Clavier*

Titles of short works—individual dances and songs, for instance—are placed in quotation marks:

> the "Gypsy Song" from *Carmen*
> "On the Trail" from the *Grand Canyon Suite*
> the "Waltz of the Flowers" from Tchaikovsky's *Nutcracker*
> "Me and Bobby McGee" from the Album *Pearl*

Titles formed from the name of a type of work, such as a symphony or a fugue, with a musical designation or opus number are always capitalized but not italicized (underlined); descriptive titles of these works, whether added by the author or by later critics, are set in italics (underlined) or placed within quotation marks, depending on the length of the work.

> Prelude and Fugue in C Major from *The Well-Tempered Clavier*
> Mahler's Symphony No. 2, *Resurrection*
> Beethoven's Ninth Symphony

Man-Made Objects: Buildings to Battleships

Buildings, dams, and monuments are capitalized but not placed in quotation marks or set in italics (underlined).

> the Guggenheim Museum
> the L.A. Memorial Coliseum; the Memorial Coliseum; the Coliseum; the stadium

the Washington Monument
the Capitol (at Washington, D.C.)
the state capitol (building)
Hoover Dam; the dam at Boulder City
the Statue of Liberty (considered a monument)

The specific names of individual ships, spaceships, and airplanes should be italicized (underlined). The generic names, such as *missile* and *bomber* below, including type and number designations, are simply capitalized. The name of a class of ship or vehicle is in lower case unless it is an initialism (an abbreviation made up of single letters).

ICBM; intercontinental ballistic missile
Minuteman III
Titan
the *Spirit of St. Louis*; Lindbergh's Ford tri-motor
Lucky Lady; a B-17; the Flying Fortress; a World War II
    bomber
the *Spirit of America*
Lady Helmsman; a C-class catamaran
Apollo XI spacecraft; the command ship *Columbia*; the
    lunar module *Eagle*
U.S.S. *Chawonoc*
the aircraft carrier *Kitty Hawk*

Movies, Television Shows, Comic Strips

Put the names of motion pictures, television series, and motion-picture-length television programs into italics (underlined). Put the names of individual episodes or segments into quotation marks. Put the name of a comic-strip series into italics (underlined).

Gone with the Wind
All in the Family
America, "The More Abundant Life, Part I"
Doonesbury

More Information

For more detailed discussions and examples, see the University of Chicago Press *Manual of Style*, on which much of this *Handbook* is based, and the United States Government Printing Office *Style Manual*.

PART THREE

The Work
of Writing

13

Writing: Getting Started and Keeping Going

A few people know exactly what they want to say when they first put pen to paper or paper to typewriter. But most of us struggle to find the precise words we want and to organize those words into a coherent piece of writing. Sometimes the struggle goes well, but too often we get stuck. It happens to the best of us and to the worst. A scientist may write lengthy research reports with ease but freeze up while writing a letter of recommendation. A social worker may write grant proposals quickly and effortlessly, only to be stymied when writing a presentation for a city-council meeting. A research engineer, having written reports all day, may suddenly go dry when asked to explain a pet project to a lay audience. And everyone has an off day occasionally.

But some people are stuck so often that they say they have a mental block against writing. Eventually they may convince themselves that they cannot write at all. Whether a writer is blocked all the time or only occasionally, there are several remedial steps that can be taken.

Getting Stuck

Most people get stuck when they begin to worry about last things first. Instead of writing down ideas (a first thing), they worry about spelling and punctuation (some last things) and the boss's attitude (almost a last thing). They paralyze themselves with their own fear of not doing as well as they think they should. Worse, they fear they will not do as well as they think someone else thinks they should. That's real paranoia. Don't wait until you have panicked to act.

Learn to recognize the early signs of getting stuck. It is easier to get yourself moving before you are up to your eye-

brows in the mire. You may be getting bogged down if you
are doing anything other than working on the words in front
of you. When you begin to stall, you will use any excuse to
leave your work area: Empty coffee cups and office football
pools will tantalize and enchant you. Eventually, with a deadline bearing down, you begin to wonder whether you will be
able to complete the project at all. That's fear.

Getting Started

To get started, you will have to learn to put aside the
worries and temptations that distract you. Each time something bothers you, you have two choices: deal with it in some
way, or—gently, but firmly—put it out of your mind. If you
are worried about the way the boss wants the report written,
ask about it. If you can't ask, or if the boss doesn't know, put
the worry aside and focus on your writing. A telephone call
may be quickly disposed of with an "I'll call you back after
lunch." If you are uncomfortable, you may need to take a
walk to wake up, or you may even need to stand up at a file
cabinet to write. But dwelling on your discomfort will simply
make you more uncomfortable and less productive.

Many people worry about noise. They are distracted by
typewriters, secretaries grousing about bosses, piped-in music,
kids yelling at each other—whatever noise is around. When
they are working well, these noises are not distracting. But
when their writing is going slowly, each noise chafes their
nerves. Some noises can be toned down by a polite request;
other noise will have to be ignored. Remember that most
people become fidgety in absolute quiet. And fidgety people
are not very productive. Apparently a little noise helps a
person focus attention on the work at hand.

In general, be wary of everything that gives you an excuse
to postpone writing. Guard especially against two time-
honored excuses—the need to clear your desk and the need
for more information. If you tell yourself that you are going
to get down to some serious writing as soon as the paperwork
is caught up, you are fooling yourself. Long before your mail
is sorted and the dusty letters are answered, the ideas you had
will flutter off, leaving only an approaching deadline.

The need for more information may be real, but more often

it is simply a way of saying, "I'm afraid to start writing." If you are convinced that you need more information, go get it. But if you are hoping that reading another article or taking another survey will help you fit everything together, forget it. You will fit everything together by writing, not by postponing. Examine your "need" for more information with great suspicion.

You can learn to set aside distractions and worry. Don't tense up and try to ignore them; that will only give them more strength. Make a note to check something later or tell yourself that this is something that can be safely ignored for now. When a new distraction enters your mind—and distractions will continue to arrive until you are writing well—set it aside. Let it out the back of your mind just as it came in the front.

Getting Words on Paper

Putting words down on paper is the best way to set distractions and worries aside. You may not like the words you put down at first (you can always change them), you may not know right off what goes into the introduction (you can rewrite it later), and you may not know how to spell *develop* and *separate* (circle them now and check them later). But when you begin to put words down, you begin to make progress.

Making Notes

Brainstorm to get your mind moving; take notes while you brainstorm. Use note cards or sheets of paper, whichever you prefer, and start jotting down ideas. Without making judgments, write down everything that comes to mind: illustrations, anecdotes, ideas and parts of ideas, phrases, titles for subsections, words and terms you want to define—everything and anything. Let your mind freewheel while you take notes. Later on, when your mind has slowed, you will pick, choose, and discard.

You may find that this note-taking leads you directly into the writing. Sometimes, if you understand the subject and your point clearly, if you know your audience well and know why you are writing, you may simply write up your notes and have your project ready for the final rewriting and editing. But don't be disappointed if this does not happen.

Really Writing

Whether you make extensive notes or not, you are going to be faced with actually putting sentences down on paper. Your real problems may begin at this point. As the first phrase goes down, you start to wonder whether it is the right phrase or not. By the end of a couple of sentences, you are wondering about the correctness of some commas and a semicolon. Gamely you plod on, wondering whether you should be using *compare with* or *compare to*. By the end of the paragraph, you have stopped to check the spelling of two words and have hunted up three synonyms, one of which you have already discarded. By the end of a page, you are searching for any excuse to leave this agony of writing.

These distractions, and dozens like them, are often left over from worrying in school about being correct. Be correct, of course. Be correct, or the frustrated office grammarian will haunt your dreams, but put off worrying and checking until your project is almost finished. When your ideas are set down fully, when your arguments and details are arranged, there will be time to check spelling, to find synonyms, to check the correctness of a comma, and to choose between *affect* and *effect*. These are editing tasks. Put off editing until near the end of the writing process. For now, write.

Write. Before you can judge the accuracy of a phrase, the phrase must have a context. It must be in a sentence, in a paragraph, in a report or article. Only then can you know whether it is a useful phrase or not. So write. Get your ideas down. When you come to a word or a punctuation mark you feel uncertain about, mark it. If it is marked, you will remember to check it later. You can forget it for now.

Begin at the beginning or at the end. Begin in the middle. Begin writing anywhere you feel comfortable. When you are finished with one section or one thought or one set of ideas, go on to another. Perhaps you will write in order, perhaps not. Write wherever the ideas seem clearest to you.

Discovery and Rewriting

As you write, quickly and without worrying about extraneous matters, surprising things will emerge. You will have ideas you did not expect. Illustrations and examples you had forgotten about will come to mind along with new ones. Don't agonize because these things are disrupting your writing; enjoy the thrill of discovery. Follow the new idea to see where it leads. You may throw it out later, but it may lead you to new insights and a stronger presentation.

If a new idea threatens to distract you, make a note or two about it, and go on with the writing at hand. The note allows you to recover the idea later, and because you know you can recover the idea, you do not waste effort trying to remember it while you are working on something else.

You should be glad for new ideas and observations that make you uncomfortable, for you are finding holes in your arguments and new thoughts that you must consider. At least be glad that you are finding these things for yourself instead of having someone else point them out later.

When you have written down most of your ideas or when you are ready to reformulate your thinking, it is time to rewrite. Put your first draft aside and write a new draft. This new draft may bear little resemblance to the first. It blends your early ideas with your more recent thoughts and sharpens the whole presentation. You will probably introduce different examples and rearrange thoughts. That's fine. You may do this once or twice more before you are finished.

Outlining

As you develop a feel for the dynamic process of writing—when thoughts grow and mature as they are being written down—you may develop disdain for outlining.

Perhaps outlining, when you learned it, was not an aid in writing; it was a chore. You learned it for the teacher's benefit. You learned neatness and form—never to have an *A* without a

B, a *1* without a *2*, and always to have parallel grammatical headings. Sometimes you were required to turn in your outline a few days before your paper was due. If you were like a great many students, you simply wrote the paper and *then* the outline. You felt that you were circumventing the assignment, but you already knew to trust your writing more than any outline arbitrarily made up ahead of the writing. Naturally, as soon as you could, you discarded outlining as a waste of time.

Yet, at the very least, you have a mental outline whenever you sit down to write. You have some understanding of the problem before you and of how you are going to tackle it. This mental outline is rearranged and refined as you write. Even though you may never make a written outline, your writing reflects your mental outline.

Most people outline on paper but still stop far short of a formal schoolroom outline. You probably begin with a few scratch notes. As you write, you alter the notes, adding and subtracting ideas, drawing arrows to indicate things that should be grouped, and adding more notes. As you think of something that needs to be included, you find a place for it in your outline. When you were in school, thinking of something new disheartened you, for that meant you either had to change your outline or wrench your writing back to the outline. But now thinking of something new should please you. Each new idea creates new possibilities and helps you fully and accurately state your thoughts. Keep track of new ideas and their probable place in your writing with your notes and your outline. Keep in mind (that is, in your outline) your key points and allow the subordinate ones to fall into place around them. Trust your increasing understanding and your changing thoughts. The outline will help steer you through the possibilities. So change your outline as your thinking changes, but don't discard it. Let it steer you in the direction you want to go.

Instead of jotting down an outline, you may decide to physically rearrange your writing. Cut out paragraphs and portions of paragraphs that seem out of place for some reason, and tape or paste them where they seem to belong. You will probably not write down a new outline in so many words, but it should be obvious to you that you are making a *de facto* outline. Your outline may change again, but you are on your way.

Your Audience

As you continue to write, organize, and rewrite, patching together bits and pieces written at various times, you will find significant variations you must deal with. For instance, you may find that you have explained some technical terms in detail but have introduced others without comment. You will need to decide which terms must be defined and which can be used without definitions. This will depend on your audience, of course. You may find that you wrote a few pages while in a joking, facetious, or even a sarcastic mood, while the rest of the writing is straightforward. You will need to decide what tone is appropriate for your audience and for your subject. Will a facetious remark enliven the report, or will it merely turn the audience sour? A joke which is misunderstood or which falls flat is worse than no joke. Gauge your audience. If your audience seems vague and nebulous, visualize two or three particular people—even if you must create them in your own mind. Write to their level of knowledge. Write to their interests and in a tone that will win you a fair hearing. Lead your audience to your point and through it—not condescendingly, but as you yourself would want to be led—clearly and directly.

With your audience firmly in mind, with your thoughts developed and organized, it is time for the final rewriting. You are ready to make the final push.

The Final Push

If you have done your work well, your final rewriting should involve little more than thorough editing. You may find that you have a hole or two to patch in an argument, or you may find that a paragraph or two must be shifted and rewritten, but all this can be quickly done. In addition, now may be the time to reexamine your introduction and possibly rewrite it.

Even as you do this final rewriting, remain alert to ideas that need sharper focus and to anything that may distract the reader. Making major changes at this stage of the writing is time-consuming, but it is better to take the time now than to wish later that you had.

Editing

Finally we come to what you wanted to do when you first sat down to write: editing. Now is the time to check the spelling of troublesome words, to search out a synonym that you have had on the end of your pencil, and to decide whether you mean *affect* or *effect* and whether *politics* takes a singular or a plural verb. Now is the time to check out the punctuation you had questions about—the colons, commas, and dashes that were trying to bother you while you were writing. If you have been thorough in the writing process, editing should be a matter of small things.

Reading your paper again, preferably aloud, often enables you to catch broken sentences and to sharpen your language. You should also be able to recognize words and phrases that contain misleading nuances and unwanted connotations. Now you should be ready for the final typing and proofreading. Don't forget the proofreading; no matter who does the typing, you, the writer, are responsible for the proofreading. It is your name on the report; you will be blamed for the typos.

Getting Stuck Halfway Through

At some point in this writing, rewriting, and organizing process, you will get stuck. The juices will stop flowing in midsentence, in midthought. But don't panic. Don't run screaming from the room for a coffee and self-flagellation break. In fact, don't take a break of any kind. If you walk away from your writing now, when you are stuck, you will return to your writing still stuck. You may stand up and stretch, but get your coffee after you have gotten unstuck.

To get unstuck, use essentially the same steps you use for getting started.

1. Put things into perspective. This is not the end. You have been stuck before and have survived. Other writers—more

efficient, more productive, and more famous—have also been stuck.

2. Examine your world for distractions that you can get rid of, and remember that most distractions are problems only when you let them be. If you have begun worrying about the reaction of the boss, your grammar, or the approaching deadline, relax and let these distractions out of your mind. Get back to your words.

3. Perhaps your mind has suddenly filled up with thoughts about the introduction, the conclusion, or some section you are not working on at the moment. Don't fight these thoughts. Make a note about your ideas and get back to your writing. Or perhaps you need more than a note; perhaps you need to work for a while on a different section of the report. Remember: always write where the writing seems easy and productive.

4. If you are still stuck, give yourself this assignment: begin writing with the words "I am stuck . . ." and go on from there. Write quickly, without making judgments, without deliberating—just write. You will probably write first about where you are stuck or why you feel you are stuck. But soon you will be writing about the point you are trying to make or about things you have left to say. Within a few minutes, you will generate an idea or two, and you will want to charge back to your main project.

Don't. Stay on your "I am stuck" assignment until you feel *compelled* to return to your main writing. If you run back to the main writing too quickly, you will quickly run out of ideas again.

5. Brainstorming will often help you get unstuck. Make notes about anything that you have not covered yet—statistics, examples, illustrations, an anecdote, a major point, an apt phrase—anything. As with writing about being stuck, don't return to the writing too soon. When you feel compelled to return to the main writing, do so.

Now, if you know what you are going to write next, if you feel completely unstuck, take a short break.

Taking Breaks

You should take breaks. Writing is hard work, and you need to stretch your arms, your legs, and your back. You need to pump some fresh blood into your leaden brain. But before you go on a break, always know what you are going to write about when you get back.

It is a natural desire, when we stall, to walk away in frustration. If you quit while you are stuck, you *may* think of ways to get unstuck, but most of your energy will be focused on negative thoughts about your writing—being aggravated because you are stuck again and dreading the approaching deadline. When you force yourself through your "stuckness" before you take a break, you leave your writing knowing what comes next, and during your break, you will focus on your success, not your failure. While you are relaxing, your mind is likely to be full of things to come. During your break, you are actually getting ready to get back to work, as well as relaxing.

Getting Stuck at the End

Even during the final revising and editing, you can get stuck. Now, instead of running out of things to say, you may find that you have said things that do not relate to the point. You may be cutting a favorite phrase or joke, but if you can't justify it, cut it. Or you may find you have explained the same point two or three times in an effort to make it clear; while none of the explanations by itself is complete, there is a great deal of overlapping. Try rewriting the section one more time. Make a note about the point you want to make, and rewrite without looking at your previous draft.

Nor should you allow yourself to be stuck by apparent gaps between ideas or paragraphs. A transition does not need to be cute or clever. If your ideas are logically arranged and logically related to an overall plan, a simple statement that you have finished with one item and are moving on to the next should work well. (For examples of such transitions, see the first sentence of this section and the last one on page 259.) If you need to explain why you are taking things up in a particular order, do so without making a fuss about it. If you cannot construct a logical transition, reexamine the arrangement and focus of your ideas.

As you finish up, you may find yourself staring at a sentence or paragraph and saying "Something's wrong here, but I can't quite put my finger on it." Read a problem sentence or paragraph aloud. Sometimes listening to your voice struggle through a sentence will alert you to possible ways of making the sentence more idiomatic. You may discover a structure that should be parallel or a word you have left out. You may find a grammatical or logical problem that you have overlooked. Having someone else read your paper may also be helpful. Take seriously any remark that indicates your reader is lost or puzzled. But look at more than the word or sentence your reader complains about. The reader may have been misled by an earlier sentence.

If, after all this, your writing still seems overly complex and difficult to follow, then work through some of the suggestions in Chapter 14.

And Good Luck

The way to get started is to start: Settle in, and admit that distractions are primarily in your mind and that the ones you cannot shunt aside will fade as you get involved with your words. Then write without worrying about the boss, the grammar, the punctuation, or the words. Write.

As you write, discover your ideas. Read what you have written, not to edit it, but to refine and develop ideas.

Continue to write, read and discover, and rewrite until you have slipped into organizing your material. Soon you will be ready to fill gaps in your arguments and provide transitions between ideas. By then you will have found the tone you are going to use. You should also have decided how much technical detail to include.

Soon you will be ready to edit the manuscript. At this point, you can worry about grammar, spelling, punctuation, and usage. Take the time to be certain that you are correct.

When you get stuck at any point, simply clear your mind

again, settle down, and write some more. This time, write about your being stuck until you have stopped being stuck.

"Sounds easy," you say.

Take it one step at a time and it is. Writing can actually be very satisfying and even—do we dare say it?—fun.

Good luck.

14

Writing Well:
It Doesn't Come Naturally

Gobbledygook. Doublespeak. Gibberish. Academese. Bureaucratese. No matter what you call it, it's easy to spot. It's language that has become more involved and more complicated than the ideas being expressed. It's language that conceals and obscures instead of making clear. It's language like this:

> TWA is required by the federal government to ensure compliance with the regulations concerning smoking on board its flights. For the comfort and safety of all, we earnestly solicit each passenger's cooperation in strictly observing these rules. Persistent disregard could result in the offending passenger's disembarkation.

The statement can be translated "If you insist on violating the smoking regulations, you may be put off the plane." But someone at TWA was overly circumspect; the result is a regulation that is verbose and unclear. The statement recently was runner-up in the doublespeak competition of the National Council of Teachers of English.

The winner in the same year's competition was the nuclear-power industry for its reporting of the Three Mile Island accident, where there was no accident but a "normal aberration," and no danger of explosion and fire but of "energetic dissassembly" and "rapid oxidation." Nor, the world was pleased to learn, was there a chance of contamination, although it was possible that plutonium might "infiltrate" and "take up residence" in some undesired places.

Usually, we recognize gobbledygook because we are bewildered by what we thought should have been a straightforward statement. This is what happened to the hotline caller who asked about a letter she had received from a lawyer. What did the lawyer mean by saying, "I hope this letter is dispossessive of your fears"? After scratching our heads for a moment, we realized that the lawyer had simply meant, "I hope this letter disposes of your fears." Instead of reassuring his reader, the lawyer had thoroughly confused her by coining a strange adjective from a perfectly good verb.

Most of us recognize the gobbledygook of officials and bureaucrats easily; indeed, we are developing a general distrust of them and their language. We could happily herd all the bureaucrats into a corner—a large corner—of the United States and ship them out to sea. But many of us would be out there adrift with them, for many of us write gobbledygook ourselves. And our own gobbledygook is harder and more painful to recognize than someone else's, and it is harder to correct.

Of course, there are those who write and speak gobbledygook for a living. These are the experts in every field and profession whose greatest expertise is their ability to speak and write in a distinguished-sounding fashion. If these experts ever eliminate gobbledygook from their writing, they may no longer have jobs.

But most of us develop our gobbledygook "skills" without being aware of them. We began in school when we had only little to say and a thousand-word assignment to write. Instead of finding things to say, we gobbled; we hesitated and backtracked, used filler phrases, and repeated ourselves. But we filled the paper and we were rewarded, perhaps not with an A—after all, as the teacher noted, the paper did not say much—but we received a decent grade because our gobbles were organized, spelled, and punctuated correctly. And thus we went through college and perhaps professional school, where almost no one really cared whether we could write simply and clearly, as long as we could write in the language of the trade. Eventually we reached the "real world," where our writing attracted "corrections" by the boss and "suggested changes" from our co-workers. Here we learned to imitate, without actually being taught, the memos and reports that came across our desks. And by now we have grown so comfortable with this language that direct, clear prose seems stark and bare.

Psychologists, sociologists, and English teachers would each offer a different analysis of the reasons why we write gobbledygook. But analysis is less important than correction. Most often, turning bad writing into good writing—writing that is effective, clear, and perhaps vigorous—is a matter of editing. Good writing does not simply happen. Admittedly, it takes dedicated effort to break longstanding gobbledygook habits, but it can be done. We offer in this chapter a number of "rules," guidelines actually, for writing more effective sentences. The various guidelines and examples should help you first become more sensitive to the various problems, and then they should help you eliminate the problems. Confirmed gobblers will, of course, always find excuses and justifications for keeping on as they are.

Directness

Almost all of the following rules and guidelines are variations and specific applications of one rule: Be direct. Your overall writing plan should be direct. Make a point and then get to it, directly and succinctly. Make each paragraph contribute to your single overall point. Make each sentence—itself direct and concise—contribute to the point of the paragraph.

Keep yourself in the background; allow the reader's attention to focus on the ideas or the observations you are presenting. Unless you are a rock star or a great adventurer telling a true-life experience, the reader is interested in your thoughts, not in the agony you went through to create those thoughts.

Verbs and Subject

Verbs dominate sentences. Active, forceful verbs contribute to direct, forceful sentences. Passive verbs encourage inefficient, indirect sentences. Overusing *is* and other forms of the verb *be* encourages the overuse of nouns and prepositional phrases. If you do nothing more to your writing than exchange your passive, static verbs for active, forceful ones, you will improve your writing greatly.

Use the Active Voice

Avoid passive verbs when possible. Write *The police stopped the disturbance*, not *The disturbance was stopped by the police.*

Original

The accident was caused by three mechanical failures.

Revised

Three mechanical failures caused the accident.

Original

The decision was made by the board of directors acting at its November 23 meeting.

Revised

The board of directors made the decision at its November 23 meeting.

Original

Verbs are transformed into adjectives by the addition of suffixes like *ful* and *ent.*

Revised

Gobbledygook writers transform verbs into adjectives by adding suffixes like *ful* and *ent.*

Use Strong, Forceful Verbs

Turn nouns and adjectives back into active verbs. By adding suffixes like *ment, tion, ance, ive,* and *ful,* we transform active verbs into abstract words: *punish* turns into *punishment, determine* into *determination, destroy* into *destruction, attend* into *attendance,* and *resent* into *resentful* or *resentment.* Occasionally such a noun or adjective is useful or even necessary—occasionally. But gobbledygook writers grow to prefer these transformed nouns and adjectives. Then, having put the nouns and adjectives into place with weak, colorless verbs such as *be, seem,* or *appear,* they add intensifiers like *absolutely, definite,* and *very* (see pages 288–89) in a pallid attempt to give their sentences force.

Original

> Many writers show a definite preference for using nouns made from verbs.

Revised

> Many writers prefer using nouns made from verbs.

Original

> Such experiences bring about an absolutely total transformation of one's philosophy.

Revised

> Such experiences transform one's philosophy totally.

Original

> In the experiment, it was assumed that workers would be resentful of a capricious supervisor.

Revised

> The experimenters assumed that workers would resent a capricious supervisor.

Original

> We are often fearful of things and situations that are unknown.

Revised

> We often fear the unknown.

Original

> Mr. Osing's work is representative of the best the company has to offer.

Revised

> Mr. Osing's work represents the best the company has to offer.

Original

> Her excellence as a supervisor cannot be denied.

Revised

> No one can deny that she excels as a supervisor.

Or better

> She excels as a supervisor.

Original

> Our group is seeking money for the establishment of a legal-defense fund.

Revised

> Our group seeks money to establish a legal-defense fund.

Original

> We ask for deliverance from the evils of gobbledygook.

Revised

> Deliver us from the evils of gobbledygook.

Reading through something you have just written, you may not notice the many passive verbs and the many verbs that have been turned into nouns and adjectives. After all, the memo sounds all right, that is, about as good as usual. But if you are interested in improving your writing, go through it sentence by sentence and force yourself to justify any form of the verb *be* that you find. Eliminating *is, was,* and *were* throughout your writing will go a long way toward eliminating passive sentences and weak verbs. Even if you overlook an occasional *appears, seems,* or *causes,* you will be making progress.

Avoid Overusing *would*

Would is now often needlessly added to verb phrases in an attempt to make the verbs more circumspect and polite. This usually makes sentences tentative and ineffective. If you actually wish to be circumspect, use some other method. Using *would* just adds an extra, meaningless word. Do use *would* to express condition and habitual action. However, if the habitual action is expressed by a phrase such as *every day*, using the past tense of the main verb, without *would*, is usually more accurate and more direct.

Original

It would appear that there is a discrepancy between these accounts.

Revised

It appears (or *seems*) that there is a discrepancy between these accounts.

Or more directly

There is a discrepancy between these accounts.

Original

Our preliminary studies would suggest that wood cannot be burned efficiently.

Revised

Our preliminary studies suggest that wood cannot be burned efficiently.

Original

Having this additional experience, a college professor would probably find his occupation more enjoyable.

Revised

Having this additional experience, a college professor usually finds (*or* will probably find) his occupation more enjoyable.

Original

Every Saturday night the cowboys would stream into town looking for baths and hell-raising.

Revised

Every Saturday night the cowboys streamed into town for baths and hell-raising.

Put the Logical Main Thought into the Main Grammatical Clause

Rid your writing of empty main clauses; they only take up space and help you avoid direct statements. Clauses like *the reason is that, the reason is because, it is a fact that,* and *it is easily seen that* usually form the main grammatical clause of a sentence, yet they add little to the thought or tone. In speaking, we use these constructions to give ourselves a moment to think before we get into the main thought. We use them in writing because we think that they add the sound of authority, but they add only words and tedium. Notice that weak verbs (*is* in the examples below) are usually at the center of such clauses.

Original

> The reason the foreman was fired was that he failed to see that all machines were properly maintained.

Revised

> The foreman was fired because he failed to see that all machines were properly maintained.

(*The reason is that/because* clauses should be reduced to *because*.)

Original

> An accepted fact of political life is that satirical newspaper comics, such as *Doonesbury,* can be potent political forces.

Revised

> Satirical newspaper comics, such as *Doonesbury,* can be potent political forces.

Original

> I firmly believe that the XYZ copier is the better machine.

Revised

> The XYZ copier is, I firmly believe, the better machine.

(The judgment being put forward is more forceful since it is now in the main grammatical clause of the sentence.)

Begin Sentences with the Logical Subject

We commonly postpone the logical subject of a sentence by beginning sentences with the words *there* and *it*. More direct sentences begin with the logical subject. In the sentence *There are three women waiting in the hall*, the word *there* does not function as an adverb. It doesn't point out where. It's an expletive, serving only to fill space. The grammatical subject, *women*, follows the verb. In the sentence *It is possible that airline profits will suffer further*, although *it* does serve as the grammatical subject of the sentence, the word doesn't refer to anything, and its primary purpose in the sentence is to postpone the logical subject, *profits*. In speaking, these sentence patterns gives us a moment to collect our thoughts while we continue to talk. But in writing, these sentence openers often lead us into verbose and unwieldy sentences built around passive verbs and forms of *be*. Occasionally, for the sake of rhythm or for sentence variety, you may choose to delay the subject of the sentence by using *there* or *it* or by inverting the usual word order of the sentence. A good writer will choose such occasions carefully.

Original

There are three women waiting in the hall.

Revised

Three women are waiting in the hall.

Original

It is possible that airline profits will suffer further.

Revised

Airline profits will possibly suffer further.

Original

There are many reasons why students fail.

Revised

> Students fail for many reasons.

Original

> It is vitally important to gauge the temper of the audience accurately.

Revised

> Accurately gauging the temper of the audience is vital.

Original

> What is obvious about this plan is that it is ill-conceived and ill-timed.

Revised

> This plan is obviously ill-conceived and ill-timed.

Explanations and definitions should begin with the key item or word. Burying the term to be defined under such phrases as *the concept of* or *the nature of* diverts the reader's attention and destroys the crispness of the sentence.

Original

> The concept of freedom is sometimes difficult to explain.

Revised

> Freedom is sometimes a difficult concept to explain.

Original

> The nature of man's intellect is impossible to define uniquely.

Revised

> Man's intellect is impossible to define uniquely.

The Shape of the Sentence

Be Positive

State positive information and positive ideas in positive ways. Avoid unnecessary negative constructions, negative qualifications, and the *not un* construction.

Original

> The instructor seldom arrived for the beginning of the class.

Revised

> The instructor was usually late for class.

Original

> No shoes except tennis shoes may be worn on the playing floor.

Revised

> Only tennis shoes may be worn on the playing floor.

Original

> The paintings from this stage in his career are not unlike (*or* not dissimilar to *or* do not fail to remind one of) early Picasso.

Revised

> The paintings from this stage in his career are like (*or* are similar to *or* remind one of) early Picasso.

(To rid yourself of *not un* sentences, memorize the following from George Orwell's "Politics and the English Language": *The not unblack dog chased the not unsmall rabbit across the not ungreen field.*)

Be Concise: Keep Sentences Brief and to the Point

Avoid complex sentences. Qualify your sentence by a following sentence, not in a subordinate clause. Avoiding complex sentences will force the main thought of your sentence into the main clause of the sentence. Even some sentences with compound predicates should be divided into two sentences.

This is extreme but effective advice. Of course, you won't want to avoid complex sentences forever. But if you do this for a week or two, or if you simply try to avoid them, you will begin treating them with much more respect. You will no

longer string clauses together; you will shape thoughts and
sentences.

Original

> These goals will be attained by having our company serve
> as intermediary between these special customers and
> the various agencies and by establishing, where
> necessary, special credit, deposit, and cutoff arrange-
> ments on an individual basis.

Revised

> Our company will serve as intermediary between these
> special customers and the various agencies. We will
> establish, where necessary, special credit, deposit, and
> cutoff arrangements on an individual basis.

Original

> The reason for what appears at first to be madness is a
> theory, which has been shown to have validity, that
> extended endurance training perfects the ability of the
> muscles to use energy and actually results in greater
> endurance capacity.

Revised

> The reason for this apparent madness is a proven theory.
> Extended endurance training perfects the ability of the
> muscles to use energy and so results in greater en-
> durance.

Or better

> What appears to be madness is based on a proven theory:
> Endurance training perfects the ability of the muscles
> to use energy and so results in greater endurance.

Cure yourself of the long sentence habit by adopting an
arbitrary maximum sentence length, say thirty words or three
typed lines. Any sentence that is longer than your maximum
should be trimmed down or cut in two. Many of your sentences, of course, should be much shorter than your maximum
length.

An arbitrary maximum sentence length will reduce the
length of your finished sentences, but it may not lead you to

stop writing such sentences. It is interesting to speculate why hotline callers, who are writers actively interested in their language, sometimes write long, clumsy, overly complex sentences. Perhaps we writers are too self-conscious about our words and so choose to qualify and overqualify our thoughts. Perhaps we are lazy and choose to leave two or three partial statements on the page instead of fighting to reduce our meanderings to a single, exact statement. After all, writing directly and precisely takes more work than writing longer, indirect sentences. But no matter what reasons are involved, the long sentence habit can be broken.

Use Parallel Construction to Express Coordinate Thoughts

Parallel construction may involve something as simple as a set of predicate adjectives: *Calico cats are orange, black, and white.* Or it may involve a series of independent clauses: *I came, I saw, I conquered.* In each case, the series is grammatically parallel and logically coordinated. And such constructions appeal to our ear and give our writing rhythm.

When using parallel constructions, we sometimes create problems for our readers by omitting too many words or by omitting words that have changed too greatly from one element to the next. Your ear should guide you in both cases. There are two well-defined rules of thumb regarding the omission of verbs. First, even the most conservative authorities (although not some of the more recent, more literal-minded ones) allow the omission of a repeated form of the verbs *be* and *have* even though the form in one element differs in number or person. Thus, the following sentences are correct:

The leader was impeached, his followers imprisoned.
The house was painted white, the shutters gray.

Second, the verb should never be omitted if the tense or the mood has changed. Thus, the verb in the first clause of the following sentence must be reinserted.

Original

No university has or is likely to adopt such a regulation.

Revised

No university has adopted or is likely to adopt such a regulation.

Other problems with parallelism may involve direct objects, prepositional phrases, and almost any other part of the sentence. The following sentences and their suggested revisions illustrate a variety of problems and possibilities.

Original

A new-employee orientation program is both worthwhile and a necessity.

(*Worthwhile* is an adjective, *necessity* a noun. Change both to noun phrases or, preferably, to adjectives, which are less wordy.)

Revised

A new-employee orientation program is both worthwhile and necessary.

Original

The chosen site should have adequate facilities for receiving raw materials and distribution of finished products.

(*Receiving* is a gerund followed by a complement, *distribution* a noun modified by a prepositional phrase. Both *receiving* and *distribution* are legitimate objects for *for*, but they are not parallel.)

Revised

The chosen site should have adequate facilities for receiving raw materials and for distributing finished products.

Original

As a merger prospect, the company is well capitalized, soundly managed, and a good profit potential has been demonstrated.

Revised

> As a merger prospect, the company is well capitalized, is soundly managed, and has good profit potential.

Or

> As a merger prospect, the company is well capitalized, soundly managed, and potentially very profitable.

Original

> The supervisor is industrious, intelligent, and knows how to manage personnel.

Revised

> The supervisor is industrious, intelligent, and able to manage her personnel.

Original

> This university has no such degree nor any plans for instituting one.

Revised

> This university has no such degree nor has it any plans for instituting one.

Or

> This university has no such degree and no plans for instituting one.

The parallel construction of the sentence and the parallel logic of the thought are often made clearer and more effective by including the repeated words—whether those words are helping verbs, the infinitive marker *to*, prepositions, articles, pronouns, or subordinating conjunctions.

Original

> The art department produces its own newspaper and yearbook—both on company time.

Revised

> The art department produces its own newspaper and its own yearbook—both on company time.

Original

> The father and teacher agreed that the boy was bored by his fellow students, teachers, and curriculum.

Revised

> The father and the teacher agreed that the boy was bored by his fellow students, his teachers, and the curriculum.

Original

> As a young girl, the writer had made it a practice to watch people closely, treasure the specific impressions they made on her, and generalize about the human race from them.

Revised

> As a young girl, the writer had made it a practice to watch people closely, to treasure the specific impressions they made on her, and to generalize about the human race from them.

Original

> The copywriter has demonstrated his value by his inventiveness, resourcefulness, and ability to keep clients happy and prosperous.

Revised

> The copywriter has demonstrated his value by his inventiveness, by his resourcefulness, and by his ability to keep clients happy and prosperous.

Problems in parallelism often develop when conjunctions or adverbs are placed so far from the words being joined that the reader expects a choice different from the one that is offered. The conjunctions *either* and *neither* are especially easy to misplace.

Original

> Either the products are poorly distributed or poorly advertised.

(Placing the conjunction *either* in front of the subject leads a reader to expect a sentence such as this: *Either the products are . . . or the management is . . .*)

Revised

> The products are either poorly distributed or poorly advertised.

Original

> The board of directors is neither responsible to the public nor to the government.

Revised

> The board of directors is responsible neither to the public nor to the government.

Original

> Hotline callers not only want good advice but also quick answers.

Revised

> Hotline callers want not only good advice but also quick answers.

In these last examples, the preferred, revised versions are balanced correctly. The adverbial modifier is placed directly in front of the two balanced and parallel elements.

Judiciously Use Absolute Constructions and Appositives

An absolute construction modifies an entire sentence without being linked to it grammatically. Absolutes can take a variety of forms, but typically an absolute consists of a subject and a participle, either past or present, such as *the contract having been lost, night falling, the job finished, weather permitting,* and *this done.* Absolutes generally, but not necessarily, come at the beginning of the sentence. Used sparingly, absolute constructions increase the readability of your writing.

Original

> Since the company had lost the contract, it found itself unable to meet the payroll.

Revised

> The contract lost, the company found itself unable to meet the payroll.

Or

> Having lost the contract, the company found itself unable to meet the payroll. (The sentence may also be written using a participial phrase)

Original

> Since they have completed the orientation, the employees now understand the insurance business more fully and can be expected to work more efficiently.

Revised

> Their orientation complete, the employees now understand the insurance business more fully and can be expected to work more efficiently.

Original

> When all things are considered, the success of the department bowling team has been phenomenal, although this success may be attributed more to the beer drunk and the consequent loose, relaxed bowling than to the innate skills of the players.

Revised

> All things considered, the success of the department bowling team has been phenomenal, a tribute more to the beer drunk and the consequent loose, relaxed bowling than to the innate skills of the players.

Relative clauses can often be changed to appositives, usually by omitting the relative pronoun and the form of the verb *be*. (Appositives are words or phrases that rename and further describe the noun or noun clause they follow. They can be substituted for the noun or the noun clause without altering the logic of the sentence.)

Original

> Bread flour, which is a recent addition to grocery shelves, is selling well.

Revised

> Bread flour, a recent addition to grocery shelves, is selling well.

Original

> Generic food products, which are known as no-name brands, are usually packaged with black-and-white labels.

Revised

> Generic food products, the no-name brands, are usually packaged with black-and-white labels.

Finish Comparisons

Our exposure to advertising language leads many of us to write dangling comparisons. "These cotton swabs are 50 percent softer," we are told, and we forget to ask, "Softer than what?" Be careful to complete sentences that contain comparative forms (*better, longer, more confused*). If the comparison cannot be completed, write the sentence another way.

Original

> These cotton swabs are 50 percent softer.

Revised

> These cotton swabs are 50 percent softer than polished cotton cloth wrapped around a toothpick.

Original

> The XYZ copier is better.

Revised

> The XYZ copier is better than the QRS copier.

Or

> The XYZ copier has been improved.

Original

    This annual report is more confusing.

Revised

    This annual report is more confusing than last year's.

Or

    This annual report is more confusing than that one.

(As you can see, revising incomplete comparisons often requires additional information. Many times a vague comparative word, such as *better,* is best replaced by a more precise description of what is supposedly "better." The new model copier can be described as faster or more versatile, for instance, than its predecessor.)

Place Modifiers near the Words They Modify

Be certain that your modifiers, particularly adverbs, modify the words or phrases you want them to modify. Accurate placement is more of a problem in writing than in speech, since in speaking we use stresses and pauses to group words and their modifiers. Look what happens to the simple sentence *The boy loved his dog* when we add the word *only* to it.

    Only the boy loved his dog. (probably an ugly, vicious dog)
    The only boy loved his dog. (a boy alone among men, women, or girls)
    The boy only loved his dog. (but never fed him, perhaps)
    The boy loved only his dog. (but not his father or mother)
    The boy loved his only dog. (who lived in his bedroom with three cats, a goldfish, and twelve gerbils)

While other adverbs cannot be shifted as easily as *only* to create as many differences in meaning, be careful with their placement. Your sensitive ear should be your guide.

Compare

    Security has been almost breached at all the plants.
    Security has been breached at almost all the plants.

For the person responsible for security in a multinational corporation, the difference between these two sentences is enormous. (See pages 275–79 on parallel construction for additional examples of misplaced adverbs.) Sometimes modifiers may "squint," or look in two directions.

Original

> Turning a large profit often calms irritable stockholders.

(Does the profit need to be turned often, or does turning a profit once usually calm the stockholders?)

Revised

> Turning a large profit can often calm irritable stockholders.

Or

> Turning large profits quarterly keeps irritable stockholders calm.

The term *dangling modifiers* refers to phrases and clauses that seem to refer grammatically to something in the sentence when, in fact, they refer either to something not mentioned in the sentence or to nothing at all. These sentences contain obvious dangling modifiers: *After eating, the bus left. While climbing into the boat, the camera fell into the water.* Such dangling modifiers can be corrected either by including a subject in the phrase or by making the phrase refer to the subject of the sentence.

Original

> When searching for a good job, a college degree is often helpful.

Revised

> When searching for a good job, a college graduate often finds a degree helpful.

Original

> Losing the game by a 35-to-7 score, the streets were soon empty and quiet.

Revised

> Since we lost the game by a 35-to-7 score, the streets were soon empty and quiet.

Even a prepositional phrase can dangle and mislead, as in this example from a newspaper story.

Original

> Besides the Browns, the center receives funds from United Way, the March of Dimes, and several other federal agencies.

(The context of the sentence, in its original news story, lets the reader know the meaning. Along with the Brown family, several foundations and agencies support this treatment center.)

Revised

> In addition to receiving funds from the Brown family, the center receives money from United Way, the March of Dimes, and several federal agencies.

The Words We Choose

Use Concrete Words

Of course, we often need to discuss abstractions. But abstractions must be defined, explained, and illustrated with concrete language to make sense. When abstractions are defined by other abstractions, the discussion floats off into smoke, and fog, and often thin air. Sometimes the writer does not want to be pinned down to the real world, preferring to pile up such phrases as *thoughts of freedom, the willingness to work,* and *the love of duty.* But readers attach specific meanings to such words. If the writer doesn't supply concrete definitions, readers will, and readers' definitions may not be those the writer has in mind. What, for instance, is a *living wage*? What are *reasonable working conditions*? What does it mean to say *treat clients like human beings*? Each of these has an enormous range of possible and reasonable meanings.

If you want phrases like these to have *your* meaning, *you* must get away from lofty abstractions and define your terms.

Use the Right Word; Use Plain Words

Books are housed in "media centers"; surgical operations have become "procedures"; and a building is part of a "complex of facilities." "Why," a typical caller asks, "has the simpler word *building* been displaced by *facility*?" We seem to have fallen in love with inflated words. Little words frighten us; they are plain and clear. When we want to impress people, we run to our thesauruses and dictionaries and start hunting for long words, impressive words, erudite words—any word but the simple word. The right word is sometimes the long word, but usually the short, plain word makes the greatest impact.

Some writers get caught up hunting for synonyms for words they have used "too often," whether "too often" is twice in a sentence or twice in five lines or on a page. Out comes the thesaurus and the dictionary again. Short, clear words are tossed aside, and polysyllabic, "elegant" words are sprinkled across the page. A "diligent" writer may rival the broadcaster giving baseball scores. Not content with merely giving scores, the announcer takes the listener into the world of sports clichés where no one beats anyone: A team may be *drubbed, clipped, stomped,* or *punished* but never *beaten.* One team may *scrape, squeak, squeeze, ease,* or *get past* another team, but it never beats a team by just one run. The sports announcer's synonyms are innocent enough, but variation for the sake of variation in writing often creates confusion. When you feel the need to use a synonym, be sure to use words with similar meanings and connotations. If you are actually over-using a word or phrase, perhaps a pronoun will ease you through the problem. But remember, there is nothing wrong with repeating a word or phrase occasionally. Indeed, repeated words and phrases are necessary to coherent writing.

Do not treat words like ornaments to be paraded and displayed. Words are tools for communicating clearly and for explaining and persuading. Short words are forceful.

Original

> The problem seems to have many unique facets, and each aspect of the situation must be addressed.

Revised

> The problem has many sides to it, and we must consider each one. (Or better yet, eliminate this vague introduction and name the problems you want to discuss.)

Original

> Most employers agree, but a few factory owners in the East remain adamantly opposed.

(Do the words *employers* and *factory owners* refer to the same group or not?)

Revised

> Most employers agree, but a few in the East remain adamantly opposed.

Original

> In general, most regions east of the Rocky Mountains would not be drastically influenced by a small climatic variation, but river basins west of the Mississippi River Basin . . .

Is *river basin* simply a fancy term for *region*? Are *river basins/regions* that are west of the Mississippi east or west of the Rockies? Is the sentence actually about Texas and the great basins west of the Mississippi River Basin?

Revised

> In general, most regions east of the Rocky Mountains would not be drastically influenced by a small climatic variation, but Texas and the Great Plains . . . (If that is actually what is meant.)

Avoid Jargon, Vogue Words, and New Coinages

Jargon is the shorthand of a particular trade or group. Each group—nuclear physicists, physicians, English professors, sociologists, and drug pushers—has its own jargon. When dealing with members of one's group, jargon may be useful, but jargon, especially in writing, often puts readers at a distance and serves to block them from the message.

Vogue words seem to sweep through business and scholarly writing and speech for a few years and then die out to be replaced by other, newer, vogue words. Current (as of this writing) vogue words include *parameters* (for *guidelines*), *the bottom line* (for *ultimate cost* or *the most important point*), *syndrome* (*symptoms* or *characteristics*), *ball-park figure* (*estimate*), *in the ball park* (*close*), *game-plan* (*plan*), *quarterback* (as a noun, *leader*, and as a verb, *lead*), and *in the neighborhood of* (*about*).

When first used metaphorically, a few of these words added vigor to the language, but now they should be dumped into the slagheap of worn-out linguistic curiosities and clichés.

New coinages, particularly words made with the vogue suffixes *ize* and *wise*, should generally be avoided. You can find a perfectly good word or phrase that does not call attention to itself to fill the need.

Original

    Game-planwise, we are in deep trouble.

Revised

    Nothing is going according to plan.

Or

    Everything has gone wrong.

Original

    When finalized, the building will contain seven floors of office suites above a modest two-story shopping mall.

Revised

    When complete, the building will contain seven floors of office suites above a modest two-story shopping mall.

Original

    The revised ball-park figure for the cost of construction within the parameters outlined in your letter of January 12, 1980, is enclosed.

Revised

    The construction cost estimate has been revised according to the guidelines furnished in your letter dated January 12, 1980.

Original

> We want your input on our needs assessment to set
> priorities for the upcoming school year.

Revised

> We want your thoughts about our needs for the coming
> year so that we can set priorities.

Choose Short Variants; Beware of the Love of the Long Word

Given two variants of one word, we seem to choose the
longer, hoping that it is more impressive than the shorter one
but forgetting that it often seems more abstract. We choose
membership instead of *members,* *leadership* instead of *leaders,*
and *preventative* instead of *preventive.* We substitute *percentage* for *some,* *proportion* for *part,* and *protagonist* for
leader, hero, or *champion.*

Original

> The party leadership wants to maximize input from the
> entire membership.

Revised

> Party leaders want ideas and suggestions from every
> member.

Original

> The new drug has been a preventative in a slight percentage of cases.

Revised

> The new drug has been a preventive in a few cases.

Words to Cut

Avoid Vague, Needless Intensifiers

Absolutely, comparatively, definitely, pretty (meaning *very*),
quite, rather, relatively, somewhat, very, and words like them

are usually unnecessary. We add these to our colorless, flat bureaucratic language so that people will pay attention to our half-formed ideas and our otherwise weak sentences. It seems easier to add one of these words than to think of the right word in the first place.

Original

> He is definitely the sort of manager that is necessary in these quite perilous times.

Revised

> He is the sort of manager that is necessary in these perilous times.

Original

> The management is quite delighted with the absolutely fine showing of the lingerie division in spite of the relatively unsettled economy.

Revised

> The management is delighted with the excellent showing of the lingerie division in spite of the unsettled economy.

Rephrase Sentences That Compare Absolutes

Adjectives like *infinite, exact, impossible,* and *unique* refer to extreme, absolute qualities. They should be compared with great caution and only on rare occasions. Formal written usage allows something to be *nearly impossible* and *quite unique* but not *more impossible, more unique,* or *more infinite* than something else. Common absolutes include the following:

absolute	exact	inevitable	total
correct	fatal	infinite	ultimate
equal	final	perfect	unanimous
eternal	impossible	supreme	unique

Generally, writers compare these words in an effort to make a strong point, but they usually end up with empty, vague overstatements.

Sentences containing compared absolutes can always be rephrased and improved by adding detail or choosing more precise words.

Original

> The Chagnon typewriter is the most unique machine currently on the market.

Revised

> The Chagnon typewriter has a special self-correcting key and typeface options that no other machine currently on the market has.

Original

> Hitler was a more absolute dictator than Mussolini.

Revised

> Hitler allowed less political dissent and persecuted minorities more than Mussolini did.

Original

> This painting style is more unique than that one.

Revised

> This painting style shows a greater mastery of contour than that one.

Some words, such as *round, smooth,* and *precise,* often act like absolutes but may sometimes be compared, depending on the context. For instance, in describing a person's face, to say that one person's face is rounder than another person's may be very useful. Or one might say that one table has a smoother finish than another. One set of equations may yield more precise answers or be a more accurate model than another set. Such uses are both idiomatic and practical, but be careful with absolutes. An accident is fatal or not; a way of doing something is unique or not. It may be *nearly unique,* but it will not be *more unique than* something else. At best it will be *more nearly unique.* But watch out for *unique.* Of all the absolutes, it is currently the most abused. Even when used correctly, as in the following example, it seems like hyperbole and is best eliminated.

Correct but weak

> An erupting volcano is an almost unique phenomenon seldom viewed by mainland Americans.

Revised

> An erupting volcano is an exceptional natural phenomenon seldom viewed by mainland Americans.

Avoid Strings of Prepositional Phrases

As useful and necessary as they are, prepositional phrases are not prefabricated sentence units that can be hooked together until one's thought is more or less expressed. Sentences that wander in and out of prepositional phrases are verbose and tiresome to read.

Original

> Many of the members of the club will be available for the official photograph of the club during the party on Wednesday evening.

Revised

> Many club members will be available for the club's official photograph during the party Wednesday evening.

Original

> Many of the senior officers of some of the leading corporations in this city are among the staunchest of supporters of this bond issue.

Revised

> Many senior officers of this city's leading corporations staunchly support this bond issue.

Avoid Pleonasms

Pleonasms are brief bits of redundant language that many writers mistakenly think add precision or emphasis to their writing. They do not add more accuracy to writing; they add only words.

Original

The receptionist wanted the walls painted blue in color.

Revised

The receptionist wanted the walls painted blue.

Original

The manager agreed to charge $1.37 per each for the sandwiches.

Revised

The manager agreed to charge $1.37 for each sandwich.

Original

In my opinion today's modern executive seems overly concerned many times with what are probably minor logistical problems, problems which, it should be apparent to most of us, should not be taking executive time.

Revised

The contemporary executive is often overly concerned, I believe, with time-consuming, minor problems.

Original

In design, the mall will be rectangular in shape with regard to its appearance, but in function, with regard to the smooth, unimpeded flow of pedestrian traffic, it will act as if it were circular in shape due to the internal layout and design.

Revised

The mall will be rectangular, but because of the internal design, the mall will handle pedestrian traffic as efficiently as a circular design.

Original

> Prices will continue to fluctuate periodically from month to month.

Revised

> Prices will continue to fluctuate from month to month.

Original

> Often people feel that it is usually useless to complain to a large corporation.

Revised

> Often people feel it useless to complain to a large corporation.

Eliminate Compound Prepositions

Compound prepositions (prepositions of more than one word) allow writers to pile up vague, abstract nouns. The use of compound prepositions leads to all sorts of problems in sentences. Substitute the simple, direct word for the compound preposition.

FOR	SUBSTITUTE
along the lines of	like
as of that time	then
at that point in time/ at this point in time	then/now
by means of	by; which
in light of the fact that	because
in terms of	(usually omit; see Glossary of Usage)
in view of	because
on the part of	by; for
in a number of	some
with regard to/ with respect to	about; concerning (or omit entirely)

There are many more such phrases, of course. Sentences containing compound prepositions can always be improved.

Original

> In connection with the original investigation, a number of welds were reinspected with regard to the composition of the weld material and to check the integrity of the welds.

Revised

> During the original investigation, several welds were reinspected to check the composition of the weld material and the integrity of the welds.

Original

> In light of the nature of the charges and in view of their seriousness, the Congress has decided to conduct a full-scale investigation.

Revised

> Because of the nature and seriousness of the charges, the Congress has decided to conduct a complete investigation.

Original

> In terms of (or with respect to) productivity, the industry made little improvement in the 1970s.

Revised

> The industry's productivity improved little in the 1970s.

What Now?

Reading about gobbledygook is one thing; eliminating it from your writing is something different. You may have noticed that many of the sentences in the chapter have more than one problem. The problems we have been discussing often do come in groups. A passive sentence invites academic verbiage. A sentence beginning with an empty main clause invites nouns and adjectives that should be turned back into verbs.

If you begin with three related editing tasks, you can eliminate much gobbledygook from your writing. First, eliminate weak verbs, particularly forms of *be*. Eliminating most instances of *is, are, was,* and *were* should eliminate sentences in the passive voice and will allow you to transform many nouns and adjectives back into verbs. Second, break the long sentence habit by adopting and enforcing a maximum sentence length. This will eliminate excessive subordination in your sentences and will give your writing more force. Finally, make checklists of jargon, academic verbiage, and compound prepositions that you often use. Edit them out of your writing. If you begin to edit these problems out of your later drafts, you will soon be putting fewer of them into your rough drafts.

With a couple of friends who also want to eliminate gobbledygook from their writing, you could form a chapter of Gobbledygookers Anonymous. You might get together on Friday afternoons and edit goobledygook out of the memos that have crossed your desks during the week. You might comment on each other's writing, too. Then, in the future, when tempted to dump a *due to the fact that* into a sentence, you'll have someone to call for help.

15

Letters: What the Etiquette Books Don't Say

The Writer's Hotline was never intended to answer etiquette questions. But we have been asked about the wording of wedding invitations and about the choice of paper for thank-you notes. As gracefully as possible, we try to sidestep such questions and have found that callers usually make their own decisions as they explain their choices to us. Callers who insist on more than a sympathetic ear are referred to Amy Vanderbilt, Emily Post, and other standard etiquette guides.

We do attempt to puzzle out one etiquette problem, however, the salutations of letters. We have been asked how to address a prime minister, and we once spent several hours searching for the proper form of address to use in writing to a sheik. Although seldom needed by most of us, lists of salutations for religious, political, and military leaders are included in some dictionaries (in a special table) and in most yearly information almanacs (look under *addresses* or *letters*), secretarial guides, and letter-writing guides. No list is all-inclusive, and you may need to check several to find a particular salutation. (We never did find a listing for a sheik.)

But typical hotline callers are not writing to sheiks. They want to know how to address a complaint department, or they want an alternative to *Dear Sir or Madam*. We will take up such problems in this chapter, and because salutations aren't the only part of the letter that concerns our callers, we also discuss several other aspects of letter writing.

Tone and Other Considerations

The tone of your letter is more important than the salutation, the paper you write on, and whether or not your letter is typed. These things should support and aid your letter, rather than being distractions, but it is the tone that is remembered and that helps your message get through.

The tone should fit the occasion. Letters to friends are chatty and personal. Business letters are businesslike. That doesn't mean that business letters must be stiff and lifeless, but rather that a business letter should take care of business. Your letter has a point to make. Make your point: explain it quickly and thoroughly, and then close.

Even if you are angry about poor service or shabby merchandise, there is no reason to berate your reader. The person reading your letter is, in all likelihood, not responsible for your problem but may be in a position to help correct the problem. You want the reader on your side. Explain how the service or the merchandise was unsatisfactory, explain that you are worried about the company's reputation, but don't call names.

If you are offering a service or product to someone—perhaps you are looking for a job—offer the service and the product. Explain how you or your product can be of assistance. Explain the qualities of the product or your credentials, but don't go on interminably. Endless letters are filed away, and if they are responded to at all, they receive a "Thank you for thinking of us" form reply.

Relevant Details

Be sure in any letter to include the relevant details the reader needs in order to respond. Relevant details may be simply your name and address. (Don't expect someone to read the return address on your envelope.) Or relevant details may include invoice numbers, account numbers, social security numbers, serial numbers, or identification numbers. If previous correspondence is alluded to, include the date and, if it has one, the file number. Without details and information, the most cooperative reader can do little or nothing about your request or problem.

Desired Outcome

If your letter is a complaint or a request, be sure to include what you want the company to do. What should be the result of this letter and request? Tell your reader, and briefly justify it, if necessary.

Format

If you are writing to a company as a private individual, you will usually be forgiven if your letter does not physically conform to the style of standard business letters. Make your letter attractive and complete. If you are typing letters for a company, your company probably follows a standard guide; if not, consult one of the standard secretarial guides. (See Chapter 18.)

Guides to Corporate and Government Addresses

In writing letters of complaint or inquiry, the first problem is finding the address of the company or government agency and, if possible, an appropriate person to write to.

The names and titles of a corporation's officers and its address are generally available in such standard business references as the *Standard and Poor's Register* or one of the Dun and Bradstreet directories. These guides attempt to keep current on mergers and exchanges of subsidiary companies as well as changes in corporate officers. They are generally available in public libraries. (Most libraries will answer requests for addresses and names over the telephone.)

The *United States Governmental Manual* contains the addresses of most federal government agencies. Addresses are also available from Federal Information Centers around the country. (The Federal Information Centers have local telephone numbers in all areas of the country.)

Addresses for state agencies are available through the office of the governor. Many states also compile state directories, registers, or blue books which list such information. These should also be available in most libraries.

Salutations

Writer's Hotline callers most often call about the salutation of the letter. They seek alternatives to *Dear Sir* or to *Dear Sir or Madam.* They ask about the salutation to a corporation or to a department and about omitting the salutation. They ask about addressing their colleagues and about the use of *Ms.*

Actually, the salutation of a letter, particularly one being sent to a group of people, a company or agency of some sort, is more of a problem for the letter writer than it is for the receiver. Therefore, we try to help letter writers find or devise openings that they feel comfortable using.

In general, finding an appropriate salutation involves finding a salutation you are comfortable with. Consider the traditional salutations, since they are less likely to call attention to themselves than more creative salutations do, but always use a salutation that you would not mind receiving.

Addressing a Company or Group of Unknown People

When writing to a company or an agency to request information or to complain about products or services, letter writers have traditionally used *Dear Sir* or *Dear Sir or Madam* as a salutation. These remain appropriate.

But some callers want alternatives. They object to *Dear Sir* because they know that a woman is as likely as a man to handle their request or complaint. They seek an alternative to *Dear Sir or Madam* because it seems overly formal and because of the negative connotations of *madam.* (However, in such a well-defined context as a letter to a company, the meaning is never likely to be confused.)

One simple alternative is to use plural forms: *Dear Gentlemen* or *Dear Ladies and Gentlemen.* These seem a bit less formal, and they avoid the *madam* "problem." However, they also seem to involve a great number of people in what may be a simple request. *To Whom It May Concern* is also an option.

The simplest, but perhaps most useful, alternative to *Dear Sir or Madam* is to address the department or the office as a whole, *Dear Complaint Department, Dear Bancroft Library,* or even *Dear Members of the Board of Directors.* In informal letters, a simple *Greetings* is occasionally used.

Omitting the Salutation

Some callers want to omit the salutation altogether, writing simply *Complaint Department* or *Bancroft Library*. Such letters take on the form of memos. This is becoming more common, although we prefer salutations directed at people.

Salutation to a Person of Unknown Sex

An awkward situation arises when you have a name to write to, but the name is not clearly either masculine or feminine, as Terry Jones or Pat Brown.

Dear Mr. or Ms. Jones is an unappealing solution; it sounds as if the letter is addressed to *occupant. Dear Mr./Ms. Brown* seems equally inelegant, but it is, perhaps, an option. Then too, one can always guess.

Two better solutions are possible. Whenever the person has a title which can be used, there is a simple and elegant salutation: *Dear Professor Jones* or *Dear Foreman Brown.* A less formal solution, but one which is always available, is to use the full name, *Dear Terry Jones, Dear Pat Brown.*

Salutations to Newspapers, Television Shows, and So On

In writing to the editor of a newspaper or magazine, one begins *To the Editor* or *Dear Editor.* In the case of a television or radio program, the name of the program is used, *Dear 60 Minutes* or *Dear Meet the Press.* Your salutation will be changed to conform with the practice of the newspaper or program if the letter is used.

Addressing Co-Workers

The way you address your co-workers may have political and social implications. If you have doubts about choosing a salutation, choose a traditional one. *Dear Colleagues, Dear Co-Workers,* and *Dear Fellow Social Workers* are all practical alternatives. In general, follow the existing practice in your office. In all cases, it is better to err on the side of the conventional rather than to be cute, clever, and misunderstood. Even if you are addressing invitations for an office Christmas party, being cute and clever often calls more attention to itself than to the message being sent.

If you are uncomfortable with the logical choices for the salutation, consider sending a memo. Most interoffice correspondence is handled by memo without salutations, *To: The Public Relations staff*, *To: Customer Relations*, or *To: All Office Memo Writers*.

Addressing a letter or memo to the lawyer upstairs who occasionally shares a table in the lunchroom with you may seem like a problem, but it can be handled easily. Decide what level of formality is appropriate, perhaps by deciding how you would wish to be addressed, and select from these alternatives (arranged from the most formal to the least formal): *Dear Ms. Davis*, *Ms. Sandra Davis*, *Dear Sandra Davis*, and *Dear Sandra*.

When you are unsure about how formal to be, it is usually better to err on the side of formality.

The Use of *Ms.*

Ms. is often a convenient title of respect for addressing a woman regardless of her marital status. It is now accepted almost everywhere in the business and professional worlds. For a writer who does not know whether or not a woman has a married name, *Ms.* frequently comes in handy. However, some women vehemently object to the use of *Ms.* If a writer is aware of it or can discover it, a woman's personal preference for a title and name should by all means be honored, as should a man's.

A writer who doesn't know the woman being addressed thus takes a chance whether *Ms.*, *Miss*, or *Mrs.* is used. A way to avoid the choice is to use a professional title, when possible (e.g. *Dr.* or *Professor*).

Even though *Ms.* is not an abbreviation, use a period with it, in conformity with *Mr.* and *Mrs.*

Plurals of Titles

The plural of *Mr.* is *Messrs.;* of *Mrs., Mmes.;* of *Miss, Misses.* A plural of *Ms.* has not yet been settled on. If there is more than one woman you wish to address, repeat *Ms.* before each name.

Complimentary Closings

Apparently Writer's Hotline callers are satisfied with the closings they select, since they rarely ask about them. For the record, however, a good closing should reflect the tone of the letter. A love letter should be full of love; a business letter should be businesslike. Do not be presumptuous in the close. Closings for business letters and other formal situations are generally built around one of four adverbs: *respectfully, truly, sincerely,* and *cordially.* Of the four, *respectfully* is most formal, *cordially* the least. Usually, *yours truly* or *yours sincerely* seems appropriate for a business letter containing a polite request. As with the salutation, always choose a closing which you would be comfortable receiving and one which fits the letter.

Opening and Closing Punctuation

The salutation is customarily followed by a colon in formal letters and by a comma in informal letters. Commas are displacing colons in many situations. The key words in the salutation are capitalized.

The complimentary closing is followed by a comma. Only the first word of the closing is capitalized.

Other punctuation formats are sometimes used in business correspondence. But the only variation the general reader is likely to encounter is the "open-punctuation" style. In this pattern, the punctuation following both the salutation and the closing is omitted. (For other details on punctuation formats, see a secretarial guide; for a list of these, see Chapter 18.)

Appendices

16

Glossary of Usage

This glossary of usage directly tackles many of the most common and persistent problems of word choice and of phrasing that writers of English face. Its entries are based on questions Writer's Hotline callers ask, on the questions most frequently discussed in other usage guides (we've consulted dozens of them), and on our own experience as English teachers and as observers of the language. Here we give advice that will enable writers to handle usage problems authoritatively and confidently and to express themselves in the best, the clearest, and the most accepted way.

Anyone who advises writers on how to use English realizes that correctness and incorrectness are not watertight categories, so we have explained to writers, wherever possible, what choices they have for different kinds of writing and what effects their choices will have on their readers. Many of the usage rules that writers learn have unremembered exceptions, so writers who try to apply them simplistically sometimes write unidiomatically and overcorrectly. In this glossary, we show writers how far they can apply rules and how to avoid the complications that can arise in using them. In a few instances, we explain the difference between what is acceptable in speech and acceptable in writing. In general, writing tends to be more formal than speech and tends to keep older usages and distinctions.

Our advice on usage is based on three principles.

1. If a distinction between two words still makes a difference in clear communication, we point it out. In other words, whenever two words are confused or are used for one another, we tell you whether they represent a useful distinction that writers should adhere to. *Imply* and *infer* should be carefully distinguished because their confusion can create misunderstanding; *shall* and *will*, however, no longer represent a meaningful distinction and can be used interchangeably.

2. If a usage may meet the disapproval of critical readers, we point this out also. Let's face it: There are some usages (such as *like* as a conjunction) that are justified by history and are listed in all dictionaries but that a writer may be condemned for using. In such cases, we instruct writers how to avoid the usage altogether, usually by writing around it.

3. Our standard for the acceptability of words is the normal usage of educated writers of English. Rather than automatically repeating rules of usage from other handbooks, we tell writers in this glossary, as we have throughout this book, what is acceptable both in general writing and in formal writing. General writing and formal writing, as explained in the Introduction to this book, differ in their intended audience and purpose. General writing is appropriate for all interoffice and interpersonal communication as well as for most writing for the general public. Formal writing is reserved for those occasions when writers want to have a special effect on their readers, as in a public announcement, a scholarly article, or other formal situation.

Some usage questions are not listed in this glossary because they come up in the course of covering other subjects. (For example, the *who/whom* question is discussed with pronouns in Chapter 4.) Writers should consult the Index to find where a specific usage question is covered.

a, an

The choice between *a* and *an* depends on the sound that follows, so a writer can be sure about making the correct choice by reading a sentence aloud. Use *an* before a vowel *sound;* but note that not all vowel letters make vowel sounds: *a* (not *an*) *unified approach to the problem* (a *y* sound begins *unified*); *a* (not *an*) *one-in-a-thousand chance* (*one* begins with a *w* sound). Be especially careful before abbreviations and numerals: *an NLRB directive, an M.B.A. degree, an 812 vote margin, a PSA jetliner*. The key in these cases lies in the sound immediately following, just as it does in the use of *a* before *savings and loan association* and *an* before *S&L association*. One hotline caller insisted that *a* should precede *S&L* because *S&L* stands for *savings and loan*. But the words are not *savings and loan,* and *an* is correct because the first sound of the abbreviation is "es."

The use of *an* before unstressed syllables beginning with the letter *h,* as in *an historical survey,* is now old-fashioned and has an academic ring to it. Of course, *an* is used before a silent *h*, as in *an honorable mention*.

affect, effect

Although they never overlap in meaning, *affect* and *effect* are often confused because they are often pronounced alike. When used as verbs, *affect* means "to influence," "to have an effect on," or "to pretend," and *effect* means "to bring about" or "to result in." Therefore

> The changes in our policy will *affect* fourteen employees.

but

> The new chairman *effected* drastic policy changes.

When used as a noun, *effect* means "a result or outcome" (*The cutbacks had no effect on the production schedule*). The noun *affect* is a technical term restricted in usage to the mental-health field and to social scientists, and it refers to human emotions and feelings. The noun *effect* is nearly always desired over the noun *affect*.

The adjective *effective*, meaning "producing an intended result," is used far more frequently than *affective*, meaning "having to do with human emotions." *Affective*, lately a popular vogue word, is still best restricted to mental-health and social-science circles.

all right

Always spell as two words. *Alright* is an informal variant, probably influenced by *already* and *altogether*. Avoid *alright* altogether.

a lot

Always spelled as two words. But *a lot of* and *lots* are very informal and very vague. Use them only in writing casual notes and letters.

among, between

The traditional rule of thumb is to use *between* with two objects and *among* with more than two. However, this rule often gives way to the facts of English usage. *Between* is used with more than two objects when they are being considered one at a time or when each object is being viewed in relation to the others.

The choice in the '68 Presidential election was *between* Humphrey, Nixon, and Wallace.

The Tri-Cities Airport lies midway *between* Bristol, Johnson City, and Kingsport.

There is no longer a difference in pronunciation *between* the words *to, too,* and *two.*

Between is also the proper choice when a mutual relationship exists between (not among) the objects following that preposition, especially after such nouns as *conference, agreement, meeting, negotiations, alliance,* and *treaty.*

A satisfactory agreement *between* the parents, the students, and the teachers cannot be reached.

A treaty *between* Britain, France, and the United States gave West Germany its independence in 1949.

When several or an undetermined number of objects are viewed together or are referred to as a group, use *among.*

The profits were divided *among* the accounting, the public relations, and the service departments.

Among the steel industry's chief problems is the increasingly aggressive foreign competition.

In summary, the use of *between* with three or more objects indicates a tighter, more direct relationship. *Among* indicates a looser relationship.

Between is also used idiomatically with only one singular object.

Between each act of the opera, the audience applauded wildly.

Between each house on the boulevard was a six-foot-high hedge.

Such sentences are improved either by replacing *between* by *after* (*After each act of the opera . . .*) or by making the object of the preposition plural (*Between acts of the opera . . .*). But the second sentence can be revised only by rephrasing it.

Six-foot-high hedges separated the houses on the boulevard from one another.

Between each house on the boulevard and the next was a six-foot-high hedge.

and/or

Although *and/or* is thought to be a convenient shortcut, its use frequently leads the writer into unnatural and confused syntax. There's no wonder that one writer couldn't pick the correct verb in *The amount of residue and/or the depth of water is/are important factors.* Most sentences are clearer if the more accurate of the two conjunctions is chosen (usually *or*).

> The amount of residue and the depth of water are important.

Or

> Either the amount of residue or the depth of water is important.

These two sentences, of course, have different meanings.

In stock legal and business phrases (*The penalty is thirty days in jail and/or a fine of five hundred dollars*), *and/or* has a place, but it is usually best to revise it out of a sentence.

archive, archives

A place where documents and public records are kept on deposit is usually called an *archives.* It may also be called an *archive,* but archivists, the people who work there, prefer the form *archives.* Both the National Archives and the Archive of Folk Song are in Washington, D.C.

as follow, as follows

As follows is always the correct form.

as to, as for

The prepositions *as for* and *as to* are not only vague and unnecessary, they also damage sentences. Any sentence containing one of them should be rewritten.

Thus,

> The subcontractors were required to maintain detailed records *as to* the usage of the materials.

is slightly improved by replacing *as to* by *of* or *regarding.* But it is a new and stronger creation if the prepositional phrase is revised out.

The subcontractors were required to record their use of materials in detail.

Original

> *As to* who will be affected by the layoffs, we do not know at this time.

Revised

> We do not know yet who will be affected by the layoffs.

Original

> *As for* permanent damage, the hurricane had little effect.

Revised

> The hurricane caused little permanent damage.

As to before *whether, how, when, where,* and *why* is always superfluous.

Original

> The rescue team was undecided *as to* how to proceed.

Revised

> The rescue team was undecided how to proceed.

Better

> The rescue team could not decide how to proceed.

a while, awhile

Awhile is an adverb. *A while* is the article *a* with the noun *while* and is used after a preposition. When the writer uses a preposition, the space should be placed between the words.

> Come to beautiful San Juan and stay *awhile*.
> Come to beautiful San Juan and stay for *a while*.

bad, badly

In writing, *bad* is an adjective and *badly* is an adverb. These two words are rarely troublesome except when used after verbs that convey no action, including the verb *be* and the verbs associated with our five senses, especially *feel*. In these cases, the accepted form in writing is *bad*.

I felt *bad* that she had to give up her job.

John looked *bad* long after his bout with pneumonia.

In speech, a distinction between *I feel bad*, meaning "I feel ill," and *I feel badly*, meaning "I feel sorry" or "I regret" is slowly gaining currency, but in writing, *I feel bad* is still the preferred usage for both meanings. To indicate regret or sympathy, write *I feel sorry* or *I am sorry* rather than *I feel badly*.

biweekly, bimonthly, biyearly

The useful prefix *bi* means "two" or "twice" (*bifocals, bicycle*), but when attached to words referring to periods of time, it often becomes a source of devilish confusion and sometimes missed deadlines. Modern dictionaries without exception report the contradictory and seemingly impossible fact that *biweekly* is used to mean "every two weeks" or "twice a week," *bimonthly* to mean "every two months" or "twice a month," and *biyearly* to mean "every two years" and "twice a year." (At present, *biannual* can mean only "twice a year"; *biennial* means "every two years.") Whatever the source of this split in meanings for *biweekly, bimonthly,* and *biyearly,* and whichever meaning you prefer, avoid these words. Choose either forms with the prefix *semi* (*semiweekly, semimonthly, semiyearly, semiannually*), which means "occurring twice within a period of time," or choose longer alternative expressions that can never be misinterpreted: *twice a week, every two weeks, twice a month, every two months, twice a year,* or *every two years.* You do yourself and your readers a service by avoiding the possibility of misunderstanding.

If you insist on using forms with *bi,* spell them without a hyphen or a space, and use them to refer to every two weeks, months, or years (except, of course, for *biannual,* which means *semiannual*).

can, may

These words are not interchangeable in most instances. Only *can* refers to ability or capability and is equivalent to "be able to."

The design branch *can* have the plans finished by Friday.

To express possibility, *may* is normally used.

The design branch *may* have the plans finished by Friday.

The problems in using *can* and *may* arise in choosing which one to use to express permission. As children, how many of us have been instructed to use *may* and not *can* to make a request? But despite the efforts of schoolteachers and parents, *can* is customarily used today for permission in all but formal and the most polite contexts. When a class of second-graders from Baltimore phoned the hotline one day, we told them that they should use *may* when wanting to be courteous, especially in making a request.

In formal writing, *may* is still preferred to *can*, but in general writing, *can* for permission is well established and is as acceptable as *may*.

All employees *can* (or *may*) take an extra day off for Christmas.

cannot
Cannot is always spelled as one word.

compare to, compare with
These two phrases are often used interchangeably with no confusion and no ill effects, but a few commentators on English usage maintain that they represent a useful distinction. To them, *compare to* states a general similarity or likeness between two things in the same category, and it is equivalent to *liken to*.

Critics *compared* Memphis State's production of *Jumpers to* Broadway's. (That is, they viewed them as similar.)

Compare with indicates that two things are being examined generally for likenesses and differences.

Critics *compared* Memphis State's production of *Jumpers with* Broadway's. (They examined the two closely for differences and similarities.)

Compare to, but not *compare with*, is usually used for figurative comparisons.

The sentence *compared* NRC regulation of the nuclear-power industry *to* a game of Russian roulette.

comprise, compose

Traditionally, a whole *comprises* its parts but the parts *compose, constitute,* or *make up* a whole. Thus

> The agenda *comprises* five items of business.

but

> Five items of business *compose* (or *constitute* or *make up*) the agenda.

But *comprise* has now come to be used in both contexts. Although this has apparently led to little confusion in meaning, some writers may want to follow the traditional distinction. The frequent use of *is comprised of* for *comprise,* as in

> The agenda *is comprised of* five items of business.

further obscures the word's traditional meaning. Writers who adhere to the distinctions should use *comprise* or *consist of* to express the relationship of a whole to parts; use *compose, constitute,* or *make up* for the relationship of the parts to a whole; and avoid *is comprised of* in favor of *is composed of.*

consensus

Consensus refers to a general agreement or concord of opinion. Therefore, *consensus of opinion* is redundant, and *partial consensus* is a mistake (use *partial agreement*). *Consensus,* related to *consent,* is often misspelled *concensus.*

continual, continuous

Continual means "happening frequently or periodically."

> Edmonton's *continual* snowfall keeps many residents indoors all winter. (There are breaks in the snowfall.)

Continuous means "happening without a break or interruption."

> Three days of *continuous* snowfall buried Edmonton's residents indoors.

convince, persuade

These words are frequently interchangeable. In formal writing, either can be followed by an *of* phrase or a *that* clause, but only *persuade* can be followed by an infinitive. A person is *convinced* (or *persuaded*) of the rightness *of* a belief, *of* a cause, or *that* a course of action is correct. A person is *persuaded to* perform an act.

> After four hours of negotiating, the police *persuaded* the sniper *to* surrender.
> After four hours of negotiating, the police *convinced* the sniper *that* she should surrender.

Persuade thus implies a consequent action. *Convince* usually involves the rightness or wrongness of a belief or action.

criterion, criteria

Criteria is the original and still the preferred plural of *criterion,* a noun English has inherited from Greek. The alternate plural form *criterions* is also acceptable in all kinds of writing, but writers should avoid using *criteria* as a singular, and they should avoid *criterias* altogether.

data

Originally the plural of *datum, data* in general usage is now primarily a singular noun meaning "a mass of information" and requiring a singular verb. (But the plural form *datas* does not exist.) The use of *data* as a plural is restricted to formal scholarly and scientific writing, where it means "a number of pieces of information" and its singular is *datum* ("a piece of information").

Whether you use *data* as a singular or as a plural, be sure your pronouns agree in number with it.

> Our *data* is incomplete. We cannot put *it* in the computer yet.
> Our *data* are incomplete. We cannot put *them* in the computer yet.

different from, different than

The use of *from* after *different* or *differently* is always acceptable. The status of *than* is less secure. If a full, a condensed, or even an implied clause follows, then *than* is recognized as acceptable. Using *from* in such cases requires the insertion of *from what, from that which,* or another phrase.

> The final score was *different than* (or *from what* or *from that which*) I had expected.
> Capital punishment is administered *differently* today *than* (or *from what*) it was in the eighteenth century.

The intersection at Pine and Battle Avenues seemed *different than* (or *from what it had been*) earlier.

If only a word or a phrase follows, with no clause implied, then *from* is the preferred usage.

A microcomputer is *different from* (not *than*) a mini-computer in many instances.

The procedure for product X was *different from* (not *than*) that of product Y.

The usage issue aside, sentences with either *different from* or *different than* usually express vague, unspecified contrasts and should be rephrased with more explicit ones. Here are improved versions of some of the sentences above.

The final score was much closer than I had expected.

Capital punishment is administered primarily by electro-cution today, whereas in the eighteenth century people were usually hanged.

A microcomputer is smaller and less expensive than a minicomputer.

discreet, discrete

These words are often confused in writing. *Discreet* means "judicious in one's behavior," and the noun formed from it is *discretion,* for Falstaff the better part of valor. *Discrete* means "separate and distinct," as in discrete parts or *discrete ideas.*

disinterested, uninterested

According to the traditional distinction, *uninterested* means "not interested, having no feeling or concern."

Despite our recent advertising campaign, the public is still *uninterested* in our products.

And *disinterested* means "impartial, neutral, unbiased."

The two neighbors sought a *disinterested* third party to settle their dispute.

But both words have a long history of being used for both meanings. Indeed, both have been used with both meanings since at least the mid-seventeenth century. Any writer wanting to be unambiguously understood and fearing that the context may be unclear should use a synonym or a paraphrase.

due to

Although some continue to disfavor its use in formal writing, *due to* as a preposition meaning "because of" or "owing to" has now become widely established.

> *Due to* circumstances beyond its control, the company had to declare bankruptcy.
> *Due to* the icy streets, traffic moved slowly throughout the afternoon.

A writer wishing to avoid all possible objections can always replace *due to*.

> *Because of* (or *Owing to*) the icy streets, traffic moved slowly throughout the afternoon.

either, neither

Generally, *either* and *neither* should be restricted to two alternatives. But when more than two alternatives are cited, using *either* or *neither* is often the only idiomatic way of expressing the idea.

> Neither the DeLoach plan, the Feehan plan, nor the Newcomb plan is feasible.

But with a choice between two or more unspecified alternatives, *any one* or *each* is preferable to *either,* and *not any* or *none* is preferable to *neither.*

> *Either* of the plans is feasible.

Better

> *Each* (or *Any one*) of the plans is feasible.

Nor, but not *or,* may follow *neither.*

In sentences with subjects joined by *either . . . or* or *neither . . . nor,* the verb agrees with the part of the subject closest to it, no matter how many parts the subject has and even though some of the parts are singular and some plural.

> If either prisoner or both prisoners are paroled, the public will stage a protest.

When two or more singular nouns are joined by *neither . . . nor,* a singular verb is usually preferred.

Neither the generator nor the carburetor *is* (or *are*) in
working condition.

etc.

Since *etc.* stands for the Latin *et cetera* ("and others"), it
should never be preceded by *and*. Nor should it end a series or
a list introduced by such a phrase as *for example* or *such as*.
A comma should precede *etc.* but should not follow it unless
the structure of the sentence otherwise demands it.

Normally *etc.* is suitable for technical contexts such as lists,
tabular materials, and other places where a reader can easily
infer the rest of the list. Sometimes the use of *etc.* shows a
writer unwilling or too hurried to complete a series, and this
use asks an unsure reader to fill a blank in the writer's mind.
Rather than overusing *etc.*, complete the series, and thus the
thought if possible, with specific information.

Original

Our firm desperately needs clerks, typists, *etc.*

Revised

Our firm desperately needs clerks, typists, and other office
personnel.

Original

Sailboats, yachts, *etc.* thickly dotted the inlet.

Revised

Sailboats, yachts, and other pleasure craft thickly dotted
the inlet.

It is often preferable to rephrase the sentence, introducing
the list with such words as *including, such as,* or *for instance.*
Etc. is no longer placed in italics (underlined). Spelling it out
in full is an affectation.

except, accept

Except, usually a preposition, is occasionally used as a verb.
In speaking, it may be confused with the more common verb
accept. To *except* means to "exclude" or "leave out"; to *accept*
means to "receive," "admit," or "welcome."

Please *accept* (not *except*) our apologies for the error.

Correct, but awkward

> We can *except* your case from the rule.

Improved

> We can make an exception in your case.

farther, further

In reference to distance, *farther* and *further* are equally acceptable.

> two miles *farther* (or *further*) down the road
> The escapee fled *farther* (or *further*) into the woods.

Only *further* can refer to time or degree and have the general meaning of "additional" or "more."

> a *further* delay
> without *further* delay
> Our firm will not discuss the matter *further*.

fewer, less

In formal writing the distinction between *fewer* and *less* is observed, although in speech and in general writing *less* is increasingly displacing *fewer*.

Fewer is used for items that can be counted (*fewer* dollars, *fewer* calories, *fewer* people). *Less* is used for quantities that can be measured and amounts that cannot be easily counted (*less* money, *less* sugar, *less* weight). A person losing weight, thus, carries *less* weight than yesterday but *fewer* pounds.

Fewer is not always required before a number, since nouns expressing specified sums, measurements, and quantities are singular. These nouns express indivisible blocks and units and require *less,* not *fewer.*

> Little Rock averages *less* (not *fewer*) than ten inches of snow each winter.
> Little Rock normally has *fewer* (not *less*) than four snowfalls each winter.

Sometimes a writer has a choice between *less* and *fewer,* depending on whether or not the writer is emphasizing the collectiveness of the noun or its separate units. (The number of the verb will change also.) Either of the following is correct.

Less than ten thousand dollars was left in the campaign fund.

Fewer than ten thousand dollars were left in the campaign fund.

When in doubt, the writer should use *less*. Overusing *less* is preferable to overusing *fewer*.

finalize

Finalize, meaning "to put into final or complete form," becomes more popular each year, but there are still more reasons to avoid it than to use it. It is frequently vague, and many people regard it as a piece of gobbledygook. Be precise in your writing and use *finish, complete,* or *put in final form* instead.

Original

The committee expects to *finalize* the plans at tonight's meeting.

Revised

The committee expects to *complete* the plans at tonight's meeting.

As an example of the thoughtless use of the word and the extent of its encroachment into the language, consider the following example from a generally well-edited newspaper.

About 85 percent of construction is complete. When *finalized* it will produce ethylene and polyethylene.

The writer was apparently afraid of repeating the word *complete* from the preceding sentence and, for some reason, chose *finalized* instead of *finished*.

first, firstly

First and *firstly* are both adverbs and are both acceptable when a writer wishes to introduce or enumerate a series of ideas or facts. Grammatically there is no reason to prefer one over the other. While *firstly* is an optional variant of *first*, it is also an unnecessary one and is often stilted and unnatural.

First (preferable to *firstly*), the agency has reduced its error rate from 14 to 3 percent since October.

Be careful not to mix forms with *ly* and forms without *ly*. Use either *first, second, third, fourth* . . . or *firstly, secondly, thirdly, fourthly*. . . .

flaunt, flout

Flaunt means "to make a show of" or "to display." *Flout* means "to defy" or "to show contempt for." *Flaunt* is often misused for *flout*, especially in reference to convention or to the law. One *flouts* the law, and if bold about it, one might *flaunt* the *flouting*.

gamut, gauntlet

To *run* or *play a gamut* is to pass through a range of something, often emotions. To *run a gauntlet* is to pass through an ordeal, usually one in which the person seems surrounded and constantly harassed. These two expressions are sometimes confused because they are similar in sound and because the words *gamut* and *gauntlet* are both known primarily in these figurative expressions. The origins of the key words make the different meanings clear, however. *Gamut* derives from *gamma*, the first note of the medieval musical scale, and *ut*, the first note of the classical scale. By the seventeenth century, the word *gamut* referred to the complete scale, note by note. The phrase *running the gamut* still carries with it the idea of moving incrementally through a range or along a scale of something.

To *run the gauntlet* (or *gantlet*) is to go through an ordeal. The expression comes from a military punishment in which a man was stripped to the waist and forced to run between two lines of men who hit him with small sticks or knotted cords. The word *gauntlet* originates from a Swedish word, *gantlope*, meaning "a passage or lane."

Neither *running a gamut* or *going through a gauntlet* has anything to do with *throwing down* or *picking up the gauntlet*, meaning "to deliver or accept a challenge." This expression derives from the medieval practice of throwing down a glove as a way of extending a challenge. *Gauntlet* was the French word for the glove of a suit of armor.

good, well

In writing, *good* is only an adjective; its use as an adverb is characteristic of speech. *Well* is usually an adverb, but it is also an adjective in reference to a person's health. After verbs associated with the five senses (e.g. *feel, smell, look, taste,* and *hear*), each of the adjectives can be used, but they differ in meaning.

> I feel *well.*/You look *well.* (*well* meaning "in good health")
> I feel *good.* (*good* meaning "in good spirits")
> You look *good.* (*good* meaning "attractive")

Thus writers can make the proper choice between *good* and *well* by determining whether a noun is being modified (in which case *good* is required) or some other part of the sentence—the verb, an adjective, an adverb, or the entire sentence—is being modified (in which case *well* is required).

historic, historical

Historic means "of special significance in history." *Historical* means "occurring in the past" and refers to events that do not necessarily have any special significance. Sites and landmarks are normally *historic,* not *historical.* A novel is *historic* if its publication made history, but *historical* if its plot is set in the past.

hopefully

Despite its condemnation by many contemporary commentators on usage, there is no point in denying that *hopefully* is too widely used and too rarely misunderstood to be stamped out. Occasionally *hopefully* is used in a vague and ambiguous way, as in

> *Hopefully* the children are looking forward to Christmas. (Who is hopeful—the children or the writer of the sentence?)

but it usually means "I hope" or "it is to be hoped that."

Careful writers will avoid the word because of the prejudice against it and because it is better to specify who is doing the hoping.

imply, infer

Infer is often misused for *imply,* but these two verbs carry an important distinction that careful writers will observe. *Imply* means "hint" or "suggest a conclusion without stating it." *Infer* means "draw a conclusion from facts or evidence." Thus, writers and speakers *imply*, but readers and hearers *infer*. The two verbs indicate two different sources of a person's knowledge, as in

> The senator *implied* that there was going to be a tax cut.
> The senator *inferred* that there was going to be a tax cut.

In the first sentence, the senator is the source of the information. In the second, someone else is; the senator is drawing a conclusion from what someone else has said or written.

The two verbs thus refer to opposite ends of the communicative process. As everyone knows, the *implication* of a writer or speaker and the *inference* drawn by a reader or hearer are not necessarily the same.

in regard to, in regards to, regarding

In regard to and *regarding* are both acceptable in writing. *In regards to* is not.

in terms of

In terms of is a wordy and vague substitute for *in* and other simple prepositions. Rephrase and strengthen a sentence by incorporating the object of *in terms of* into the main part of the sentence.

Original

> *In terms of* productivity, the industry made little improvement in the 1970s.

Revised

> The industry's productivity increased little in the 1970s.

Original

> *In terms of* balancing the budget, Jones's administration was a success.

Revised

> Jones's administration succeeded in balancing the budget.

irregardless

Unacceptable. It is either a careless redundancy for *regardless* or a mistake for *irrespective* and should be replaced by one of these two words.

its, it's

Its is a possessive pronoun. Like other possessive pronouns such as *theirs, your, his,* and *whose,* it has no apostrophe. *It's* is the contraction of *it is* or *it has* and is never a possessive. *Its'* is a mistake.

lay, lie

The accurate use of the verbs *lay* and *lie* in writing is often considered a mark of education. The two are frequently confused because the verbs are similar in sound and in their principal parts.

Lay (principal parts *lay, laid, laid, laying*) is a transitive verb, which means that it always takes a direct object (except when one is discussing chickens that are laying.) One *lays* something down or *lays* it aside.

> Someone *laid* the report on her desk.
> He often *lays* himself open to criticism.
> The parents have *laid* down the law to their children many times.

Lie (principal parts *lie, lay, lain, lying*) is an intransitive verb, which means that the action of the verb is self-contained. *Lie* never takes a direct object. One *lies* down for a rest, *lies* low for a while, or complains that something has been *lying* on the boss's desk for a week.

> Reports used to *lie* on his desk for a month or more.
> The monthly sales figures *lay* on her desk for less than a day.

Some additional illustrations of the two verbs:

> He *laid* (past tense of *lay*) the trash at the curb, where it *lay* (past tense of *lie*) for a week.
> After the shortstop and the second baseman collided, they *lay* (past tense of *lie*) on the field unconscious until their teammates *laid* (past tense of *lay*) them on the stretchers.

like, as

The fuss over the use of *like* as a conjunction to introduce a clause has been so great since the Winston commercials of the sixties (*Winston tastes good like a cigarette should*) that this usage issue can no longer be objectively discussed. Even though *like* as a conjunction can be defended on historical (Shakespeare used it) and other grounds, writers who use it should be prepared for criticism because there is such prejudice against its use in writing. We present here the guidelines for writers who want to avoid possible disapproval in using *like* and *as*.

Use *like* as a preposition with a noun, a pronoun, or a noun substitute that is not followed by a verb. Use *as* as a conjunction before clauses and phrases that contain verbs. If a following verb is implied but not stated, use *like*.

> The new Trident automobile looks *like* (not *as*) a Polaris, but drives *as* (not *like*) a San Marino does (or drives *like* a San Marino)

Writers who are uncomfortable with both *like* and *as* before a clause can use *the way* instead.

> The new Trident looks *the way* a Polaris does, but drives *the way* a San Marino does.

In writing, *as if* and *as though* as conjunctions are also preferable to *like*.

> The apartment looked *as if* (or *as though*, but not *like*) a violent fight had taken place there.

The fear of misusing *like* sometimes leads writers to use *as* when there is no following verb. *Like* is the only acceptable form if no verb follows.

> Texas and Tennessee, *like* (not *as*) several other Sunbelt states, gained congressional seats as a result of the 1980 census.

loan, lend

The idea that *loan* is not an acceptable verb is a superstition held by latter-day commentators who, in quest of neatness, wish to restrict *lend* to use as a verb and *loan* to use as a noun. Yet *loan* (principal parts *loan, loaned, loaned, loaning*) has been a verb for at least eight centuries, especially in financial and commercial contexts (*The bank loaned the publisher two million dollars*). The verb *lend* (principal parts *lend, lent, lent, lending*) is used in most other contexts and also has the sense of "grant" or "furnish," as in *Friends, Romans, countrymen, lend me your ears*.

Loan, unlike *lend*, can also be a noun.

media

Media, the plural form of *medium*, refers to the agencies of mass communications, especially to television, newspapers, and radio. Like *data*, another plural from Latin, *media* is becoming a singular noun referring to mass communication agencies or to the press collectively. But unlike *data*, the use of *media* as a singular is not yet widely accepted in writing.

Avoid the use of *medias* altogether.

> Representatives of the various news *media* attended the governor's press conference.

The plural *mediums* refers to middle points, to sizes, and to spiritualists.

militate, mitigate

Militate means "to work or fight against."

> A dense fog and oncoming darkness *militated* against the finding of any survivors.

Mitigate is frequently confused with *militate* and mistakenly used with *against*. It means "to make milder" or "lessen the severity of."

> A sudden downpour *mitigated* the midafternoon heat.

Ms.

Ms. is often a convenient title of respect for addressing a woman, regardless of her marital status. It is now accepted almost everywhere in the business and professional worlds. For a writer who does not know whether a woman has a married name or not, *Ms.* frequently comes in handy. However, many women object sometimes vehemently to the use of *Ms.* for one reason or another. If a writer is aware of it or can discover it, a woman's personal preference for a title and name should by all means be honored.

A writer who doesn't know the woman being addressed must choose among *Ms.*, *Miss*, or *Mrs.* To avoid the choice, use a professional title (*Dr., Professor*, etc.) when possible. Even though *Ms.* is not an abbreviation, use a period with it, in conformity with *Mr.* and *Mrs.* A plural of *Ms.* has not yet been settled on. If there is more than one woman you wish to address, repeat *Ms.* before each name.

on, upon

The shorter form *on* is normally preferred when there is a choice between *on* and *upon.* *Upon* is often a stilted.

oral, verbal

The question about the distinction between these two adjectives arises because *verbal* is often used to mean "oral" or "spoken," especially in the phrase *a verbal agreement.* *Verbal* also has the general meaning "pertaining to words." *Verbal* is thus potentially ambiguous (is a *verbal* contract one arrived at in speech or in writing?). A *verbal* agreement is thus distinct from one arrived at by gestures or some other means, but it may be either a written or a spoken agreement. *Oral* means only "spoken" or "pertaining to the mouth."

When writers have a choice between *oral* and *written* or between *spoken* and *written,* they should avoid *verbal* altogether.

orient, orientate

These two variants have the identical meaning "to adjust to surrounding or existing circumstances." *Orient,* the shorter, simpler form, is always preferred.

> Sergeant Castille's assignment is to *orient* new recruits to camp rules and regulations.

phenomenon, phenomena

Phenomena is a plural form and should be used only with a plural verb. The singular form of this noun, inherited from Greek, is *phenomenon.* The use of *phenomena* as a singular is sometimes heard but is unacceptable in writing.

preventive, preventative

Preventative is a needless variant of *preventive.* Write *preventive* (not *preventative*) *medicine.*

principal, principle

Principle is a noun referring to a rule of conduct, a belief, or a general truth.

Principal, usually an adjective meaning "chief" or "main," is sometimes a noun meaning "the chief one" (as the *principals in a legal action,* the *principal in a play,* and the *principal of a school*). *Principal* also refers to a sum of money on which interest is paid.

prior to, before

When they refer to time or order, these two words are interchangeable. But *before* is preferable; *prior to* often seems affected.

> *Before* (not *prior to*) taking this job, I had been unemployed for nine months.

proved, proven

Proved and *proven* are both acceptable as the past participle of *prove. Proved* is generally the more common form, but *proven* is frequently used in legal contexts.

> Energy legislation has *proved* (or *proven*) to be a political football.

As an adjective, *proven* is more widely used than *proved* (e.g. *proven oil reserves, a proven remedy*).

provided, providing

Provided and *providing* are both acceptable in writing; *provided* is more common in formal usage.

> *Providing* (or *Provided*) the weather remains clear, Riverfest will attract more than ten thousand people this weekend.

But there is no reason to use either if the word *if* will do.

> *If the* weather remains clear, Riverfest will attract more than ten thousand people this weekend.

reason . . . is because

Sentences employing the *reason . . . is because* construction are indirect and redundant. In formal writing, *that* is always preferred to *because.* Sentences using either *the reason . . . is that* or *the reason . . . is because* are easily improved by getting rid of *reason* and the form of the verb *be.*

Original

> The reason our profits have increased is that we have implemented better cost-accounting procedures.

Revised

> Our profits have increased because we have implemented better cost-accounting procedures.

set, sit

Set (principal parts *set, set, set, setting*) is usually a transitive verb (takes a direct object) and means "to place." One *sets* a package on a shelf and a report on a desk. One *sets* hair, tables, and time limits. *Set* also has a few very specific intransitive (without a direct object) meanings. Hens *set*, the sun *sets*, and glue and concrete *set*.

Sit (principal parts *sit, sat, sat, sitting*) is an intransitive verb (does not take a direct object) and means "to be seated or to rest."

> No conventionally built house can sit on the slope.
> The table sits twelve.
> The assembly is not sitting now.

shall, will

These two words once had a list of prescribed uses that did not overlap, but today most of the distinctions between *shall* and *will* no longer exist. In using them, the contemporary writer should go by the following basic rule: If it sounds natural, use *will*.

To express simple futurity, *shall* was at one time commonly used with first-person subjects and *will* with second- and third-person subjects. A remnant or two of this distinction remains, but *will* has almost entirely displaced *shall* in this use (although this distinction is still often made in Britain). *Will* is now the normal future form for all levels of writing. *Shall* can still be used to express futurity when an especially formal effect is desired, as in legal documents. But use *shall* for the future conservatively; it often sounds affected.

Shall usually conveys more than simple futurity. It asks for permission in formal or polite first-person questions (where *will* is unidiomatic): *Shall we meet tomorrow at ten?*

To express obligation, warning, determination, or prohibition in statements about the future, both *shall* and *will* are acceptable. *Shall* is more forceful and is typically used in government and legal documents.

> At the end of each quarter, division chiefs *will* (or *shall*) submit inventory statements.
> The accused *shall* stand trial on March 15.
> Picket lines *will* not be crossed.

Often there is a fine line between simple futurity and obligation. What kind of statement is the following?

> All employees with more than two years of service *shall* (or *will*) receive a longevity payment on September 30.

In such a case, a writer will be safe in using *will*.

slow, slowly

Both of these words have a long history as adverbs and are equally acceptable in writing, even though controversy continues to be generated over the supposed "incorrect" use of *slow* as an adverb. The choice between the two depends on the rhythm and force a writer wishes to adopt, and it has nothing to do with grammar. *Slow* is often preferred in direct commands, but *slowly* is usually preferred in other cases.

> Go *slow*. (*but* All condemned men go slowly to the gallows.)
> Drive *slow*. (*but* To pass the driver's test, drive slowly around the block and execute all turns cleanly.)

Many other pairs of adverbs like *slow* and *slowly* are distinguished by one having the ending *ly* and the other not having it. (For a discussion of these, see pages 83–85.)

speak, talk

There seems to be a phantom "rule," learned by many hotline callers in their schooldays, that *with* is the correct preposition to use after *speak* and *to* is correct after *talk*. Actually, both prepositions are entirely acceptable after each verb. *Speak to* and *talk to* connote a one-sided activity, something close to a monologue. *Speak with* and *talk with* connote a give-and-take conversation.

split infinitive

An infinitive is split when an adverb comes between *to* and the following verb. The rule prohibiting split infinitives is an arbitrary taboo and a thing of the past. Sometimes splitting an infinitive is unavoidable.

> In the 1980s, Exxon expects to more than triple its efforts to search for new sources of oil.

When the adverb is short (no more than one word), splitting an infinitive often produces the smoothest, most natural phrasing.

> The mission of the *Enterprise* is to boldly go where no man has gone before.
> The commission chose to completely disregard the findings of its research staff.

In general, avoid splitting an infinitive when the adverb is two or more words long and when the adverb seems to interrupt the flow of the sentence.

Original

> The judge had to on more than one occasion excuse the jury.

Revised

> The judge had to excuse the jury on more than one occasion.

stationary, stationery

Stationary means "standing still." *Stationery* refers to paper goods. Remember the spelling difference by remembering that the e*arth* seems station*ary*, and that station*ery* refers to pap*er*.

that, which

These two relative pronouns overlap in usage, so writers often can choose either one. *Which* is used to refer to things but not to people. *That* can refer both to things and to people; in reference to people it is acceptable in general writing.

> The typewriter *that* (or *which*) the company ordered is an IBM.
> The man *who* (or *that,* but not *which*) was driving the red Toyota had no insurance.

Nor are *that* and *which* used in rigidly distinct places. Some other usage guides urge that *that* be used in defining (restrictive) clauses (those essential to the meaning of the sentences in which they appear) and that *which* be used in descriptive (nonrestrictive) clauses (those not essential to the meaning of sentences). This rule may have some value for writers who keep such clauses straight (defining clauses should not be set off by commas, descriptive clauses should be set off) and for those who use *which* at the expense of *that* in restrictive clauses. But on the whole, this rule has very little basis in usage and writers should feel free to use *which* with defining clauses (*the house which we own, the book which we wrote*).

That is used in defining clauses. The word *that* seems to have an emphatic thrust to it inappropriate to descriptive clauses, but good writers have used *which* with defining clauses since the thirteenth century. The choice between *that* and *which* in defining clauses depends primarily on emphasis, rhythm, and personal preference. Neither is more formal nor more cultured than the other.

> The materials *that* (or *which*) were ordered yesterday arrived this morning.

In summary, *which* is used with either defining or descriptive clauses. You may or may not need commas to set off a clause beginning with *which*. *That* is used only with defining clauses. You never need commas to set off a clause beginning with *that*.

thus, thusly

Thusly is an unnecessary variant of *thus*, which is already an adverb.

to, too, two

To is the preposition and the marker of the infinitive, *two* is the numeral, and *too* is the adverb meaning "also" or "an excessive amount."

The only way to write that these three words are pronounced identically is *To, too, and two are all pronounced "tu."*

17

Glossary of Grammatical Terms

This following glossary briefly defines and explains the more common grammatical terms. Since many of them are discussed at several points in this book, consult the Index for all the material on a particular term.

absolute constructions

Absolute constructions modify entire sentences or clauses without being grammatically linked to them. Usually they consist of a noun or substitute and a participle.

> *The telephones having rung constantly all morning,* the secretaries took a long lunch break.
> *The room being jammed with people,* latecomers found themselves unable to find a seat.

adjective clauses

See clauses.

adjectives

Adjectives modify and describe nouns and pronouns. Adjectives that precede what they modify are called attributive adjectives:

> *unruly* children
> the *last* one
> the *crucial* vote
> the *impossible* dream

Adjectives that follow a form of *be* and modify the subject are called predicate adjectives:

> the vote was *crucial*
> the dream was *impossible*

Adjectives may be transformed into nouns by adding suffixes like *ness* (good, *goodness;* bright, *brightness*) or into adverbs by adding *ly* (blithe, *blithely;* foolish, *foolishly*).

Adjectives are sometimes used as nouns:

> Only the *brave* deserve the *fair.*
> The *poor* are always with us.

Some adjectives are inflected (change their forms) to show degrees of comparison: good, better, best; small, smaller, smallest.

The words *a, an,* and *the* are a type of adjective called articles (see articles).

adverb clauses
See clauses.

adverbs
Modifying words that are not adjectives are adverbs. Adverbs generally indicate when, where, how, or to what degree something happens. Adverbs may modify verbs, adjectives, other adverbs, or sentences or clauses as a whole.

> Go *quickly.* (modifying a verb)
> That runner is *very* fast. (modifying an adjective)
> She appeared *quite* suddenly. (modifying another adverb)
> *Finally* the mail arrived. (modifying the sentence as a whole)

A phrase or subordinate clause acting as an adverb is called an adverb phrase or clause.

> We went *on Sunday.* (prepositional phrase used as an adverb stating when)
> *Although we feared the outcome,* we went to the game. (subordinate clause used as an adverb, telling how or in what manner, i.e. fearfully)

Adverbs are often formed from adjectives by the addition of the *ly* suffix (fearful, *fearfully;* haughty, *haughtily;* swift, *swiftly*). But some adverbs and adjectives have the same form (*leisurely* and *fast* for instance), and many common adverbs have alternate forms (*slow/slowly; tight/tightly*).

Adverbs that modify verbs can show degrees of comparison: closely, *more closely, most closely.*

agreement

Agreement is the correspondence between forms of words that reflects the grammatical relationships. Subjects and verbs agree in number (Chapter 3); pronouns and their antecedents agree in number and gender (Chapter 4); and demonstratives agree in number with following nouns (*this kind, those kinds*).

antecedents

Words or groups of words that pronouns refer to are called antecedents. Antecedents generally precede the pronoun but can sometimes follow it.

> Jill thought that she was God's gift to the company. (*Jill* is the antecedent of *she*.)
>
> Since he had already been reprimanded, the supervisor was immediately suspect. (*Supervisor,* the antecedent of *he,* follows it.)

appositives

Appositives are nouns or noun substitutes that follow and rename or describe other nouns or noun substitutes. They may follow subjects or objects. Unlike relative clauses, appositives can substitute grammatically for the noun being modified.

> Smith, the new chairman of the board, dislikes Jones, an incompetent and a bumbler. (*The new chairman of the board* is in apposition to *Smith,* and *an incompetent and a bumbler* is in apposition to *Jones.*)

For how to punctuate appositives, see pages 139–41.

articles

The articles *a, an,* and *the* are a type of adjective and are sometimes called noun determiners or noun markers. *A* and *an,* the indefinite articles, precede many singular nouns (*a* car, *a* house, *an* employee). *The,* the definite article, precedes either singular or plural nouns (the man, the coast, the trees).

attributive adjectives

See adjectives.

attributive nouns

See nouns.

auxiliary verbs

Auxiliary verbs, also called helping verbs, precede main verbs and indicate their tense, voice, and mood. Auxiliary verbs include *be, do,* and *have* and the modal verbs *can, could, may, might, must, shall, should, will, would, ought to,* and *need (to).* Of these, only forms of *be, do,* and *have* can ever be used by themselves. The others are always used with main verbs or implied main verbs:

> "If I want to do it, I *can* (do it)," the little girl pouted.

case

Case refers to the grammatical form a noun or pronoun takes according to its function in a particular sentence. The nominative or subjective case form is used for subjects of sentences and clauses and for predicate nominatives, the objective form for objects, and the possessive or genitive case form for ownership and similar meanings.

Nouns have only two cases, nominative and possessive. They are possessive when they add an apostrophe or apostrophe *s: members, members'; child, child's.* Personal pronouns and *who* have three cases: nominative (*I, she, they, who*), objective (*me, her, them, whom*), and possessive (*my* and *mine, her* and *hers, their* and *theirs, whose*). Some pronouns (*which* and *that,* for instance) do not have case forms.

clauses

Clauses are groups of words containing both a subject and a complete predicate (not simply an infinitive or a participle). Clauses may be either independent or dependent. Independent clauses can stand alone in complete sentences. Dependent clauses (also called subordinate clauses) rely on another clause to complete their meaning. They function as adjectives, adverbs, or nouns.

Adjective-dependent clauses, usually called relative clauses, modify nouns and are usually introduced by relative pronouns (*who, whom, which, that*).

> Jack, *who voted against the incumbent only as a protest,* was stunned at the governor's defeat. (relative clause modifying *Jack*)

Adverb-dependent clauses tell when, to what degree, or under what conditions the main clause is done or is true. They are introduced by subordinating conjunctions (e.g. *if, when, because, although*).

> *When we chose your company as primary contractor,* we did not anticipate the extent of design changes. (adverb-dependent clause)
> *Although we have tentatively offered the job to Marks,* we have had second thoughts about her qualifications. (adverb-dependent clause)

Noun-dependent clauses function as subjects or objects within independent clauses.

> *Whoever wants the job of coordinating the conference* may have it. (noun clause functioning as a subject of the sentence)
> The company knows *that hard times are coming.* (noun clause functioning as direct object of the sentence)

collective nouns
See nouns.

common nouns
See nouns.

complements
Complements are words or groups of words that complete another part of a sentence. Direct and indirect objects complete verbs. Predicate adjectives and predicate nominatives are subject complements because they complete subjects. Object complements complete direct objects.

> Fifteen employees used the *company.* (direct object)
> The assistant managers gave their *boss* a new car. (indirect object)
> He is the *man* for the job. (predicate nominative here completes the subject)
> Her story seemed *convincing.* (predicate adjective here completes the subject)
> They chose Sam Jones *treasurer.* (*Treasurer* completes the direct object *Sam Jones.*)
> His mother made him *what he is today.* (*What he is today* completes the direct object *him.*)

conjugation

A conjugation is a list of the forms that a verb takes to show changes in number, person, tense, mood, and voice. An example of a complete conjugation appears on page 8 of Chapter 1.

conjunctions

Conjunctions link related words, phrases, and clauses.

Coordinating conjunctions link equal grammatical elements, whether clauses, phrases, or words. Coordinating conjunctions include *and, but, or, nor, so* (when it means "therefore"), *yet* (when it means "but"), and *for* (when it means "because"). When *so, yet,* and *for* are used as conjunctions, they are always preceded by commas. Well-entrenched myths notwithstanding, coordinating conjunctions may begin sentences.

Subordinating conjunctions express many relationships, including time (e.g. *after* and *before*), cause and effect (e.g. *because* and *since*), and condition (e.g. *if* and *unless*). They also link clauses that are not grammatically parallel: *If she is not promoted, I will resign.* Common subordinating conjunctions include the following:

after	so that
although	that
as	though
as . . . as	till
as if/as though	unless
because	until
before	what
even though	when/whenever
how	where/wherever
if	whether
in order that	while
once	why
since	

Correlative conjunctions are coordinating conjunctions made of two or more words (*either . . . or; neither . . . nor; both . . . and; not only . . . but also*): *Not only was he sick, but he was also poor.*

conjunctive adverbs

Adverbs that connect and relate two independent clauses are called conjunctive adverbs. They can usually be moved around in sentences without affecting the grammar. Commonly used conjunctive adverbs include the following:

accordingly	likewise
also	meanwhile
besides	moreover
consequently	namely
finally	nevertheless
first	next
furthermore	otherwise
hence	still
however	then
indeed	therefore
instead	thus
last	

Many conjunctive adverbs are used as transitional phrases. Common ones used transitional phrases include the following:

after all	in other words
as a result	in the first place
at the same time	on the other hand
by the way	that is
for example	what is more
in addition	

coordinating conjunctions
See conjunctions.

correlative conjunctions
See conjunctions.

count nouns
See nouns.

defining and descriptive modifiers
Appositives and modifying clauses and phrases are said to be defining (restrictive) or describing (nonrestrictive). Defining (restrictive) words and clauses limit or further define the words they modify. Descriptive (nonrestrictive) words and clauses may add further information, but they do not limit what is being discussed or change the grammar of the sentence. (For examples and a fuller discussion, including punctuation with such appositives and clauses, see pages 139–41.)

demonstrative adjectives

Demonstrative pronouns (*this, that, these, those*) are often used as adjectives. When they are, they agree in number with the nouns immediately following them.

> *This* kind of report is unacceptable.
> *That* applicant is the best of the four.
> *Those* salaries are out of line.

dependent clauses

See clauses.

descriptive modifiers

See defining and descriptive modifiers.

descriptive nouns

See nouns.

direct object

The WHO or WHAT that receives the action of a transitive verb is called a direct object. Nouns, pronouns, phrases, and clauses may function as direct objects.

> The bureaucratic structure has swallowed your *application*. (noun)
> The bureaucratic structure has swallowed *it*. (pronoun)
> Not everyone enjoys *flying at night*. (gerund phrase)
> He likes *what many people hate*. (noun clause)

Generally, the direct objects of active sentences can be made the subjects of passive sentences.

> Your application has been swallowed.
> Flying at night is not enjoyed by everyone.

exclamations

See interjections.

finite and nonfinite verbs

Finite verbs are verbs that show tense and that have subjects (e.g. *go, was placed, has been gone*). Nonfinite verbs (participles, infinitives, and gerunds) do not show tense and may or may not have a subject.

> After *swimming* for twenty minutes, she *felt* refreshed. (*swimming* is a gerund functioning as the object of the preposition *after* and is a nonfinite verb; *felt* is a finite verb in the past tense)
>
> He wants *to go.* (*to go* is an infinitive, a nonfinite verb, functioning as the direct object of *wants*)

genitive case
See case.

gerund
Gerunds are verb forms (such as *swimming* and *working*) that end in *ing* and function as nouns.

> *Swimming* is a favorite summer pastime. (as a subject)
> The old man loved *working* in his garden. (as a direct object)
> She believes in *working* only until five o'clock. (as an object of a preposition)

helping verbs
See auxiliary verbs.

imperative mood
See mood.

independent clauses
See clauses.

indicative mood
See mood.

indirect object
The indirect object is the TO WHOM or FOR WHOM the action in a sentence is done and names the WHO or WHAT that receives the direct object.

> The critic gave the entire *cast* excellent reviews.
> Elaine gave *Matthew* a present.

infinitives
The plain form of the verb, often preceded by the word *to* (the infinitive marker) is the present infinitive. It carries

no tense; that is, it conveys no time other than the time of the main verb of the sentence. The perfect infinitive (e.g. *to have gone*) conveys a time previous to the main verb of the sentence.

Infinitives cannot convey the tense of the sentence and so cannot function as verbs. Like other verbals, however, they can function as other parts of speech.

> *To win* was his only goal. (*To win* functions as a noun and is the subject of the sentence.)
>
> He wanted *to win*. (*To win* functions as a noun and is the direct object of the sentence.)
>
> The important thing *to do* is *to survive*. (*To do* functions as an adjective and modifies *thing*; to *survive* functions as a noun and is the predicate nominative.)

The prohibition against splitting infinitives reflects Latin grammar, not English. The grammarians who patterned English grammar after Latin first dictated that infinitives in English should not be split. As a matter of style, and for ease of reading, one should avoid splitting infinitives with phrases or clauses. But inserting a single-word adverb between the infinitive and its marker *to* seldom creates a problem.

inflection

The change of a word to show different grammatical properties is known as inflection. Nouns are inflected to show number (singular and plural) and to show possession. Verbs are inflected to show number, person, tense, and mood. Adjectives and adverbs are inflected to show degrees of comparison.

interjection

Words that by themselves express strong emotion are interjections or exclamations (*oh, pshaw, what a man, damn*). These words have no grammatical relationship to the rest of the sentence.

Interjections are sometimes punctuated as complete sentences. When they are attached to sentences, they are punctuated as interrupters—set off by commas, dashes, or parentheses.

intransitive verbs

See verbs.

linking verbs
    See verbs.

mass nouns
    See nouns.

modal verbs
    Modal verbs are auxiliary (helping) verbs that indicate possibility, necessity, willingness, and other conditions. Modal verbs in English are *can, could, may, might, must, shall, should, will, would, ought to,* and *need (to)*.

mood
    Verbs in English have three moods that express a writer's attitude toward the action of a sentence. The indicative mood, by far the most common, is used for ordinary statements and questions.

> The giant *approached* the castle.
> *Will* you *run* home?

The imperative mood is used for commands and requests.

> *Look.*
> *Come* here.

The subjunctive is used for contrary-to-fact statements and for wishes.

> If wishes *were* horses, beggars would ride.
> I wish that wishes *were* horses.

nominative case
    See case.

nonfinite verbs
    See finite and nonfinite verbs.

nonrestrictive clauses and modifiers
    See defining and descriptive modifiers.

noun clauses
    See clauses.

noun determiners
   See articles.

noun markers
   See articles.

noun substitutes
   Words or groups of words that take the position of nouns and function like nouns are called noun substitutes. Pronouns, gerunds, infinitives, noun clauses, and other phrases and clauses are noun substitutes when they function as subjects, direct objects, indirect objects, objects of prepositions, and appositives.

nouns
   Words that name things are nouns. Common nouns include the names of unspecified persons, places, organizations, and things. Proper nouns include the names of specific persons, places, organizations, and things. (For the capitalization of proper nouns, see Chapter 8.)
   Count nouns can be counted and divided into units; they have singular and plural forms: *chairs, gallons, animals, speeches.* Mass nouns cannot be divided into discrete units: *gasoline, sugar, freedom, music.* Collective nouns group together several like things or people: a *flock* of geese, a *committee,* a *team.*
   Nouns can function as subjects (The *car* was red), as direct objects (We pushed the *car*), as indirect objects (We gave the *car* a tune-up), as appositives (Our car, a *Toyota,* is red), and as objects of prepositions (We sat in the *car* for an hour).
   Nouns sometimes modify other nouns. When they do and are marked with a possessive (the *child's* toys), they are called possessive nouns; when they modify a noun but are not marked with a possessive (*state* hospital, *wall* calendar), they are called descriptive or attributive nouns.

number
   Number refers to whether a noun, pronoun, or verb is singular or plural. Some nouns are singular in meaning but act as plurals grammatically (*scissors* and *trousers*). Others can be construed as singular or plural only from their contexts.

His *politics* place a priority on fence-sitting. (plural
   subject and verb)
Politics is statesmanship at close range. (singular subject
   and verb)

(Number is discussed with verbs in Chapter 1, on page 3,
with nouns throughout Chapter 2, as part of subject-verb agreement throughout Chapter 3, and with pronouns in Chapter 4,
on pages 69–74.)

object complements
   See complements.

objective case
   See case.

participles
   Among the principal parts of a verb are the past and present
participles. The past participle is formed in a variety of ways,
most often by adding *d* or *ed* to the infinitive (*climbed, chafed*).
The present participle is always formed by adding *ing* to the
infinitive (*climbing, chafing*). Participles are nonfinite verbs;
that is, they do not have tense and cannot serve as verbs by
themselves. The present participle conveys action that is incomplete; the past participle conveys completed action.
   Participles can function as adjectives (a *snarling* dog, a
broken mirror), and like other verbals, they may sometimes
take subjects and objects.

   The order having been filled, the mailroom was alerted.
      (*Order* is the subject of the participle *having been
      filled.*)
   Having filled the order, we feel we are not responsible for
      delivery problems. (*Order* is the direct object of the
      participle phrase *having filled.*)

parts of speech
   Grammarians customarily divide words into eight groups
or parts of speech based on the meaning, the position, or the
function of a word in a sentence. The eight parts of speech
are noun, pronoun, verb, adjective, adverb, preposition, conjunction, and interjection (each of these is defined separately
in this glossary).

A word may belong to more than one part of speech because its function may differ from sentence to sentence.

> A law *that* is not supported cannot be enforced. (*That* is a pronoun.)
> *That* book needs to be revised. (*That* is an adjective.)
> She stated *that* she would not release the information. (*That* is a conjunction.)
> Is the manuscript *that* late? (*That* is an adverb modifying the adjective *late*.)

phrases

Phrases are groups of grammatically related words not containing both a subject and a verb. Phrases function as single parts of speech and are of many different types.

> *Running for office* is fun. (gerund phrase used as noun)
> *To dance* is *to live*. (infinitive phrases used as nouns)
> *By the time* the spring rains begin, it is too late to plant English peas. (prepositional phrase used as adverb)
> When the parts finally arrive, we *will have grown* old and gray. (verb phrase)

possessive case

See case.

predicate

A predicate is the verb or verb phrase, along with the objects, complements, and modifiers that indicate the action, condition, or state of being of the subject. Every clause has a predicate. It is sometimes useful to distinguish between the complete predicate and the simple predicate. The simple predicate is the verb or verb phrase without object, complements, or modifiers. In

> The company has already ordered, for delivery on the first of the month, three cubic yards of certified fluff.

the complete predicate is everything except the subject, *the company*. The simple predicate is *has ordered*.

predicate adjective

A predicate adjective is an adjective (or phrase used as an adjective) that follows a linking verb and describes the subject.

The coffee smells *good*.
The performance was *stupendous*.

predicate nominatives

Predicate nominatives are nouns or pronouns that follow
linking verbs and rename or define a subject. Phrases and
noun clauses can function as predicate nominatives.

One of the bystanders was a *doctor*.
The most populous state is *California*.
His presentation was not *what we expected*.

prefixes

Prefixes are word elements that are attached to the
beginnings of word roots or words to form new words: *re*play,
*un*couth, *multi*national.

prepositions

A preposition links a noun or pronoun (the object of the
preposition) to a sentence. A preposition and its object form
a prepositional phrase, which may function as either an adjective or an adverb.

For three months he lived in the house on the corner.
(*In the house* is an adverb prepositional phrase; *on
the corner* is an adjective prepositional phrase.)

principal parts (of verbs)

Every verb has four principal parts used to express its
many grammatical properties. These are the present or infinitive form (*look, see*), the form listed in dictionaries; the past
tense form (*looked, saw*); the past participle (*looked, seen*);
and the present participle (*looking, seeing*). The present
participle, because it is always regular (present form + *ing*),
is often omitted from dictionaries.

pronouns

Pronouns are the words that take the place of and refer to
nouns and noun substitutes. There are seven different types.
Personal pronouns stand for and refer to persons or things.

I gave *it* to *her*.
She gave *me hers* and *yours*, too.

Interrogative pronouns are those used in asking questions:

What time is it?
Who is responsible?

Demonstrative pronouns (*this, that, these,* and *those*) point things out: *this* book, *that* kind of people, *those* beliefs.

Indefinite pronouns refer to one or more unspecified persons or objects: *everyone, some* (of the books), *each* (of the children).

Reflexive and intensive pronouns are those ending in *self* or *selves,* such as *myself, ourselves, himself, itself,* and *herself.* A reflexive pronoun refers and reflects back to the person(s) who or object(s) that are the subject of the sentence or clause (*The senators voted themselves a raise*). Intensive pronouns strengthen or emphasize a statement (*The children decorated the tree themselves*).

Relative pronouns (*who, whom, that, which, whose, whoever, whomever,* and sometimes *when* and *where*) relate one clause either to a noun (*The corporation that lost money was Chrysler*) or to the rest of the sentence (*Chrysler lost millions, which was surprising*).

proper nouns
See nouns.

relative clauses
See clauses.

restrictive clauses and modifiers
See defining and descriptive modifiers.

subject
The subject is the WHO or WHAT of the verb of a sentence or clause. All clauses, whether independent or dependent, have subjects, although the subject may be only implied, as in a command. Phrases and clauses can function as subjects, as can single nouns, pronouns, and adjectives being used as nouns. Verbals may also have subjects.

The *invoices* were sent out last week. (noun as subject)
They were mailed on time, as usual. (pronoun as subject)
The *rich* get richer every day. (adjective as subject)
To eat, for some, is to live. (infinitive as subject)

Running for office is an obsession for some. (gerund as subject)

What the chairman has requested is reasonable. (subordinate clause as subject; *chairman* is subject of the subordinate clause)

The *president* wants *him* to visit the field offices. (*president* is subject of *wants*, *him* the subject of the infinitive *to visit*)

Sometimes a writer must distinguish between the simple subject and the full or complete subject. The simple subject is the single element that names the WHO or WHAT of the verb. The complete subject includes the words and phrases that modify the subject word or element and that appear on the same side of the verb as the subject. In

The recently hired executive vice-president for public relations has quit.

the complete subject is everything except the verb phrase, *has quit*. The simple subject is *vice-president*.

subject complements
See complements.

subjective case
See case.

subjunctive mood
See mood.

subordinate clauses
See clauses.

subordinating conjunctions
See conjunctions.

suffixes
Suffixes are word elements that are attached to the ends of words either to show grammatical relationships (cat/cats, run/running, small/smaller, walk/walks) or to change one word into another, usually a different part of speech (holy/holiness, critic/criticize).

tense

Verbs are inflected (change their forms) to show the time of their action or their state of being.

> She *walks* home. (present tense)
> She *walked* home. (past tense)
> She *will walk* home. (future tense)

The present and the past tenses are called simple tenses because they are expressed by single words. Other tenses, including the future, the perfect tenses, and progressive tenses, are formed with auxiliary or helping verbs.

The tense of the verb also shows whether or not the action was completed. Perfect tenses show completed action; progressive tenses show uncompleted action.

> She *had walked* home. (past perfect—completed action)
> She *is walking* home. (present progressive—uncompleted action)

The tense of the verb does not always indicate the time of action, however. Future action is often expressed through the present and the present-progressive tense and adverbs of time.

> The train leaves tomorrow.
> The train is leaving tomorrow.

Tense is thoroughly discussed in Chapter 1, pages 7–11.

transitive verbs

See verbs.

verbals

Verbals are verb forms used as other parts of speech, usually as nouns or adjectives. Gerunds, infinitives, and participles are all verbals.

> The *snarling* dog attacked the man who loved *to dance*. (*snarling* is a participle used as an adjective; *to dance* is an infinitive used as a direct object)

verbs

At the heart of every sentence lies a verb, the word or series of words that conveys the action (He *acts*), the condition (The smoke *smells* acrid), or the state of being (The order *is* lost) of the sentence.

Through inflections (changes in their forms), verbs indicate tense, mood, voice, and sometimes number. (See Chapter 1.)

A transitive verb takes a direct object to complete its meaning.

> She *gave* him a *surprise.*
> The *company* ordered a *gross.*

An intransitive verb does not take a direct object.

> She *will sit* there all day.
> The company *folded.*

Linking verbs are intransitive verbs that take a complement to complete their meaning. They link the subject of the sentence with the noun, pronoun, or adjective that renames or describes the subject. These verbs include *be, seem, appear, become, remain,* verbs with similar meanings, and the sense verbs *look, feel, smell, taste,* and *hear.* Linking verbs express a state of being or a condition.

> He *was* (*seemed, became, appeared to be*) an honest man.
> She *looked* (*felt, was, became*) angry.

voice

Verbs are said to be in the active or passive voice. In the active voice, the grammatical subject is the doer of the action.

> The *police caught* the suspect.
> The *company ordered* a gross.

In the passive voice, what was the direct object in the active sentence becomes the grammatical subject; the agent or doer of the action may be omitted or expressed by a prepositional phrase.

> The suspect *was caught* (by the police).
> A gross *was ordered* (by the company).

18

Reference Works:
For More Information

The following highly selective list contains the names of many standard sources of information useful to writers.

Unabridged Dictionaries

Unabridged dictionaries are treasuries of information about the meanings and uses of words through much of the history of English. They are too large and detailed to be practical for most office work. They are available in most libraries, and any student of the English language should spend time getting to know them.

The Oxford English Dictionary. Oxford, 1933.

This thirteen-volume dictionary, available in most libraries, is the most comprehensive dictionary of the language. It traces the developments in pronunciation, spelling, meaning, and usage of every word in English since the eleventh century. Changing forms are illustrated with numerous quotations. The dictionary has been reissued in full size and in a two-volume, reduced-type edition. An extensive supplement is currently being completed. A number of useful abridgments have also been made.

Webster's Third New International Dictionary of the English Language, Unabridged. Springfield, Mass., 1961.

The most comprehensive dictionary published in the United States, this is the authority for American spelling. It contains no proper nouns. Its decision to drop many usage labels (such as "colloquial") and report how the language is actually used created a furor. This dictionary gives historical coverage of words and illustrates usage through quotations. The previous edition, *Webster's Second*, remains valuable for its many geographical and biographical entries.

The Random House Dictionary of the English Language. New York, 1973.

The smallest, least expensive, and most recent of the unabridged dictionaries. It has fewer entries than *Webster's Third* but is an excellent dictionary. It includes many proper nouns.

Abridged or Standard Dictionaries

A good desk dictionary is an indispensable tool for a writer. Besides indicating meanings, spellings, syllabication, and pronunciation, a standard dictionary includes etymological information and discussions of synonyms and notes on usage. Read the introduction of the dictionary to see how the editors have arranged meanings—oldest or most frequent first?—and how they have dealt with slang and colloquial words. Do not mistake a small paperback for a good desk dictionary. The dictionaries we list here each have about 1,500 pages and about 150,000 entries.

The American Heritage Dictionary of the English Language. New College Edition. Boston, 1969.

Contains extensive usage notes and has an attractive design. Some of its definitions are noticeably weak.

Funk and Wagnalls Standard College Dictionary. New York, 1963.

Contains many usage notes. One of the better abridged dictionaries.

The Random House College Dictionary. Revised Edition. New York, 1980.

More entries than other desk dictionaries. Also contains more proper nouns. Type size is slightly smaller than usual but is still very readable.

Webster's New Collegiate Dictionary. Springfield, Mass., 1976.

Has fewer usage notes and labels than most dictionaries but

has more information on word meanings than other comparable dictionaries. Used as the standard for spelling by many publications. Word definitions in chronological order.

Webster's New World Dictionary of the American Language,
    Second College Edition. Cleveland, Ohio, 1970.
    Has simplified definitions. Omits Latin plant and animal names but includes large number of Americanisms. Good etymological information.

Thesauruses

These are books of synonyms and antonyms. Two things need to be said about using them. First, do not let a thesaurus seduce you into affecting long, "impressive" words. Second, know the meaning and connotations of the words you select from a thesaurus. (Desk dictionaries contain many lists of synonyms with discussions of shades of meaning.)

Lewis, Norman. *Roget's Thesaurus in Dictionary Form,* rev.,
    New York, 1973.

Rodale, J. I. *Synonym Finder,* rev. ed., Emmaus, Penn., 1961.

Roget's II: The New Thesaurus. Boston, 1980.

Usage Guides

These books deal with problems and debates in usage. Some of the writers are more prescriptive than others, but each of these books presents interesting viewpoints and advice on writing.

Bernstein, Theodore M. *The Careful Writer: A Modern Guide
    to English Usage.* New York, 1965.
    The most useful of Bernstein's many books.

Bryant, Margaret M., *Current American Usage: How
    Americans Say It and Write It.* New York, 1962.

Addresses usage questions based on extensive field research —both in spoken and written language—and distinguishes among formal, informal, and colloquial use.

Copperud, Roy H. *American Usage and Style: The Consensus.* New York, 1980.
A combination and revision of two earlier Copperud books, including *American Usage.*

Copperud, Roy H. *American Usage: The Consensus.* New York, 1970.
Surveys the responses of well-known dictionaries and usage guides to the usual problems, sometimes presenting a discussion and sometimes a consensus.

Evans, Bergen, and Evans, Cornelia. *A Dictionary of Contemporary American Usage.* New York, 1957.
Comprehensive guide to American usage and grammar. Entries are thorough and informed. There are few quick answers; there is much interesting reading.

Flesch, Rudolph. *The ABC of Style: A Guide to Plain English.* New York, 1964 (since reprinted).
Very useful guide concentrating on doing away with set phrases, clichés, and jargon. Some of the judgments seem hasty, but they are always lively.

Fowler, H. W. *A Dictionary of Modern English Usage,* 2d ed., revised by Sir Ernest Gowers. Oxford, 1965.
One of the standards. While it is British and sometimes old-fashioned, it is always interesting.

Strunk, William, Jr., and White, E. B. *The Elements of Style,* 3d ed. New York, 1979.
A standard. Sometimes too brief to be useful, but it does highlight many important points.

Self-Help Grammar Books

These are self-teaching books. They use relatively little terminology and thoroughly define what they do use. They cover basic grammar and punctuation and include many sets of exercises. They are good as far as they go, but they are basic and simplified. All are available in paperback.

Flesch, Rudolf, and Lass, A. H. *A New Guide to Better Writing.* New York, 1949 (originally published, 1947, as *The Way To Write*).
A self-help writing book; it also deals with grammar problems.

Lewis, Norman. *Better English.* New York, 1961.

Nurnberg, Maxwell. *Questions You Always Wanted To Ask About English, But Were Afraid To Raise Your Hand.* New York, 1972.

Shaw, Harry. *Punctuate It Right!* New York, 1963.
Punctuation reference only; no exercises.

Shefter, Harry. *Shortcuts to Effective English,* rev. ed. New York, 1976.

Walpole, Jane. *A Writer's Guide: Easy Ground Rules for Successful Written English.* Englewood Cliffs, N.J., 1980.
No exercises.

Reference Grammars

These grammars deal much more extensively with the language than the self-help grammars. The books listed use, for the most part, traditional grammatical categories in their discussions.

Curme, George O. *A Grammar of the English Language,* 2 vols. Boston, 1931.

A paperback one-volume abridgment, *English Grammar,* is available.

Jespersen, Otto. *Essentials of English Grammar.* Tuscaloosa, Alabama, 1964.
A reprint of Jespersen's 1933 abridgment of his seven-volume *A Modern English Grammar on Historical Principles.* One of the standard English grammars, but not for beginners.

Opdycke, John Baker. *Harper's English Grammar.* New York, 1941.
Revised edition by Stewart Benedict, New York, 1966. In paperback.

Summey, George, Jr. *American Punctuation.* New York, 1949.
One of the few systematic studies of the use of punctuation in printed American writing.

Writing Handbooks

These handbooks were written for the college classroom. They contain a little of everything—grammar, usage, writing and rhetoric, and an introduction to library research and research writing. Because they cover so much, they often simplify, but they are extremely handy. One or more of them may be available at a local college bookstore.

Brusaw, Charles T., Alred, Gerald J., and Oliu, Walter E. *Handbook of Technical Writing.* New York, 1976.
Alphabetized handbook includes usage, punctuation, and writing, in addition to extensive coverage of formats for reports, letters, charts, and other technical writing tasks.

Ebbitt, Wilma R., and Ebbitt, David R. *Writer's Guide and Index to English,* 6th ed. Glenview, Ill., 1978.
The most recent edition of the book originally edited by Porter G. Perrin. One of the best of the composition handbooks.

Fowler, H. Ramsey. *The Little, Brown Handbook.* Boston, 1980.

Hodges, John C., and Whitten, Mary E. *Harbrace College Handbook*, 8th ed. New York, 1977.

Millward, Celia. *Handbook for Writers: Grammar, Punctuation, Diction, Rhetoric, Research*. New York, 1980.

Style Guides

These guides are intended to assist writers and editors in specific fields prepare papers for journal and scholarly publication. They focus generally on matters of footnotes and bibliographies. Most deal slightly or not at all with punctuation, grammar, and usage.

American Chemical Society. *Handbook for Authors of Papers in American Chemical Society Publications*. Washington, D.C., 1978

American Institute of Physics. *Style Manual for Guidance in the Preparation of Papers*, 2d rev. ed. New York, 1967.

American Medical Association, Division of Scientific Publications. *Style Book and Editorial Manual*, 4th ed. Chicago, 1966.

American Psychological Association. *Publication Manual*, 2d ed. Washington, D.C., 1974.

Council of Biology Editors. *CBE Style Manual: a Guide for Authors, Editors, and Copywriters*, 4th ed. Washington, D.C., 1978.

Government Printing Office. *Style Manual*, rev. ed. Washington, D.C., 1973.
The "GPO" is most useful as a supplement to other manuals. It can be consulted at most libraries.

Harvard Law Review Association. *A Uniform System of Citation and Abbreviations*, 12th ed. Cambridge, Mass., 1976.
Also known as the "Harvard Blue Book."

Modern Language Association. *The MLA Style Sheet,* compiled by William Riley Parker, rev. ed., 3d printing with corrections. New York, 1971.

Turabian, Kate L. *A Manual for Writers of Term Papers, Theses, and Dissertations,* 4th ed. Chicago, 1973.
Known to users simply as "Turabian," this manual is an abbreviated Chicago *Manual of Style;* it is directed toward typists rather than printers.

University of Chicago Press. *A Manual of Style, for Authors, Editors, and Copywriters,* 12th ed., rev. Chicago, 1969.
One of the standard style manuals. Many specialized style manuals add a note that anything not covered in their manual or style sheet should be handled as Chicago handles it.

Secretarial Handbooks

These manuals include information on business correspondence, letter formats, filing systems, and on and on.

Doris, Lillian, and Miller, Bessemay. *The Complete Secretary's Handbook,* 3d ed. Englewood Cliffs, N.J., 1970.

Hutchinson, Lois. *Standard Handbook for Secretaries,* 8th ed. New York, 1969.

Webster's Secretarial Handbook. Springfield, Mass., 1976.

Spelling Aid

Lewis, Norman. *Correct Spelling Made Easy.* New York, 1963.
One of the better self-help spelling programs.

Spelling Lists

These books (and others like them) contain lists of words without definitions, except to distinguish very briefly between words often confused. They provide very quick spelling references.

Gleeson, Ruth, and Colvin, James. *Words Most Often Misspelled and Mispronounced*. New York, 1963 (paperback).

Louis, A. Leslie. *20,000 Words*, 7th ed. New York, 1977.

Webster's Instant Word Guide. Springfield, Mass., 1980.

Webster's Legal Speller. Springfield, Mass., 1978.

Webster's Medical Speller. Springfield, Mass., 1975,

Webster's New World Speller-Divider Book. New York, 1971.

Index

Ethnic groups, names of, 193–94
Evans, Bergen, 72n
Evans, Cornelia, 72n
Even, evenness, 211
Every, 72
Everybody, 49, 72, 73
Every day, 269
Everyone, 49, 61, 72, 73
   possessive of, 94
Everything, 49
Exact, 289
Except, accept, 317–18
Exclamation point, 121–22
   overuse of, 121
   and parentheses, 154
   with question mark, 121
   with quotation marks, 158
Exclamations, as sentence frag-
   ments, 113
   see also Interjections
Ex, compounds with, 209
Exhibit, exhibits, 23
Exotic, forms of, 86
Expository writing, exclamation
   point in, 121

Fictitious names, 179–80
Fair, fairly, 84
Fanatic, fanatically, 211
Fancy, forms of, 213
Farther, further, 318
fast, 83
Father, capitalization of, 181–82
Federal, 183
Federal Information Centers, 298
Feel, 310–11
   forms of, 80, 82
Fewer, less, 318–19
Figures
   plurals of, 23–24
   vs. words, 230–33
   see also Numbers
*Finalize, finish, complete, put in
   final form*, 319
Finite verbs, 339–40
Finnish, case in, 57
First, firstly, 84, 319–20
First letter of sentence, capitaliz-
   ing, 171–72
Fish, plural of, 26
Flaunt, flout, 320
Flock, 44
Flu, 227
Fly, forms of, 5, 214

Focus, plurals of, 30
Foot, plural of, 25, 33, **34**
Football, 204
Footnote references
   colon in, 130
   period in, 120
For, 117, 337
Forbid, forms of, 5
Foreign countries, names of, 190–
   91
Foreign/English plurals, 29–30
Foreign plurals, preserved, 28–29
Foreign words
   in italics, 165
   plurals of, 27–32
For example, 133, 317
   semicolon preceding, 124–25
For instance, 317
Formal letters, salutation in, 302
Formal usage, 57
   vs. general usage, 66
   and *whom*, 67
Formal writing, 166, 244, 306, 313
   capitalization styles in, 170
   and sentence fragments, 113
   that for *because* in, 327
Form, forms, 23
Formula, plurals of, 28, 30
Fowler, F. G., 15
Fowler, H. W., 15, 75, 77
Fractions
   decimal, 231, 233
   hyphenation in, 207
   slash for, 168
Fragmentary quotations, 172–73
Fragments, sentence, 113
French, 200, 201
From what, from that which, 314–
   15
Ful endings, 266
Fungus, plurals of, 30
Further, farther, 318
Future perfect tense, 8
Future tense, 8, 16, 349
   main-clause verb in, 11

Gallon, 33, 34, 102
Gamut, gauntlet, 320
Gas, forms of, 210
Gay, forms of, 214
Ge endings, 212
General usage, vs. formal usage, 66
General writing, 306
Generic terms, 184–85